Improvising on a Theme

This book is dedicated to the memory of Michael Lloyd, Brian Loane, David Perkins and Paul Slater, all of whom made invaluable contributions – sharing with me their experiences of music education in Birmingham – but sadly passed away before the book's publication.

Improvising on a Theme

The story of the Birmingham Music Service

Cormac Loane

To Roy,

With best wishes,

Cormac

First published in 2020 by the UCL Institute of Education Press, 20 Bedford Way, London WC1H 0AL

www.ucl-ioe-press.com

British Library Cataloguing in Publication Data:
A catalogue record for this publication is available from the British Library

ISBNs
978-1-78277-286-6 (paperback)
978-1-78277-302-3 (PDF eBook)
978-1-78277-303-0 (ePub eBook)
978-1-78277-304-7 (Kindle eBook)

Typeset by Quadrant Infotech (India) Pvt Ltd
Printed by CPI Group (UK) Ltd, Croydon, CR0 4YY
Front cover image © Fran Slaughter. The author conducting the Birmingham Schools' Training Wind Orchestra at the Midlands Arts Centre, *c*.1989.
Back cover image by Michael Bates, © Birmingham Music Service. The author conducting the Birmingham Schools' Training Wind Orchestra outside Birmingham Town Hall, *c*.1989.

Contents

Dramatis personae

City of Birmingham Education Department Music Advisers and Inspectors

Desmond MacMahon (Music Adviser: 1937–1962)
Stanley Adams (Music Adviser: 1962–1975)
Peter Davies (Senior Inspector for Music: 1975–1983)
Linda Gilbert (General Inspector for Music: 1983–1990)
Lewis Coley (Schools Adviser [with responsibility for music]: 1990–1991)
Mark Wyatt (Schools Adviser for Music: 1991–1998)
Robert Bunting (Adviser for Music: 1998–2007)

Birmingham Music Service Heads of Service

Keith Allen (Head of Instrumental Staff: 1977–1987; Head of Service: 1987–1991)
David Perkins (Acting Head of Service: 1991–1992; Head of Service: 1992–2000)
John Clemson (Acting Head of Service: 2000–2004; Head of Service: 2004–2014)
Cormac Loane (Acting Head of Service: May–August 2000)
Ciaran O'Donnell (Head of Service: 2014–2018)
Stuart Birnie (Interim Head of Service: 2018–2019; Head of Service: 2019–)

Services for Education Chief Executives

David Perkins (2012–2016)
Charles Elvin (2016–2017)
Martyn Collin (2017–2019)
Sharon Bell (2019–)

List of figures

List of figures

List of abbreviations

A-level	General Certificate of Education Advanced Level qualification
AST	Advanced Skills Teacher
BCMG	Birmingham Contemporary Music Group
BSBO	Birmingham Schools' Baroque Orchestra
BSC	Birmingham Schools' Chorale
BSCO	Birmingham Schools' Concert Orchestra
BSDO	Birmingham Schools' Dance Orchestra
BSJE	Birmingham Schools' Jazz Ensemble
BSJO	Birmingham Schools' Jazz Orchestra
BSSO	Birmingham Schools' Symphony Orchestra
BSTO	Birmingham Schools' Training Orchestra
BSTWO	Birmingham Schools' Training Wind Orchestra
BTEC	Business and Technology Education Council qualification
CBSO	City of Birmingham Symphony Orchestra
DfE	Department for Education
EBacc	English Baccalaureate
GCSE	General Certificate of Secondary Education
GMS	grant-maintained status
HEAR	Higher Education Achievement Report
HMI	Her Majesty's Inspector
ILEA	Inner London Education Authority
LMS	local management of schools
MAC	Midlands Arts Centre
Ofsted	Office for Standards in Education, Children's Services and Skills
PPA	planning, preparation and assessment
PSV	professional support visit
ROMA	Record of Musical Achievement
S4E	Services for Education
SATs	Standard Attainment Tests
SEND	special educational needs and disability
SMART	specific, measurable, achievable, realistic and time-measured

Acknowledgements

After retiring from the Birmingham Music Service in 2013 I began, more so than ever, to reflect upon and hold conversations with people about the extraordinary achievements of that organization. It was these reflections and conversations that led me to the decision to write this book, and I would like to express my gratitude to the following people who gave me the initial encouragement and practical support that I needed, in order to embark upon the project: Professors Martin Fautley and Richard Hatcher from Birmingham City University, Pauline Adams from the Institute of Education, Nicky Platt from UCL IOE Press, my brother Terry Loane, and Kim Ballard.

Between 2014 and 2019, as the major part of my research for the book, I interviewed more than 60 people. Most of the interviewees had been directly involved with the Birmingham Music Service – as teachers, managers or students – some of them as far back as the foundation of the service in the 1950s and 1960s. Nearly all of the interviews were face-to-face meetings – some taking place in Birmingham and some in other parts of the country. As well as providing me with information and understanding, which would form the basis of this book, these meetings were extremely enjoyable occasions – often reuniting me with former colleagues or students with whom I had lost touch many years previously. I would like to thank all of the people I interviewed for giving up their time to help in this way: Keith Allen, Andrew Biggs, Pat Brennan, Peter Bridle, Tim Brighouse, Robert Bunting, Heather Clemson, John Clemson, Xhosa Cole, Lewis Coley, Maggie Cotton, John Croghan, Alan Davis, Richard Duckett, Roderick Dunk, Chris Egan, Charles Elvin, Rod Evans, Martin Fautley, Angela Fenwick, Olivia Goodborn (formerly Olive Goodborn), Alwyn Green, Sandy Hay, Robert Heeks, Bernard Herrmann junior, Brian Hunt, Denyse Hyett, Chris Jones, Roger Jones, Lesa Kingham, Sneh Lata, Antony le Fleming, Peter Lee, Geoff Leigh, Bryan Lester, Julian Lloyd Webber, Debbie Loane, Terry Loane, Harjinder Matharu, Christopher Morley, Rodney Newton, Ciaran O'Donnell, David Osborne, Stephon Phillip, Rita Porzi, Richard Reakes, Linda Rose (formerly Linda Gilbert), Joyce Rothschild, Anneke Scott, Patricia Scott, Harjit Singh, Jeffrey Skidmore, Norman Stewart, Gordon Thornett, Bob Vivian, Nicola Walker, Helen Warren, Paul Wassall, Mick Waters, Alison Whatley, Bridget Whyte and Richard Worth.

I would like to thank Rupert Bond, Richard Hatcher, Terry Loane and Peter True for the invaluable feedback they gave me following their reading of the manuscript as it developed. And I would like to thank Pat Gordon-Smith and Jonathan Dore from UCL IOE Press who, with great patience, provided expert advice and guidance with preparation of the final manuscript.

I am grateful to the following people who generously provided photographs they had taken for use in the book: Birmingham Music Service brass teacher Michael Bates; Matt Chambers who, as a teenage violinist during the 1960s, was a member of the Birmingham Schools' Symphony Orchestra; Robert Nagle, husband of Birmingham Music Service teacher Sue Nagle; Fran Slaughter, mother of Jayne Slaughter, a Birmingham Music Service French horn student in the 1980s; and Nick Gilbert.

About the author

Following his graduation from the University of London Goldsmiths College, Cormac Loane worked as a saxophone player 'on the boats' and at the Empress Ballroom, Blackpool, during the late 1970s. In 1980 he started his career in music education, teaching woodwind instruments for music services in the London area, including the Inner London Education Authority. In 1984 he was appointed Head of Woodwind for the Birmingham Music Service and was later promoted to Deputy Head of Service - a role he continued to occupy until his retirement in 2013. Loane is co-author of the series of music tutor books, *Team Woodwind.*

Foreword

Sir Tim Brighouse, Chief Education Officer, Birmingham Education Authority (1993–2002)

In the early 1940s, the wartime Coalition Government began to plan for post-war reconstruction. Heavily influenced by the Beveridge Report, plans were drawn up to abolish squalor, ignorance, want, idleness and disease. In Birmingham, at the same time, a young administrative assistant in the Education Department visited Steward Street County Primary School in the inner city and witnessed an extraordinary headteacher, Arthur Stone, and his staff, who focused every afternoon's activities on the expressive arts – on performance involving drama and music. The administrative assistant was Alec Clegg who shortly afterwards became Chief Education Officer of the West Riding of Yorkshire where, for nearly 30 years, he wove educational magic both within schools and in out-of-school provision. Among Clegg's many accomplishments, one of the most far-reaching was the founding of Bretton Hall which in 1949 opened as a teacher training college committed to music, design and the creative and performing arts. It gave birth to countless performers and generations of talented teachers of the arts who themselves transformed young lives. Meanwhile Arthur Stone, at the behest of Clegg, wrote the Ministry of Education's pamphlet of guidance for primary schools (Ministry of Education, 1949), describing his beloved Steward Street School's curriculum and rationale. The pamphlet, entitled *Story of a School*, was reprinted many times and was the only guidance for England's primary schools until the Plowden Report in 1967.

Cormac Loane starts this story of Birmingham's outstanding music service with Desmond MacMahon's role in establishing a strong choral tradition in schools and more widely in Birmingham. MacMahon's work laid the foundations on which all the rest was built. Did MacMahon meet Stone and Clegg? If he did – and it seems unlikely that he didn't – every conversation must have started with exciting questions: 'What if ... ?', 'Shall we try ... ?' Cormac then describes the developments that Stanley Adams, Peter Davies, Linda Gilbert, John Clemson and many others subsequently made by standing on the shoulders of these wartime giants. Each of these music makers put their individual signature on the rich tapestry of Birmingham's music: the Birmingham Schools' Symphony Orchestra; the peripatetic music service for youngsters in challenged areas of the city; the development and celebration of music that reflected the diverse communities in a city which prided itself on welcoming, as 'Brummies', settlers first from all parts of the United Kingdom and then from all parts of the world. In the process, of course, the lives of individual young people, lucky enough to live in the city and be touched by this part of its ambitious education service, were changed for the better. Some walked more than a step or two of the way with genius, but all led more fulfilling lives as a result of their brush with the Birmingham Music Service. They had less chance of living what Thoreau, the American polymath, once described as 'lives of quiet desperation before going to their graves with the song still inside them'. The Music Service unlocked their minds and opened the shut chambers of their hearts. They found and sang their songs.

Doubtless influenced by these tunes, the city made the International Convention Centre with its Symphony Hall, home to the City of Birmingham Symphony Orchestra (CBSO), a cornerstone of the city's renewal of its infrastructure and its economic fortunes during the mid-1980s. Birmingham became a Mecca for UK music lovers, first inspired by the bold appointment of a relatively unknown but up-and-coming Simon Rattle and then by his hugely talented successors. In Cormac's story, Linda Gilbert was the animateur who connected the CBSO and the Symphony Hall to young music makers in the city.

Was it this love of music and the arts that persuaded the city to make land available at Cannon Hill Park for what was originally called the Midlands Arts Centre and now is known locally, after a £25 million facelift, as MAC? And how far did the pervasive influence of the Birmingham Music Service play its part in persuading the peripatetic part of Sadler's Wells to accept the city council's invitation to settle as the Birmingham Royal Ballet, which, with an associate school, further opened up opportunities in the arts for young people in the region?

I arrived in the city during this latter period and, even though I had experienced the Inner London Education Authority's superb music provision, I marvelled at Birmingham's music. It seemed to attract some extraordinary talents, with each individual delighting and respecting other members of the formidable team.

I have described briefly the wider backdrop to the fascinating and compelling story that Cormac Loane has assembled in this book. The wider picture, however, does not end with Birmingham's ambition to live by its motto of 'Forward' and transform its traditional boast of being a 'city of a thousand trades' into one of learning without limits on what Brummies would achieve, especially through music and the arts. It goes further afield, as we have seen from the opening paragraph of this Foreword. What happened in Birmingham had a national influence. It inspired Clegg's West Riding as it did so many music services in other local education authorities. In short, it is arguable that what this book describes provided the impetus for an emphasis on the arts, and music in particular, which has led to a flowering of the arts in the UK. This has been to the immense benefit of our civilized well-being, not to mention the invisible balance of trade earnings where the contribution of the creative arts and education is massive.

Read, enjoy, learn and be inspired.

Introduction

On Tuesday 4 September 1984, I sat with a group of about 30 instrumental music teachers in a small meeting room at the Martineau Teachers' Centre on the Bristol Road in Birmingham. This small group of people comprised the Birmingham Music Service – teachers who visited schools all around Birmingham, teaching young people to play musical instruments – and this was my first day as a member of that organization. I had just moved from being an instrumental music teacher in London to take up the post of Head of Woodwind in Birmingham.

On Friday 20 December 2013, the day of my retirement from the Birmingham Music Service, I sat with a group of over 150 teachers at their training day in a large banqueting room at Birmingham City Football Club – such had been the huge growth of the organization over those intervening 29 years. By that time, the Birmingham Music Service had developed into one of the strongest music services in England, providing a wealth of musical opportunities for Birmingham children, characterized by exceptionally high standards of performance and a breadth of musical styles, and inclusivity of participation, reflecting the city's rich cultural diversity.

My recollections of that first meeting in 1984, however, exemplify some of the disparate features that prevailed within the Birmingham Music Service at that time. In the full staff meeting, at the start of the day, I found myself sitting next to a teacher who, judging from our conversation, appeared to have little interest in teaching young people – his work for the Music Service was clearly just a means of earning some extra money to supplement an income that, reputedly, he earned from running a private sales business. During the lunch break a number of teachers, including senior staff, visited the Sir Harry public house across the road, returning slightly late and 'worse for wear' for the afternoon session. I was already familiar with this rather casual attitude among some instrumental music teachers at that time. During my Postgraduate Certificate in Education course at Bulmershe College, Reading, in 1977/78, I undertook a teaching practice placement as an instrumental teacher in the west of Berkshire. Every Friday lunchtime, while on our way to John O'Gaunt School, my teacher supervisor and I would meet up with a group of instrumental teachers in a pub on Hungerford High Street for lunch and drinks. At a certain stage in the proceedings the teachers would decide, collectively, whether to go to their afternoon schools or to remain in the pub drinking. I can remember at least one occasion when the decision was taken to remain in the pub, without even a telephone call being made to schools that should have been visited that afternoon. And, at the start of the first year of my teaching career, working for Hertfordshire Music Service, I was greeted with surprise by the Head of Music at Alleyne's School, Stevenage, when I turned up at the school in the first week of September. 'We don't normally see you people in the first couple of weeks or the last couple of weeks of any term,' he told me.

So, by lunchtime on my first day with the Birmingham Music Service, I was beginning to wonder whether I had made the right decision in moving from London to Birmingham. These doubts soon disappeared, however, once the afternoon session got under way – this involved different members of staff, none of whom were managers, sharing their teaching experiences with other colleagues. First of all, guitar teacher Bryan Lester spoke about strategies he had been using for getting pupils to compose their own music – quite a radical idea within instrumental music teaching at that time. And then Bill Hunt, who had achieved fame in the 1970s as a member of Wizzard and Electric Light Orchestra, spoke about his experimental work in introducing electric-keyboard teaching in schools. The very fact that there were teachers of guitar and electric keyboard in the room was, in itself, a sign of innovation, since instrumental music teaching in England had, up to that time, been based almost exclusively on the teaching of classical orchestral instruments. This pointed strongly to the way things were going to develop in the future, since guitar and keyboard teaching would, by the start of the twenty-first century, have grown to be among the most important areas of teaching within the Birmingham Music Service, as well as in many other music services around the country.

Later in the afternoon there were departmental meetings, and I found myself, as Head of Woodwind, chairing the meeting of woodwind teachers. There was no agenda, so I suggested that staff raised issues they wanted to discuss. There followed a vibrant discussion about the merits, or otherwise, of group instrumental tuition. Some teachers took the traditional stance that one-to-one teaching was the ideal, but that group teaching had become an economic necessity – probably the dominant view among instrumental teachers in England at that time. But others took the more progressive view that group teaching was intrinsically desirable because of its educational and musical benefits. This is an issue that I shall return to in later chapters.

So the content of the afternoon session pointed to the possibility of an exciting future of innovation and discovery in the Birmingham Music Service – in terms of both the curriculum and the pedagogy. I also saw evidence of what was, for that time, a forward-looking approach to leadership and professional development – the idea that teachers learn best through sharing ideas with one another, rather than by being told what to do by their managers. I believe that in these areas of innovation the Birmingham Music Service, throughout much of its history, has stood apart from many other English music services, and an examination of this will form a principal focus of this book.

My decision to move from London to Birmingham had been a difficult one. I loved the excitement of living in London in the 1980s, with its thriving artistic scene and its groundbreaking approach to the celebration of diversity, nurtured by the Greater London Council under Ken Livingstone's leadership and by the Inner London Education Authority. Birmingham, in comparison, seemed like an undeveloped backwater that remained, as yet, unaffected by London's more progressive attitude. This difference between the two cities was encapsulated for me by the contrast in sense of humour. I was sickened, for example, by the propensity of some of my new colleagues for telling jokes of a sexist or homophobic nature – something that I felt London teachers had long since moved beyond. This made me feel as though I had moved back to the 1970s when, working as a musician on a cruise liner, I found such jokes to be the stock-in-trade of the ship's cabaret artists. I was attracted, however, by the prospect of a career promotion so it was my intention to stay in Birmingham for a few years and then, most likely, return to London. Little did I know then, however, that within a short while, conductor Simon Rattle would transform the City of Birmingham Symphony Orchestra into a world-class orchestra, that one of the great concert halls of the world, Symphony Hall, would be built in Birmingham, that Ronnie Scott would choose Birmingham to open his only jazz club outside London, and that one of the most inspiring educational thinkers of the time, Tim Brighouse, would be appointed as Birmingham's Chief Education Officer. So, by the mid-1990s, Birmingham had become a very exciting place to live and work, and I have remained there ever since.

With its population of around one million inhabitants, Birmingham is England's second-largest city after London, and following the abolition of the Inner London Education Authority in 1990, Birmingham City Council became the country's largest local education authority. At the time of writing, the city's state-funded schools comprise 361 primary schools, 79 non-selective secondary schools and eight grammar schools. (Birmingham is one of the very few areas of the country to have retained grammar schools, most other areas having abolished the post-war system of selective education by the 1980s.)

Following the end of the Second World War, Birmingham became the home for large numbers of immigrants from many parts of the world – in particular, Ireland, the Indian subcontinent and the Caribbean. And in the new millennium the city's cultural diversity was enriched still further through the migration of people from the Middle East, African countries such as Somalia, and Eastern European countries such as Poland and Romania. As a result, Birmingham is one of the most ethnically diverse areas of the country – even more so than London. And ever since the mid-1970s, as we shall see in the course of this story, the Birmingham Music Service has led the way nationally, as it has risen to the challenge of celebrating the music of the city's increasingly diverse population. In addition, the Birmingham Music Service has been a national leader in terms of recognizing the value of musical styles that young people themselves listen to and perform outside school. Following the emergence of rock and pop music in Britain during the 1960s – a style associated with teenage rebellion at the time – it would take many decades before this would be accepted by the educational establishment as serious music. As early as the 1970s, however, the Birmingham Music Service's Consortium Music Teacher Paul Slater was engaging pupils (albeit without approval) through rock and pop music. And, by the start of the twenty-first century, all styles of music were seen by the Music Service as being of equal value.

This book tells the story of the development of the Birmingham Music Service over the 29 years that I worked for the organization, as well as its earlier and more recent history. The book also explores the possible future of English music services within a political and educational landscape that has changed beyond recognition in recent years. In the course of the book I shall explain my belief that the development of local authority music services has been one of the great educational achievements in this country, as well as one of the best examples of music education anywhere in the world. And I shall explain why I think that the Birmingham Music Service has been a particularly outstanding example – largely due to the creativity and innovation it has demonstrated throughout its history in relation to the curriculum, pedagogy, diversity and leadership.

Those who have used music metaphors to describe working together, especially jazz metaphors, are sensing the nature of this quantum world. This world demands that we be present together, and be willing to improvise. We agree on the melody, tempo and key, and then we play. We listen carefully, we communicate constantly, and suddenly, there is music, possibilities beyond anything we imagined. The music comes from somewhere else, from a unified whole we have accessed among ourselves, a relationship that transcends our false sense of separateness. When the music appears, we can't help but be amazed and grateful.

Margaret J. Wheatley (*Leadership and the New Science*, 1999)

Chapter 1

The embryonic years

During the 1920s, the Music HMI (His Majesty's Inspector) Geoffrey Shaw and his assistant, Cyril Winn, began to organize and direct Non-competitive Schools Music Festivals in different parts of England. These festivals involved children coming together from groups of schools in particular areas to rehearse and then present high-profile concerts. By the mid-1930s the Non-competitive Schools Music Festivals had become so popular and successful that Shaw and Winn, working on their own, were no longer able to meet the demand, so local education authorities began to appoint their own Music Advisers (or Music Inspectors), whose main role was to organize and conduct these events.

Figure 1.1: Desmond MacMahon conducting a rehearsal in a Birmingham school, 1945 (Photo: Mirrorpix)

One of the first authorities to make such an appointment was the Birmingham Education Committee, who appointed Desmond MacMahon (Figure 1.1) as their first Music Adviser in 1937. MacMahon was born and brought up in Sunderland, in the north-east of England, and attended

Sunderland Teacher Training College before being awarded a doctorate in music at Dublin University (now known as Trinity College Dublin). From 1921 he taught music at Firth Park Secondary School in Sheffield, where he established a thriving choir and orchestra. While in Sheffield he also worked as Musical Director for the Croft House Theatre Company, which gave regular performances of musical theatre in Sheffield's Lyceum Theatre (and continues to do so at the time of writing). In June 1924, less than two years after the birth of radio broadcasting in Britain, the newly formed BBC's radio station in Manchester, known as 2ZY, broadcast a lecture by MacMahon entitled 'Our Folk Music'. The *Radio Times*, at the time, described the broadcast as, 'A talk on the growth, construction and appreciation of our national songs and dances, with pianoforte illustrations' (Radio Times, 1924). This broadcast signalled both the start of MacMahon's interest in radio broadcasting, which was to play an important part in his future career, as well as his interest in folk song, which was to manifest itself later in a huge quantity of printed publications. Also, the fact that MacMahon was involved in a radio broadcast so early in the history of that medium demonstrates the flair he clearly possessed for innovation and for exploiting new opportunities.

In 1935 MacMahon was promoted to the post of Music Adviser for Manchester Education Committee, following in the footsteps of that city's first Music Adviser, Walter Carroll. And, two years after that, MacMahon took up the newly created post of Music Adviser in Birmingham. As soon as he arrived in Birmingham, MacMahon set up the Birmingham Children's Choir and, continuing the tradition he had inherited from Walter Carroll in Manchester, he established a pattern of regular, high-profile, massed choral concerts involving children. These occasions, which took place at Birmingham Town Hall, had accompaniment provided by the City of Birmingham Orchestra, and soon became established as a regular part of the musical life of the city. Huge numbers of children from schools all over Birmingham were involved and the Town Hall would typically be packed with parents, friends and local politicians.

MacMahon also continued the tradition that had been established in Manchester, whereby children took part in BBC radio broadcasts. During his first year in Birmingham, the BBC Regional Programme broadcast a series entitled *Songs for Schools,* presented by MacMahon himself, and featuring the Birmingham Children's Choir. Here is a description of the programme, as it appeared in the *Radio Times* at the time:

> Until recently composers have given very little attention to songs for children, with the result that teachers have been compelled to rely on adaptations of solo songs, many of them quite unsuitable for school use. The deficiency has now been adequately filled by modern composers, and it is to familiarise teachers with modern work of real worth and merit, as well as to provide a good programme for the general listener, that this monthly series has been begun. Dr. McMahon [sic], who is presenting this programme, is musical adviser to the Birmingham Education Department ... He has selected and trained two choirs, composed of boys and girls and drawn from Birmingham schools, to illustrate the series. (Radio Times, 1937)

In 1946 MacMahon nearly left the city when he applied for, and was offered, a post as Director of the New South Wales Conservatorium of Music, in Australia. But, luckily for Birmingham, MacMahon turned down the offer at the last minute and remained as Music Adviser in Birmingham until his death in 1962. In the course of his long career in Birmingham, MacMahon came to be regarded as a hero in the world of music education, both locally and nationally, and was awarded an OBE (Officer of the Most Excellent Order of the British Empire), as well as a fellowship from Trinity College London. The extremely high regard in which he was held was summed up in an article headed 'Our debt to Dr D. MacMahon' that appeared in *The Birmingham Mail* in 1949:

> If the man in the street, and more particularly the young man in the street, is not finding music more attractive today than ever he has done, it is not the fault of Dr Desmond MacMahon, Music Adviser to the Birmingham Education Committee. For years now, principally by his writings, though frequently by personal demonstration, he has been inculcating a love of music by showing that basically the art is simple and in no way terrifying; is available, indeed, to all who care to avail themselves of it. This is one of the main services rendered to music by Dr MacMahon and Birmingham is fortunate that most of his practical work in this direction – in schools and for the adolescent – has taken place within the City. Many young people who might have regarded serious music as beyond their reach have had its wonders brought home to them in the most effortless way and what at first seemed formidable has quickly become fascinating. (*Birmingham Mail*, 1949)

One example of Desmond MacMahon's high-profile children's performances was the Education Committee's Festival of Christmas Music, directed by MacMahon in December 1950 at Birmingham Town Hall, and very favourably reviewed at the time by the *Birmingham Post* (1950). The main item on the programme was *A Christmas Mystery* – an oratorio by Philipp Wolfrum in which choral parts were performed by The Birmingham Singers alongside a choir of schoolchildren, with accompaniment provided by the newly named City of Birmingham Symphony Orchestra (CBSO), and acting parts played by girls from Paget Road Secondary Modern School. My Birmingham Music Service colleague Paul Slater – whose career is described later in the book – had clear memories of taking part in choral events such as this under MacMahon's direction, while Slater was a pupil at Hall Green Junior School during the 1950s. And when I met up with Birmingham-born film music composer Rodney Newton he recalled, as a junior school pupil at around the same time, attending performances for schoolchildren at the Town Hall, given by the CBSO under the direction of MacMahon. In addition to involving the CBSO in these children's events at Birmingham Town Hall, Desmond MacMahon also established the tradition of performances given by the CBSO in schools – often members of the orchestra would travel around in small groups, visiting several different schools in the course of a day. So, by the 1950s, MacMahon had established strong links between the CBSO and the embryonic Birmingham Music Service, as well as an understanding that Birmingham's professional orchestra had an important role to play in the musical experiences of schoolchildren.

In 1952, under the chairmanship of Wilfred Martineau, Birmingham Education Committee established the Martineau Teachers' Centre on the Bristol Road, Edgbaston, in a building that had previously housed Edgbaston College for Girls. The purpose of the Martineau Teachers' Centre was to provide a meeting place for teachers close to the city centre, for social as well as professional purposes – partly with the aim of trying to attract more good teachers to Birmingham at a time when this was proving difficult. According to Wilfred Martineau, the Centre would be somewhere where teachers could 'put up their feet and let their hair down' (Martineau Gardens, n.d.). In the late 1960s and early 1970s there was a huge growth in the number of teachers' centres around the country and, according to Roland Morant, the Martineau Teachers' Centre was 'the model on which later Centres were fashioned' (Morant, 1978: 200). The Centre consisted of a fairly large hall, a number of meeting rooms, a canteen and a bar (known as the Martineau Club), tennis courts and a bowling green. Soon after the Centre opened, MacMahon established his office there and, in due course, it became the administrative base for the emerging Birmingham Music Service, which continued to be based there until 1989. From the time of my arrival in Birmingham in 1984, I have very happy memories of the Martineau Teachers' Centre: as my office base, as a venue for teachers' meetings and musical rehearsals, and as a social centre. I have particularly fond recollections of my visits to the Martineau Club on Saturday lunchtimes when teachers came together from schools all over the city to enjoy a buffet lunch together in a comfortable, relaxed environment, and to exchange stories about their week's work. To me, this seemed like extremely good value for the £1 per month that was automatically deducted from my salary to pay for my Martineau Club membership.

Within a few months of the Centre's opening, Desmond MacMahon, characteristically, saw the building's potential as a venue for musical recitals. One such recital, in July 1953, was reviewed by the *Birmingham Post*:

> That unique and enlightened creation of Birmingham's Education Committee, the Martineau Teachers' Club in Bristol Road, has a music society whose activities should be worth watching. Last night it sponsored a recital of songs, mostly of recent composition, by Desmond MacMahon, music adviser to the committee. (*Birmingham Post*, 1953)

The review goes on to describe how MacMahon's settings of 'The Owl and the Pussycat' and 'The Pelican Chorus' were 'enlivened by dance-mimes happily performed by children from Lea Village Secondary Modern School' (ibid.) – evidence of MacMahon's commitment to involving schoolchildren in high-level performances, including pupils from secondary modern schools in less advantaged areas of the city.

A colleague's recollections

I was privileged, in the course of my research for this book, to meet just one person who had worked alongside MacMahon as a colleague during his time as Music Adviser in Birmingham. When I visited 85-year-old Michael Lloyd at his home in Newcastle-under-Lyme, he told me that he first met MacMahon at the Birmingham School of Music when Lloyd was a student there in 1951. Later that year Lloyd visited Switzerland in order to attend a course that MacMahon was running there, involving a choir of schoolchildren from Birmingham. 'And in 1952,' said Lloyd, '"Doctor Mac" was instrumental in getting me my first job – as a specialist music teacher at Rednal Hill Junior School in the south of Birmingham. As a blind person, it wasn't straightforward getting a job in a local authority in those days, but MacMahon used his influence.' In 1965 Lloyd moved from Rednal Hill to take up the post of specialist music teacher at St James Junior School in the same area of Birmingham, and he remained there until his retirement in 1986. From the start of his career, Lloyd worked closely alongside MacMahon, in particular assisting him at the Schools Music Festivals, right up to MacMahon's death in 1962. Lloyd explained to me that, although the Schools Music Festivals were essentially choral events, with accompaniment provided by the CBSO, each concert also included a section of instrumental music. Sometimes this involved the CBSO playing items on their own, and sometimes the orchestra would accompany an advanced pupil playing, for example, a movement from a concerto. According to Lloyd, however, MacMahon did not always have the best of relationships with the CBSO players. 'I recall one occasion,' he said, 'when the CBSO were rehearsing with us in the Town Hall and something went wrong in the orchestra. MacMahon called out to me, "That wasn't right, was it, Michael?" I didn't want to respond so I said nothing, whereupon he shouted the question at me again and I had to respond! And it's extraordinary that, although he didn't have much rapport with the children during the Music Festivals, they always gave him a tremendous welcome – they must have sensed what a special person he was.'

'MacMahon was a great mentor for me,' said Lloyd. 'I liked him, although he could be difficult and outspoken. He was always addressed by his colleagues either as "Doctor Mac" or "Sir" – I don't think I ever heard him addressed as "Desmond". He wasn't an extrovert, but he was a very strong, influential personality – what he said went!' Lloyd went on to say that MacMahon's primary aim was to ensure that *all* children were involved in the enjoyment of music, from infants upwards. And, according to Lloyd, MacMahon went a long way towards achieving this. It was for this reason, said Lloyd, that MacMahon's main focus was on vocal music and percussion, because these were areas in which every child could participate. In summing up his own philosophy of music education, which he said owed much to MacMahon, Michael Lloyd said, 'Instead of talking to children about music, I got them to perform music.' Apparently Desmond MacMahon often visited Rednal Hill Junior School where he was highly supportive of Lloyd's practical approach to music teaching although, according to Lloyd, 'He never said "Well done" – that wasn't in his nature.'

Lloyd explained to me that another music educator who strongly influenced him towards the start of his career was Stephen Moore, a friend of MacMahon's who, in the 1950s and 1960s, played an important role nationally in developing the use of percussion instruments in school music-making and who, like MacMahon in the field of vocal music, wrote a huge amount of published material for use in schools. 'When you think of it,' said Lloyd, 'percussion instruments are real orchestral instruments, but they also have the attribute of being simple to play, so children can join in. So every child in my school got the experience of playing percussion instruments, as well as singing.'

Michael Lloyd said that he was fortunate as a teacher because, through his acquaintance with Desmond MacMahon, he was provided with whatever resources he needed. 'I could get as many sets of songbooks as I wanted,' he said, 'whatever gramophone records I wanted and whatever percussion instruments I wanted. Just when I thought I had everything I needed, I decided it would be good to have a set of chromatic glockenspiels, to make it easier to do melodic accompaniments to songs – so I put in a request to MacMahon and they duly arrived. I think this was because MacMahon was such a powerful person within the local authority.' It might be considered that such behaviour exemplified a culture of patronage that, as we shall see in the course of this book, was a strong feature of Birmingham's local authority music provision, right up to the closing years of the twentieth century.

During his lifetime and since, Desmond MacMahon was best known for the huge quantity of his publications. Particularly popular was the *New National and Folk Song Book – Part 1* (MacMahon, 1938), which comprised vocal parts with piano accompaniments for traditional songs such as 'Auld Lang Syne', 'Bobby Shafto' and 'The British Grenadiers'. MacMahon's books were written for educational use and were very widely used for class and choral singing in schools all over the country at the time. 'It was an example of MacMahon's power within the local authority,' said Michael Lloyd, 'that he was able to get away with selling huge quantities of his own publications for the Schools Music Festivals. It seemed like he brought out a new book in time for each event to ensure he got a good market for it – he was a good businessman!' MacMahon was also a prolific composer, mainly of vocal music, although his best-known work is probably the oboe concerto. This was broadcast by the BBC Welsh Orchestra with oboe soloist Evelyn Rothwell in the year of its composition, 1956, and the third movement was included on a record of oboe solos performed by one of the twentieth century's most highly acclaimed oboists, Léon Goossens. I also learnt from Michael Lloyd that MacMahon's flair for radio broadcasting extended far beyond his work as a musician. 'I turned on the BBC Home

Service one day,' said Lloyd, 'and found myself listening to a thirty-minute whodunnit radio play, which later turned out to have been written by Desmond MacMahon – he was a man of great capacity!'

A legacy of innovation

Although MacMahon had a wide range of talents – musical and otherwise – there can be no doubt that his most lasting and significant legacy was the work he did in laying the foundations for what became known as the Birmingham Music Service. He accomplished this by establishing the tradition of regular, large-scale musical events involving children at Birmingham Town Hall, for which he elicited enthusiastic support from the city's schools, councillors and education officers. It is clear from my conversation with Michael Lloyd, however, that Desmond MacMahon's contribution to music in Birmingham was much wider than just the high-profile Town Hall concerts and radio broadcasts. The spirit of innovation that he established in the city was to become the hallmark of the Birmingham Music Service for many decades to come, and was reflected in many different areas of his work. He had a deep commitment, for example, to supporting classroom music teaching and, in particular, encouraging practical approaches that involved all pupils in music-making – through singing and playing recorders and percussion instruments. In this sense, I believe that the work of MacMahon looked forward to developments that were to take place much later in the Birmingham Music Service – not under his immediate successors, but during the 1980s under the leadership of Linda Gilbert, whose work will be explained in a later chapter. Another area in which MacMahon foreshadowed developments that were to take place decades later in the Music Service was his commitment to employing the most up-to-date technology within music teaching. In 1952 the *Birmingham Mail* reported on a training session for music teachers, led by MacMahon, in which he demonstrated educational uses of some of the latest technological equipment: the Telecine, a remote-control projection television that would allow the new BBC Schools Service to be viewed in classrooms, as well as state-of-the-art reel-to-reel tape recorders (*Birmingham Mail*, 1952). And, in the same training session, MacMahon took the opportunity to demonstrate the use of recorders and percussion instruments in classroom music teaching.

Although MacMahon, while in Manchester, had continued working with the Manchester Children's Orchestra, created by his predecessor Walter Carroll, he did not attempt to start a children's orchestra at any time during his long career in Birmingham. This particular innovation, which was to signal the birth of the Birmingham Music Service proper, was left to his successor Stanley Adams to implement in the 1960s, and this crucial development will form the main focus of the next chapter.

Chapter 2

Birth of the Birmingham Schools' Symphony Orchestra

As part of my research for this book I interviewed Tim Brighouse, Birmingham's Chief Education Officer from 1993 to 2002. We met in the café of Blackwell's bookshop in his home town of Oxford, where he shared with me his recollections of working in Birmingham, as well as some of his thoughts, more generally, on education. Brighouse explained that he believed the development of music services in post-war Britain was very much due to the influence of Alec Clegg, Chief Education Officer for the West Riding of Yorkshire from 1945 to 1974. According to Brighouse, Clegg's massive influence was based on the central importance he attached to the performing arts within the school curriculum – something that is explained more fully by Brighouse in the Foreword to this book. At the time of our conversation in Blackwell's café, however, neither Brighouse nor I was aware of an interesting (albeit rather unhappy) link between Alec Clegg and Birmingham's second Music Adviser, Stanley Adams. This connection was to come to light at a later stage of my research and will be addressed later in this chapter.

Stanley Adams was born and brought up in Brierley Hill in the Black Country area of the West Midlands. From the 1920s onwards he worked, mainly in that area, as a choral conductor and accompanist and sometimes performed as a piano soloist in BBC radio broadcasts. In 1933 he founded the hugely successful Brierley Hill Choral Society, which continues to flourish, over 80 years later. The Choral Society's first-ever concert was a performance of Samuel Coleridge-Taylor's *Hiawatha's Wedding Feast* which, as we shall see, was to become a favourite repertoire item for Adams throughout his long career as a conductor. Following his wartime service with the Royal Air Force, Adams returned to the West Midlands where he undertook Emergency Teacher Training under a scheme set up by the post-war Labour Government, whereby ex-service personnel could quickly train as schoolteachers. And, upon completion of this course in 1947, he was appointed as Music Master at Moseley Grammar School in Birmingham. While in this post, he continued his work with the Brierley Hill Choral Society, as well as working as a piano soloist, and sometimes conductor, with the CBSO. Organist and conductor Roy Massey described the huge impact that Stanley Adams had on him as a pupil at Moseley Grammar School:

> In my third year (1948) at Moseley, Stanley Adams arrived and transformed my school life as he rapidly created a choir and orchestra, encouraged boys to be musicians, and even managed to persuade hardened rugby-playing types to sing. We did orchestral concerts, operas, chamber music, and took part in the Schools Music Festival which he conducted in the Town Hall. (Massey, n.d.)

Massey went on to forge an extremely successful career as a professional musician, which included being Warden of the Royal School of Church Music, organist at St Philip's Cathedral, Birmingham, and Director of Music at King Edward's School, Edgbaston.

As mentioned by Roy Massey above, by the late 1940s Stanley Adams was assisting Music Adviser Desmond MacMahon with the running of the Schools Music Festivals. In this role, Adams found himself conducting challenging repertoire at Birmingham Town Hall including his old favourite, *Hiawatha's Wedding Feast*, and Part I of Mendelssohn's *Elijah* (which had received its premiere performance at the same venue, under the baton of the composer, 100 years earlier). And in 1951 Adams trained the Birmingham Schools Music Festival Choir, which then took part in the second National Schools Music Festival at the Royal Albert Hall, performing in the premiere of Vaughan Williams's *The Sons of Light*, conducted by Sir Adrian Boult.

Transformation and conflict

In 1954 Adams left Birmingham when he was appointed by Alec Clegg to take up the post of Senior Adviser in Music for the West Riding of Yorkshire, where he was to remain for eight years. According to Paul Mann, writing in his PhD thesis 'The Development of Music Education in the West Riding of Yorkshire Education Authority: 1935–1974', Adams had a huge impact on music education in the county: he expanded the team of instrumental music teachers from one to seventeen; he increased the number of full-time music teachers in secondary schools; he established the County Schools' Orchestra for young musicians to perform in; and he established music centres with their own ensembles in Harrogate, Ripon and Stanley (Mann, 1991: 143).

Notwithstanding this transforming effect on music education in the West Riding, where Adams was greatly admired by headteachers, school music teachers and pupils, his relationship with colleagues in the education authority seemed to be fraught with difficulties. Under Adams there were two Area Music Advisers, who were already in place when Adams was appointed. In relation to these two colleagues, according to Mann, 'Adams took an authoritarian stance which led to early and serious disagreements over the policy for music in schools' (ibid.: 131). More seriously, the relationship between Adams and Clegg apparently also broke down, shortly after Adams's appointment. Under Clegg, the education authority was pioneering new, child-centred approaches to learning in the expressive arts that, according to Mann, were in conflict with Adams's more traditional approach. The County Schools Music Festivals established by Adams, although hugely popular with everyone who took part, were criticized by some within the authority as being elitist since they focused on a minority of secondary school children who had been specially selected (ibid.: 134). According to Mann, 'Adams's critics considered that he had a musical and educational philosophy which tended to encourage those who already showed musical interest and ability' (ibid.: 133). And, at a time when the West Riding was introducing comprehensive education, 'Clegg himself accused Adams of adopting methods which savoured of the grammar school' (cited in Mann, 1991: 133). According to Mann, Adams showed little interest in the child-centred, exploratory approaches to learning that were being pioneered in the West Riding at the time and, as a result, his critics considered that 'the development of important new approaches in primary school music for the broad majority of children was neglected during the period in which Adams was the Senior Music Adviser' (cited in Mann, 1991: 135). Mann summed up by saying, 'Adams's traditional philosophy ... was perceived by some as an anachronism in an education authority which was becoming known nationally as a pioneer in the development of new approaches in the curriculum' (Mann, 1991: 135).

This conflict between Stanley Adams and his colleagues in the West Riding exemplifies a tension between two different approaches to music education – one that is perceived as traditional, teacher-directed and elitist, and the other which is perceived as creative, child-centred and inclusive. It is a tension that was to become an ongoing issue within English music education for decades to come, and it is a matter that will be returned to later in the book.

Adams – the innovator

In 1962, following the death of Desmond MacMahon, the post of Music Adviser in Birmingham became vacant. Adams applied for the post, perhaps because he had had enough of the disagreements with his colleagues in the West Riding and felt that, in Birmingham, he would be freer to work in the way he wished. And perhaps he was also attracted by the idea of moving back to his homeland, the West Midlands. Adams was duly appointed as Birmingham's second Music Adviser, remaining in the post until his retirement 13 years later in 1975.

Upon his appointment in Birmingham, Stanley Adams continued to develop the tradition of children's choral music that had been established by his predecessor Desmond MacMahon. Rodney Newton, whose recollection of MacMahon was referred to in Chapter 1, spoke to me about his participation as a school pupil in Stanley Adams's first Schools Music Festival at Birmingham Town Hall in 1962 – only a few months after Adams's return to the city. Newton explained that, although the event was co-ordinated by Adams, the children's choir was trained by his Moseley Grammar School protégé Roy Massey (who also played organ in the performance), and the conductor in the concert was Douglas Guest (who was shortly to become organist and choirmaster at Westminster Abbey). Accompaniment was provided by the CBSO and the programme included a performance of Vaughan Williams's *Hodie* cantata.

Jeffrey Skidmore, who was to become Director of the internationally known Ex Cathedra choir, recalled that some of his earliest musical experiences, as a school pupil in Birmingham during the 1960s, included singing in the Grammar Schools Choral Festivals at Birmingham Town Hall under the direction of Stanley Adams. Skidmore told me that, in addition to Adams, the conductors at these events included some of the leading choral conductors of the time, such as Christopher Robinson (who was conductor of the City of Birmingham Choir) and Vernon Handley. In 1963 Rita Porzi, a 9-year-old pupil from Anderton Park Junior School in the Sparkhill area of Birmingham, took part in the Junior Schools Music Festival at Birmingham Town Hall. As part of my research for this book, I met up with Porzi who was, by then, Deputy Head of Barnet Music Service in North London. She still vividly recalled the songs that she had performed, under the direction of Stanley Adams, at Birmingham Town Hall 55 years earlier: 'Lilliburlero', 'My Love is a Rose' and Holst's 'I Vow to Thee my Country'. 'This was my first-ever visit to the Town Hall,' said Porzi, 'and my first experience of singing in a massed choir. It was an amazing occasion and I can still remember the feeling of excitement.'

Keith Allen, who was later to become Head of the Birmingham Music Service, described to me his first encounter with Stanley Adams. In 1963, Allen was on a teaching practice placement at a school in Erdington in North Birmingham, as part of his Certificate in Education course at the City of Birmingham College of Education. 'I saw Stanley Adams in the school hall one day,' said Allen, 'directing a massed choir of kids, and giving them an experience they'd never had before. The excitement of this made me think that, although I was a Londoner, I'd quite like to stay in Birmingham to start my teaching career.' So Allen got in touch with Adams who duly arranged an interview, following which Allen was placed in a pool of classroom music teachers and then appointed as Head of Music at Hartfield Crescent School from September 1964.

In addition to continuing the tradition of choral music for Birmingham schoolchildren, Adams was determined to do something that had not happened in the city up to that time, which was to create an orchestra for children to play in, just as he had done in the West Riding of Yorkshire a few years earlier. So, in the autumn of 1964, Adams held the first rehearsal of the newly formed Birmingham Schools' Symphony Orchestra (BSSO). Initially the BSSO was made up mainly of the pupils of private teachers, plus pupils from some of the city's grammar schools that bought in instrumental music teaching on a private basis. Probably the two schools with the highest representation in the BSSO at its first rehearsals were the prestigious, direct-grant King Edward's School in Edgbaston, and Moseley Grammar School, whose former music master Stanley Adams (Figure 2.1) was now the BSSO's conductor. One of the founder members of the orchestra in 1964, who would eventually go on to occupy a senior teaching position within the Birmingham Music Service, was Moseley Grammar School pupil Richard Worth, who shared the leadership of the orchestra with another pupil. 'Our music teacher at school was Barry Draycott,' said Worth, 'a well-known composer, conductor and organist, who had a long association with the London College of Music. He wanted us to make music and was very keen that Moseley Grammar School should be part of the birth of instrumental playing which was taking place in the city at that time.' So Richard Worth started having violin lessons at school and then, very quickly, found himself playing in the BSSO.

Figure 2.1: Stanley Adams conducting a rehearsal of the Birmingham Schools' Symphony Orchestra, *c.*1969 (Photo: Matt Chambers)

Also in 1964, with a view to creating a larger pool of players who could be drawn upon to join the BSSO, Adams began to introduce instrumental music teaching into Birmingham schools – appointing a small number of full-time, salaried, visiting teachers employed by the city council. In other words, he began to create the team of teachers that became known as the Birmingham Music Service and which now, at the time of writing, totals nearly 300 people. Keith Allen told me that, soon after starting his job as Head of Music at Hartfield Crescent School in 1964, he received a visit from Stanley Adams who asked him if he would like a brass teacher at the school. 'So John Lewis started coming along for an hour a week,' said Allen, 'bringing with him a few trumpets and trombones. The team of instrumental teachers was just starting off at that time and, as far as I can remember, there were just four of them: Dot Hier teaching violin, Louise Burrowes teaching cello (she was co-author of a leading series of cello tutor books at the time), Paul Griffiths teaching the flute and John Lewis teaching brass.' Another teacher who received a similar visit from Adams around the same time was Lewis Coley, Head of Maths and Music at Primrose Hill Junior School who, many years later, was to become the city's Schools Adviser with responsibility for music. Coley recalled that Adams suggested the introduction of violin and cello teaching at Primrose Hill, but that brass or woodwind teaching would not be available, because playing these instruments could cause damage to the lungs of young children!

In the summer of 1965, the BSSO gave their first-ever public performance – in the hall of Queensbridge School, Kings Heath. Adams's choice of venue for the orchestra's debut performance was an inspired one since Queensbridge School hall was considered to have the best acoustics of any school hall in Birmingham, and for this reason it was, reportedly, sometimes used by the CBSO for recording sessions. Richard Worth described the performance as being 'more like an open rehearsal than a concert' and said that the orchestra's work at that time consisted of playing 'mainly straightforward arrangements, and not at a very high standard'. Within a few months of this inaugural performance, however, the BSSO were to give their first performance at Birmingham Town Hall, taking part in the 1965 Schools' Christmas Concert. On this occasion the BSSO provided accompaniment for carols being sung by the 300-strong Junior Choir, made up of children from junior schools across the city, and the 50-strong Birmingham Schools' Choir, comprising specially selected secondary school pupils. So now, just over a year since its formation, the BSSO was well and truly established, having taken over the role previously occupied by the CBSO in providing accompaniment on such occasions. This was the first Birmingham Town Hall concert to be performed entirely by schoolchildren, establishing a pattern that was to continue in the years and decades ahead.

In 1966 there was, apparently, a falling out between Stanley Adams and the management of the CBSO, resulting from the CBSO's decision, at short notice, to cancel a school visit that they had already committed to. As a result of this, Adams decided to sever all links with the CBSO with immediate effect. Such a reaction from Adams was consistent with the description of him given by a CBSO player who knew him at the time: 'Stanley was blunt and efficient, with a bad temper – a rough diamond!' The reaction was also consistent with Adams's failure to resolve professional disagreements with his colleagues in the West Riding a few years earlier. So, buoyed up by the BSSO's recent, successful performance at the Town Hall, Adams decided that, from that point onwards, the BSSO would continue to replace the CBSO at future schools' choral events. Following Adams's decision to break the 30-year link between the local authority and the CBSO, Birmingham would have to wait another 20 years for the appointment of Linda Gilbert as General Inspector for Music, before this hugely valuable partnership would be restored. In order, however, to provide accompaniment when more challenging repertoire was being performed, and to replace the CBSO in their role of giving performances in schools, Adams formed the Birmingham Festival Orchestra, made up of teachers and freelance musicians. Rodney Newton recalled playing timpani in the Birmingham Festival Orchestra in a performance of *Hiawatha's Wedding Feast* at the Town Hall in the late 1960s. And my brother, Terry Loane, while a music student at the University of Birmingham, played percussion in yet another performance of that piece under Adams's baton in 1971. Terry recollected that, although it was a good concert, Adams (like his predecessor Desmond MacMahon) did not appear to enjoy the best of relationships with the orchestral players. The orchestra's other percussionist – a freelance, professional musician – had an altercation about payment with Adams in the stage wing immediately before the concert started, refusing to go on stage until the matter had been resolved in his favour.

After three years as Head of Music at Hartfield Crescent School, Keith Allen decided that he would like to specialize in instrumental music teaching so, in 1967, he joined the recently formed instrumental team as a clarinet teacher. 'By that time,' said Allen, 'the service had grown: the Woodwind Department now included an oboe specialist, a bassoon specialist, a flute specialist, and myself teaching the clarinet. The saxophone was not taught at that time, because it wasn't considered to be a serious musical instrument.'

We learnt earlier in this chapter about Rita Porzi who, in 1963, took part in the Junior Schools Music Festival at Birmingham Town Hall. Four years later, after her transfer to Duddeston Manor Bilateral School, Rita attained a high score in the Bentley Music Aptitude Test (a system of testing devised by Arnold Bentley in the 1960s, widely used at the time, and based on the now discredited notion that a child's level of musical ability is fixed and measurable). Accordingly, Rita Porzi was invited to start clarinet lessons at the school with Keith Allen, who was now in his first year of teaching for the Music Service. 'I'd learnt the descant recorder at primary school,' said Porzi, 'but neither my parents nor I had a clue what a clarinet was until after my first lesson, when I brought the instrument home to practise on.' Her progress on the instrument was such, however, that after only one year of tuition she was playing in the BSSO. Porzi told me that she considered herself extremely fortunate to have had such musical opportunities while still at school. One of the highlights, she told me, was attending the BSSO's first-ever residential trip, which was to Butlin's Holiday Camp in Minehead in 1971. When Rita Porzi joined the BSSO in 1968 she was part of a small minority within the orchestra, coming as she did from a school that was not a grammar school, and which was situated in one of the poorer areas of the city. But, according to Porzi, by the time she left in 1972, the orchestra was increasingly populated by pupils who had started off their lessons with Music Service teachers in non-selective schools in different areas of the city.

Figure 2.2: The Birmingham Schools' Symphony Orchestra woodwind section rehearsing at Portland Road School, with the orchestra's woodwind tutor Keith Allen seated by the window, *c.*1969 (Photo: Matt Chambers)

At the same time as becoming the Music Service's clarinet teacher in 1967, Keith Allen also started to work on Saturday mornings as woodwind tutor for the BSSO (Figure 2.2). His description of the repertoire being tackled by the orchestra at that time shows how much the standard of playing had developed since the BSSO had been formed three years earlier. 'We did ambitious programmes,' said Allen, 'which included Britten's *Young Person's Guide to the Orchestra*, Sibelius's *Finlandia* and Dvořák's *New World Symphony*.' Allen went on to explain that, right from the start of the BSSO in the 1960s, many musicians emerged from the orchestra who went on to forge extremely successful careers as professional musicians. One such player was Margaret Faultless who, as a teenager, was leader of the BSSO and whose work, at the time of writing, includes being co-leader of the Orchestra of the Age of Enlightenment and leader of Jeffrey Skidmore's Ex Cathedra period-instrument orchestra.

In 1967, upon graduating from the Royal Academy of Music, Peter Bridle took up the post of Head of Music at St Thomas Aquinas Grammar

School in Birmingham. 'When I arrived there,' said Bridle, 'there were just two visiting instrumental teachers from the Music Service – a violin teacher and a brass teacher, both of whom were brilliant.' But Bridle was determined to have more instrumental teaching at the school, in order to start a school orchestra, so he quickly got in touch with Stanley Adams. 'I was told there were no more teachers available,' said Bridle, 'so I said to Stanley, "If I suggested some teachers to you, could you then take them on as hourly-paid staff?"' Adams agreed to this suggestion so, in this way, Bridle was able to quickly build up a full, handpicked team of instrumental teachers for his school, including some CBSO players such as percussionist Annie Oakley. And, at the same time, Bridle was also helping to build up the team of sessional, hourly-paid teachers within the Music Service. 'There were some tremendous, inspirational teachers working for the Music Service at that time,' said Bridle, 'and they were producing some great young players in schools.' Towards the end of the 1960s, according to Keith Allen, 'Stanley Adams suddenly realized that he'd created the top of the pyramid – the BSSO – but he now needed layers underneath to support it.' So the Music Service's structure of Central Ensembles began to develop with the formation of the Birmingham Schools' Junior String Orchestra, directed by Dot Hier, and the Birmingham Schools' Training Orchestra, directed by Peter Bridle – in order to better prepare young musicians for entry to the BSSO. And in September 1970 the Birmingham Schools' Wind Band was created, with Keith Allen as its conductor. In July 1971 – less than a year after its formation – the wind band was to take part in the first-ever National Festival of Music for Youth performance, at the Lyceum Theatre, London. The ensemble subsequently changed its name to the Birmingham Schools' Wind Orchestra and, under the direction of Keith Allen for over twenty years, established itself as one of the country's leading youth wind orchestras, competing successfully at national festivals, touring abroad, and giving powerful performances of challenging, contemporary repertoire.

On 10 February 2017 I visited Birmingham's Symphony Hall to hear a programme of Cole Porter songs performed by four singers with accompaniment from the CBSO, conducted by Roderick Dunk. In the course of the evening, Dunk explained to the audience that working with that orchestra was a very special experience for him because the CBSO was the first live orchestra he had ever heard in his life. Apparently, when Dunk was a pupil at Our Lady and St Rose of Lima Junior School in Birmingham in the mid-1960s, the CBSO string section visited the school to give a performance, and that was the moment that sparked off his lifelong commitment to music. When I met up with Dunk some 50 years after that school visit, at the beautifully restored café at London's St Pancras Station, he took up the story from that point: 'The excitement of hearing the sound of a live string section stayed with me, so when I transferred to St Thomas Aquinas Grammar School in 1967, I decided to have lessons on the double bass. Within a few weeks,' said Dunk, 'I was playing in the School Orchestra, run by Peter Bridle who had just started teaching at the school. Peter completely inspired me – it was because of him that I got the conducting bug at the age of 11 and, from that point, I knew that music was going to be my life.' Dunk then became a regular attender at CBSO concerts at Birmingham Town Hall and, while he was still a teenager, started putting orchestras together, made up of his own friends, to perform in public concerts. Dunk's recollection of a precise moment when his passion for music was ignited, through hearing live musical performance, is echoed by other people whose stories are told in this book. It also accords with my own vivid memory of Mr Rodham, my school music teacher, walking into the classroom during my first week at grammar school (also in 1967) and performing Acker Bilk's 'Stranger on the Shore' on the clarinet. It was from that moment that I knew I wanted to be a jazz clarinettist and, at the time of writing, I continue to perform 'Stranger on the Shore' regularly at professional musical engagements.

Like Rita Porzi, Roderick Dunk found himself playing in the BSSO after just one year of instrumental lessons at school. 'I was whisked into "Stan's Band", as we used to call it,' said Dunk. 'I think they must have been desperate for double bass players.' Speaking about his recollections of the BSSO during the late 1960s and early 1970s, Dunk said, 'The standard of playing was pretty good, and we tackled some challenging repertoire like Brahms's Symphony No. 4 and Walton's *Crown Imperial* march.' Like Rita Porzi, Dunk also took part in the BSSO's first residential trip – to Butlin's at Minehead. 'The orchestra rehearsed all day, every day on that trip,' he said, 'and it was a wonderful experience.' And in 1972, Dunk took part in a memorable performance of Elgar's *Enigma Variations* at the Royal Festival Hall in London. 'I remember being part of a small deputation from the orchestra,' he said, 'who met the former Labour cabinet minister Barbara Castle at a reception during the interval.' Shortly after that performance, Dunk left the BSSO when he went to study at the Birmingham School of Music, but he came back to take part in the orchestra's first two foreign visits – to Hamburg in 1973 where the orchestra performed at the Laeiszhalle, and to Berlin in 1974 where they performed at the Berliner Philharmonie. Dunk told me he was aware that the BSSO was always regarded as being 'slightly in the shadow of the Leicestershire Schools' Symphony Orchestra', which, at the time, was regarded as England's premier youth orchestra. 'But, of course,' said Dunk, 'the Leicestershire orchestra had been going a lot longer than us and, as I remember it, by the time I left in 1972, we weren't far behind them!' After concluding his studies at the Birmingham School of Music, Dunk went on to work as a professional double bass player with orchestras in London before ending up as one of the country's leading and most versatile conductors, particularly well known for his long association with the BBC Concert Orchestra.

Dunk described Stanley Adams as 'a legend – such a powerfully driven individual. There was not a hint of democracy about his regime. It was like a kingdom of which he was the king. He was definitely the boss, and everything was always exactly the way he said it would be. Under the surface,' said Dunk, 'he had a kind and slightly cheeky nature which the kids saw, but the staff only saw the strict, authoritarian side of the man.' Dunk recalled a BSSO rehearsal where things were not going well in the brass section. Adams called out to the orchestra's brass tutor Vernon Briggs, 'I'm sorry Mr Briggs, this is just not good enough.' But then Adams looked at the children and gave them a wink. 'So his relationship with the kids,' said Dunk, 'was rather like an uncle, but his relationship with the staff was very different.'

In addition to Stanley Adams's work as a conductor, Roderick Dunk also remembered him as a very accomplished pianist. The parents' fundraising organization, Friends of the Birmingham Schools' Orchestras, established by Adams, used to organize regular recitals at the Martineau Teachers' Centre in which Music Service staff took part. Apparently pupils regularly attended these recitals as members of the audience, and Dunk described as 'breathtaking' a performance of cello sonatas by Rachmaninov and Brahms given by cello teacher Louise Burrowes, accompanied by Stanley Adams. And, according to Dunk, pupils from the BSSO sometimes took part in the recitals, performing solo pieces – again accompanied by Stanley Adams on the piano. 'These were fantastic experiences for everyone concerned,' said Dunk. 'We were so lucky to have such brilliant musicians teaching us.'

Roderick Dunk told me that, without the work of the Birmingham Music Service, he never would have become a professional musician. 'My parents came from a modest background,' he said. 'They never would have been able to pay for music lessons or for an instrument. So without the Music Service I never would have got started and, when I look back at my contemporaries in the BSSO, for many of them it was the same story and some of them went on to make careers out of music too.'

Throughout this book there are stories of people who, like Roderick Dunk, received their first musical experiences through the Birmingham Music Service and then went on to become highly successful professional musicians. There are also examples, however, of people who were introduced to music in the same way, did not pursue careers in music but for whom, nonetheless, music became a very important part of their lives. One such person was Robert Heeks, whose introduction to music was very similar to that of Roderick Dunk. As a 7-year-old pupil at Erdington Hall Junior School in the mid-1950s, Heeks fell in love with the violin when he heard a string quartet from the CBSO giving a performance at his school. Such was the impression left by that experience that, well into his adult life, upon hearing a recording of Haydn's String Quartet Op. 17 No. 5, Heeks recognized it as the piece performed by the CBSO musicians all those years before. Unfortunately Robert Heeks's parents were not able to afford to pay for violin lessons for their son, but when he moved to King Edward VI Aston Grammar School, he had the opportunity for free lessons and, as a sixth-form pupil in 1964, he became one of the founder members of the newly formed BSSO. Heeks went on to become a very successful architect and, towards the end of his career, was responsible for designing the new music department building at his old grammar school. As an adult, he did not have time to continue his violin playing, but when he retired, in his 50s, he started having violin lessons again, began to play string quartets with groups of friends and, at the time of my meeting with him in 2016, was a member of the Telford Orchestra directed by Birmingham Music Service teacher Bob Vivian.

In 1972, in order to manage the expanding team of instrumental teachers, Stanley Adams created four Head of Department posts to which internal candidates were appointed: Dot Hier became Head of Upper Strings; Louise Burrowes became Head of Lower Strings; Keith Allen became Head of Woodwind; and Vernon Briggs became Head of Brass. And in 1973, shortly before his retirement, Adams created the new post of Assistant Music Inspector – possibly the first job of its kind in the country. To fill this post, Adams appointed Antony le Fleming who had, up to then, been Director of Music at the independent Abingdon School, and who was to go on to become a highly acclaimed composer, particularly of choral music. Le Fleming's first comment when I met up with him in the café of the Wigmore Hall in London, was, 'I very much enjoyed being based at the Martineau Teachers' Centre in Birmingham because we were so close to Edgbaston Cricket Ground – I often used to spend my lunchtimes there.' Le Fleming went on to describe the nature of his job as Assistant Music

Inspector. 'I was, basically, Stanley Adams's lackey,' he said. 'I used to follow him around, helping him when he visited schools, and I also ran courses for classroom music teachers and visited teachers in schools to give support. The way of working at the time was quite old-fashioned – things were rather slow-moving and unstructured and there wasn't much accountability.' Very quickly, however, le Fleming's outstanding skills as a musician were recognized, and made good use of, for the benefit of Birmingham's young musicians. Within months of his appointment he set up a choir of schoolchildren that accompanied the BSSO on their visit to Berlin in 1974, joining forces in a performance of Vaughan Williams's *Dona Nobis Pacem*. And, around the same time, le Fleming took over the conductorship of the Birmingham Schools' Training Orchestra. This post had become vacant because, after several years of running the orchestra, Peter Bridle had had enough. 'It was frustrating,' said Bridle, 'because Stanley's main concern was the BSSO – I couldn't get him to buy music for the Training Orchestra, and sometimes he'd turn up at a rehearsal and say, "I need so and so", because his 1st-clarinet player hadn't turned up that morning. As far as Stanley was concerned, the BSSO was what mattered, and the purpose of the Training Orchestra and the Junior String Orchestra was merely to feed players into that orchestra – I don't think he saw the wider picture.'

Also in 1973 Adams appointed a group of new, young instrumental music teachers to the Music Service, signalling a significant expansion in the organization and increasing the total number of staff to approximately thirty. A number of these went on to become extremely important members of the instrumental team in the years ahead, such as oboe teacher Alison Lancaster, violin teacher Chris Bull and brass teacher Bob Vivian. These new staff were mainly people who had studied at the Birmingham School of Music and then taken the Certificate in Education course at the City of Birmingham College of Education. 'We were very lucky,' said Bob Vivian. 'The right opportunities were there for us at the right time, so after college we just walked into a job and a number of us, like me, stayed in that job for the rest of our careers. As new, young teachers, we didn't own cars, so at the start of September we were each given a bus map and a teaching timetable. We were sent off to find our schools and were told: "See you at Christmas!" So there was hardly any support for us as newly qualified teachers – we were just left to our own devices.'

Adams – the traditionalist

In addition to running the BSSO and managing the team of instrumental teachers, Stanley Adams was also responsible for appointing and supporting classroom music teachers in Birmingham schools. In 1973 he visited Jaffray School in Erdington, in order to observe the work of my brother Brian Loane, who was approaching the end of his first year as a secondary school music teacher. Brian had recently qualified as a teacher at the University of York music department where his tutor was John Paynter – author of the groundbreaking book on creative music-making in the classroom, *Sound and Silence* (Paynter and Aston, 1970), and probably the most influential of English post-war music educators. Unsurprisingly, therefore, when Adams walked into the classroom, he found that Brian – inspired by the work of John Paynter – was leading a class of 14-year-olds in small-group composition work. Birmingham's Music Adviser was not impressed and, as a result, Brian had to wait a further twelve months before passing his probationary year. In his feedback at the end of the visit, Adams suggested to my brother that his pupils would be more gainfully employed by studying music of the great composers such as Mendelssohn, rather than composing their own music. Ignoring this advice, Brian continued to develop his work on pupil composition and went on to become one of the country's leading voices in this area of music education. While Head of Music at Boldon Comprehensive School, South Tyneside, during the early 1980s, he was a founder member of the editorial board, and a contributor of articles, for the *British Journal of Music Education*. From 1985 he worked as a Divisional Music Co-ordinator for the Inner London Education Authority (ILEA) and in 1988, as well as gaining his PhD, 'Understanding Children's Music', under the supervision of John Paynter, he was appointed Senior Lecturer in Music Education at Sunderland Polytechnic (which was soon to become the University of Sunderland). Nigel Taylor, former Head of Staffordshire Performing Arts and Chair of the Federation of Music Services, reflected on his time as a teaching practice student with Brian at Boldon Comprehensive School during the late 1970s: 'He was inspirational and visionary – one of the people who helped shape me as a music teacher and as a person'. So much for Stanley Adams's assessment at the end of Brian's probationary year.

Similarly, when Stanley Adams watched Paul Slater teaching a class of 14-year-olds at Pitmaston School and found them engaged in small-group composition work, he suggested to Slater that the pupils' time would be better spent in singing traditional English folk songs in four parts. Like Brian, Paul Slater bravely ignored the Music Adviser's advice and continued to develop his creative approach to secondary school music teaching. Slater was later appointed by the Music Service as a Consortium Music Teacher, and in this role (which will be fully explained in the next chapter) the support he gave to classroom music teachers was extremely highly valued.

So it is clear from these examples that Adams had an old-fashioned approach to classroom music teaching. He was either unaware of, or did not value, the innovative practice being developed in schools at that time as a result of the work of John Paynter and others. And his lack of willingness to learn from different, more progressive approaches was, presumably, the same characteristic that had brought him into conflict with Alec Clegg and others in the West Riding of Yorkshire some twenty years earlier. On the other hand, there can be no doubt that Adams was extremely forward looking in the way he established opportunities for instrumental lessons and orchestral playing for large numbers of young people in Birmingham. And, in so doing, he laid the foundations for the huge expansion and broadening of these opportunities that were to take place in the city under his successor Peter Davies, and which will be examined in the next chapter.

Chapter 3

An emerging philosophy

From the start of Peter Davies's career as a secondary-school music teacher in Cardiff in the 1950s, he demonstrated a passion for developing instrumental and vocal teaching, always linking this to ensemble and performance opportunities and involving the wider community including other local schools. In 1954, at the age of 25, he won the first-ever competition for orchestral conductors to be held in the UK, conducting the BBC Welsh Orchestra, which he subsequently went on to conduct in a BBC radio broadcast. Davies's career as a schoolteacher, however, was short-lived because, at the age of 27, he was appointed as Music Adviser for Montgomeryshire in Wales and, soon after that, he became Music Adviser in Southampton. In this post he was responsible for a huge development in the local authority's music provision, establishing cross-phase musical collaboration between schools and a programme of regular public performances given by a wide range of orchestras, choirs, wind bands and other ensembles.

In 1975 Peter Davies was appointed Senior Inspector for Music for Birmingham City Council, taking over from Stanley Adams upon his retirement. Davies remained in this post until his retirement in 1983, but during this relatively short period of time, he made a transformative contribution to the development of children's music in Birmingham. Davies significantly expanded and broadened the work of the instrumental teaching team, as well as the range of musical ensembles available for young people to play in. He introduced innovations that set the Music Service apart from most other English music services at that time, such as the teaching of instruments outside the Western symphonic tradition, the introduction of Suzuki violin teaching, the establishment of a team of Consortium Music Teachers whose role was to support classroom music teaching, and the appointment of a full-time music therapist. And crucially, it was under the watch of Peter Davies that a clear pedagogical philosophy began to emerge within the Music Service. As we shall see in the course of this chapter, however, certain important aspects of these developments took place in spite of, rather than because of, Peter Davies. They were often the result of teachers trying out and sharing new ideas within their schools, which had the effect, in some ways, of moving the service in the opposite direction to Peter Davies's instincts. All of these innovations – those coming from the Senior Inspector and those coming from teachers at the grassroots – were to pave the way for a new, creative ethos that was to characterize the work of the Music Service in the years ahead and well into the twenty-first century.

Peter Davies was a complex character. On the one hand, he was responsible for inspired and innovative thinking. On the other hand he was, in many respects, very much stuck in the mould of the typical post-war local-authority music adviser: the male, dictatorial, boss-like figure who perceived his main role as conductor of the youth orchestra, and whose motivation, arguably, was the prestige that stemmed from that. One Music Service teacher who worked with Peter Davies described him as 'a figure of authority'; another described him as 'not the easiest of people'; a classroom music teacher described him as 'very autocratic – leading by diktat rather than co-operation'; and other colleagues to whom I spoke used much more disparaging language. Davies expected all staff – in the Music Service and in schools – to address him as 'Mr Davies'. The Music Service Head of Brass, John Lewis, who as a fellow Welshman was on good terms with Davies, once tried addressing him as 'Peter' but, according to a colleague, 'he was quickly slapped down'. A number of instrumental music teachers told me that they felt disrespected by Davies because he often arrived late for staff meetings that he had arranged, but never apologized for having kept them waiting. As soon as Davies took over as Senior Inspector, it became clear that he and the recently appointed Assistant Music Inspector, Antony le Fleming, did not have a good relationship. According to one senior colleague at the time, 'They could barely bring themselves to speak civilly to one another, let alone work together.' Le Fleming himself said, 'things became a bit more regulated under Davies,' implying that this change in approach did not suit le Fleming. So, with few exceptions, Peter Davies was neither liked nor respected by those who worked under him. And yet, despite his poor relationships with staff, we shall see in the course of this chapter how Davies continually listened to and acted upon innovative suggestions from teachers and, in so doing, developed the Music Service into a much more creative, forward-looking organization.

In the previous chapter we heard about Richard Worth who, as a school pupil in the mid-1960s, was a founder member and co-leader of the newly formed BSSO. Having left school in 1966 to study violin at the London College of Music, Worth returned to the Midlands three years later in order to take up the post of music teacher at John Willmott School in Sutton Coldfield. In 1975, after several years in this post, Worth found himself responsible for running the music department at John Willmott, since Head of Music Peter Tidmarsh was away from school, studying on a sabbatical year. The school had just moved from Warwickshire County Council into Birmingham City Council as part of the 1974 local government reorganization, and Worth had heard that a new Senior Inspector for Music had just been appointed in Birmingham. So he decided to invite Peter Davies, the new Senior Inspector, to visit the school. 'Partly,' said Worth, 'this was because I was concerned about the quality of one of the school pianos and was hoping for a replacement.' So, when Davies made his visit, Worth mentioned the faulty piano and, very soon afterwards, a brand-new replacement piano was duly delivered to the school by the education authority. 'Apparently this was Peter Davies's first visit to a Birmingham school,' said Worth. 'I think he saw the good work that was going on, and wanted to make an impression at the start of his tenure in Birmingham – so we were lucky!' This swift delivery of a replacement piano is reminiscent of Desmond MacMahon's provision of a set of chromatic glockenspiels to Michael Lloyd many years earlier, as described in Chapter 1 – both, arguably, examples of local authority patronage. Indeed, Richard Worth, referring to the new piano and to the local authority funding that enabled both Peter Tidmarsh and himself to benefit from sabbatical study leave, commented that 'patronage was rife'. Worth went on to say that 'Peter Davies was someone who was treated with great deference. Some respected him and others loathed him but, either way, he was a powerful and influential person with a budget which he could use as he saw fit.' Such patronage was certainly an important feature of local authority music provision during the twentieth century. While, on the one hand, this behaviour might be considered unfair or even corrupt, it could also be argued that the high level of unaccountable autonomy enjoyed by music advisers at the time was an essential factor in the development of flourishing, post-war English music services.

Many have suggested that, as with his predecessor Stanley Adams, Davies's overriding concern as Senior Inspector was the success and status of the BSSO, and that in his eyes – notwithstanding his innovations in other areas – the main purpose of the Music Service was to provide the necessary support for that orchestra. It has also been suggested that for Davies, and for other music advisers at that time, a principal purpose of the local authority children's orchestra was to provide a vehicle for the self-aggrandizement of its conductor. It could be considered that, for someone who enjoyed the acclaim attached to being a conductor, but who did not have sufficient expertise to work with professional orchestras, the role of music adviser (or senior inspector) provided a perfect opportunity. An instrumental teacher who worked for the Music Service at the time said to me, 'Peter Davies's main interest was in being the conductor of the BSSO and seeing his name in lights. He once told all of us at a staff meeting, "Your job is to produce players for my orchestra."' John Clemson, a cello teacher appointed early in Davies's tenure, who later went on to become Head of the Music Service, said, 'As far as Stanley Adams and Peter Davies were concerned, the main purpose of the Music Service was to produce a symphony orchestra for them to conduct.' Clemson went on to explain that it was for this reason, in his view, that instrumental teaching was initially concentrated in the King Edward VI grammar schools and schools in middle-class areas of the city like Moseley, Hall Green and Sutton Coldfield. 'This meant,' he said, 'that teachers could quickly get children up to the required standard for the BSSO.' This suggestion was, presumably, based on the assumption that children at grammar schools, or from middle-class areas, would be more likely to enjoy the parental and/or financial support that would facilitate their progress as musicians. According to Clemson, however, there were some interesting exceptions to this pattern of provision: 'Headteachers who had places on the organizing committee of the Junior Schools Music Festival often had instrumental teaching in their schools – even in the poorer areas, where no other schools nearby did.' The suggestion that certain schools might be favoured because their headteachers contributed to the organizational work of the Music Service could, perhaps, be considered as yet another example of the culture of patronage referred to earlier. Another instrumental teacher working for the Music Service at that time said to me: 'It was entirely up to Peter Davies as to which schools had instrumental teaching – very often it was just down to which headteachers or heads of music were "in with" the Senior Inspector.'

Unlike his predecessor Stanley Adams, Davies was not generally regarded by his colleagues as a good conductor. One teacher who worked with him at the time said, 'He had delusions about his abilities as a conductor – he wasn't actually that great!' Another told me that Davies would typically drill the BSSO in rehearsing the same repertoire for month after month, 'until any spontaneity in the performance had long expired'. Despite these concerns, there can be no doubt that, under his baton, the BSSO continued to develop its profile in the city, with an increasing number of foreign visits being made and a huge strengthening of the esteem in which the orchestra was held by the local authority. Many years later, in programme notes written for the BSSO's 25th Anniversary Concert in 1990, Peter Davies described the crucial role played by the local authority over the years in supporting the BSSO and the wider work of the Music Service:

> The partnership embraces more than that of conductor and players. It includes parents, teachers, schools, support organizations such as the Friends of Birmingham Schools' Orchestras and the Local Education Authority [LEA]. The confidence of the LEA in the outcome is paramount, if the future is to be assured. From 1975 until his untimely death, Councillor Neil Scrimshaw, Chair of the Education Committee, played a vital part in this development. He not only attended virtually every concert, including those in Frankfurt, but also enhanced the future of music by support for the Junior School of Music and increasing the number of key music appointments in the Music Service. (Davies, 1990)

The Junior School of Music, referred to above, was a scheme instigated by Davies whereby especially talented young musicians would attend the Birmingham School of Music on Saturday afternoons (after their Saturday morning ensemble rehearsals) for individual instrumental lessons with Birmingham School of Music teachers. Like the expanding structure of Music Service ensembles, which had started under Stanley Adams, the purpose of the Junior School of Music, according to a senior member of staff at the time, was to give young musicians the best possible preparation for membership of the BSSO.

Developing pedagogy

Following the expansion of the instrumental teaching team under Stanley Adams in 1973, Peter Davies went on to increase the size of the team still further in 1976, appointing a large number of new, young teachers. These included a number of staff who were to play an important role in the future development of the Music Service, such as cellist John Clemson, violinist Jeremy Blunt, who a few years later would be appointed Head of Upper Strings, cellist Olive Goodborn, who was the service's new Head of Lower Strings, and French horn teacher Richard Duckett. A number of these new teachers, including Clemson, Blunt and Duckett, had recently gained their Certificate in Education (CertEd) qualifications at the City of Birmingham College of Education (which, in 1975, became part of Birmingham Polytechnic). In 1977, shortly after these appointments were made and in order to help manage the increased number of instrumental teachers, Davies created the new post, Head of Instrumental Staff – to which Head of Woodwind Keith Allen was promoted.

When, many years later, I interviewed John Clemson, as part of my research for this book, he told me that, despite Allen's appointment as Head of Instrumental Staff, Peter Davies continued to run the Music Service, albeit through Allen. 'Peter Davies, in practice, was still very much the boss,' said Clemson. And when I asked John Clemson to reflect more generally on his first impressions of the Music Service at the time of his appointment in 1976, he told me, 'It was still quite a small team and the culture was far from collegiate – there was very little sharing of ideas, and no professional development or observation of one another's teaching.' Clemson then echoed the exact words of Bob Vivian, as reported in the last chapter: 'You were very much left to your own devices.'

And Richard Duckett, recollecting his impressions of the Music Service around the same time, told me, 'It was a group of people who regarded themselves, first and foremost, as professional musicians rather than teachers, whereas today it would probably be the other way around. For example, when I did my CertEd teaching practice with the service, the brass teacher who was supervising me had just been away from work for a fortnight, because he was playing on a cruise liner.' According to Duckett, 'There was nothing particularly inventive going on at that time. It was a case of going to the practice room, usually with an individual pupil, getting out the music stand and the *Tune a Day* tutor book – it was all rather stultified. And the only guidance Peter Davies ever gave us was that all instrumental lessons should be of 30-minutes duration and one-to-one.'

Duckett went on to say, 'There were certain things I couldn't change in my teaching, such as the room I was required to teach in – it might be the medical room or the PE changing room, which felt rather demeaning – or the poor quality of instruments the pupils were using. But the one thing I could change was what the pupils were actually doing in their lessons.' So, from the mid-1970s onwards, Duckett started to pioneer new approaches to instrumental teaching that were to have a huge impact on the work of the Music Service in the years ahead, as well as having a significant influence at a national level – through his publications and through training sessions he led for instrumental teachers all over the UK. I believe that Duckett's incorporation of playing by ear, improvising and composing as integral parts of his teaching had a profound effect on the culture of the Music Service as an organization: some teachers followed his example and began working in similar ways, but even those teachers who chose not to do so were influenced to the extent that they grew to respect, rather than look down on, these approaches to teaching. Such a positive response from colleagues would have been unimaginable in many other music services at that time (and even at the time of writing) where, for work to be valued, it had to be based on musical notation, rooted in the Western symphonic tradition and linked to graded examinations. Part of the reason for the respect in which Duckett was held was that his creative approaches did not detract in any way from his ability to develop pupils to the most advanced levels of playing. Throughout his career he taught pupils who progressed through the Music Service ensembles, attended music college or university, and then pursued successful careers as professional musicians.

It was at Greenmeadow Primary School and Hill West Middle School that Duckett began to experiment with group instrumental teaching, because he was becoming convinced that this was much more effective than one-to-one teaching. Since this approach, however, contravened Peter Davies's diktat that all instrumental teaching should be one-to-one, Duckett prepared official timetables for display in his schools, indicating a succession of individual lessons. 'But in fact,' said Duckett, 'I was teaching pupils in groups for longer periods of time.' (During the 1990s, by which time group teaching was officially endorsed by the Music Service, I remember seeing a teacher doing the exact opposite of this, in order to return illicitly to the one-to-one approach: four pupils had arrived together for a scheduled half-hour group lesson, but each pupil in turn ended up receiving an individual seven-minute lesson while the other three children gazed out of the classroom window!) An indicator of the great effectiveness of Duckett's group-teaching approach was the fact that many of his pupils who were taught in this way went on to become high-level performers, such as Steven James who started off having group lessons with Duckett at Greenmeadow, and then went on to pass his Grade VIII examination on the French horn at the age of 13 and to become the principal horn player in the BSSO. The ensemble arrangements written by Duckett for his early experimentation with group instrumental teaching were to form the basis for the hugely successful *Team Brass* (Duckett, 1988) series of tutor books written by Duckett, and first published by International Music Publications in 1988. (Thirty years later, at the time of writing, the *Team* series – which now also includes books for woodwind and strings – is still among the best-selling of instrumental music tutor books.)

In the early days of local authority instrumental music teaching there had been a largely unchallenged assumption that one-to-one teaching was the ideal method but that often, for financial reasons, it was necessary to compromise by teaching pupils in groups. I recall that, when I worked as an instrumental teacher for the Inner London Education Authority Music Service in the early 1980s – a service that, in many respects, was very forward looking – there was a scheme whereby particularly talented pupils being taught in groups could be nominated by their teachers for 30-minute individual lessons instead. This was based on the belief – misguided, in my opinion – that better progress would be made in this way. And, at the time of writing, some music services operate charging policies whereby parents can opt to pay a higher rate in order for their children to receive individual lessons – again reinforcing the view that group learning is a second-best option. I suspect that such assumptions may be partly based on the personal learning experiences of music service teachers and managers. Many of them may have started off by having one-to-one lessons at school or with a private teacher, and then continued to have individual lessons at music college or university. And because that method worked well for them, this may have led them to believe that it would also be the best method for their pupils. My own view, however, is that group instrumental teaching is infinitely more effective, for two main reasons. First of all, music is essentially a social activity – the most important skills we need to develop as musicians are concerned with collaborating musically with others and these skills, I believe, can only be learnt in group situations. Secondly, it is now generally accepted that, regardless of subject area, people learn best through interaction with their peers – where there are opportunities for exchange of ideas and learning one from another. I would suggest that the tradition of individual tuition is almost unique to instrumental music. In nearly every other subject area – whether it is a child learning mathematics at school or a young adult training to be an airline pilot or a surgeon – learning in groups is the norm. I once made this observation at a training course I was leading on group teaching, whereupon a teacher suggested to me that learning to drive a car was an example of one-to-one teaching. I replied that this was an excellent example of group learning since the most important aspect of driving a car was concerned with awareness of other road users – one could never become a safe driver through practising only on deserted roads, just as one could never develop as a musician without playing music alongside others.

In addition to his innovative work on group teaching, within months of starting his career with the Birmingham Music Service, Richard Duckett had begun to explore strategies for integrating instrumental music teaching much more fully into the life of his schools – a commitment that, according to Duckett, was probably rooted in his earlier, short experience as a classroom teacher. So he began organizing his pupils into ensembles to give regular school performances and, at Stanmore Secondary School, for example, he began to work closely with the school music teacher – making musical arrangements so that groups of instrumental pupils could accompany the singing of hymns during assembly, as well as making arrangements of television theme music which was, of course, a great motivator for pupils. Again, these ways of working were to have a huge influence on the future ethos of the Music Service.

In order to identify pupils for tuition, Duckett started, in a number of his schools, to present demonstrations of brass instruments to whole classes of children, followed by the opportunity for all of those children, working in large groups, to try out the instruments. This resulted in a hugely increased interest in brass tuition, meaning that in some schools, in order to meet this demand, he would be teaching much larger groups of pupils and yet there was still a waiting list for lessons. I believe that Duckett's experience in these schools demonstrated an important principle, which is that the more instrumental music teaching that takes place in a school, and the more it is integrated into the life of a school, the more popular and successful that teaching becomes. Success breeds success and there is, I would suggest, no upper limit to the number of pupils who can benefit from instrumental tuition. This principle is borne out in many private schools where the majority of pupils learn to play musical instruments, and in many state primary schools that, in more recent years, have adopted the whole-class Wider Opportunities model which will be explained in Chapter 7.

Figure 3.1: Centre Sounds Woodwind performing in a Birmingham junior school, *c*.1985. From left to right: Julie Schroder, Richard Reakes, John Dawson, Roger Tempest, Fiona Biddulph, the author, David Robinson (drawing by a school pupil, Clinton Odell Scott, who was present in the audience).

So positive was the feedback from schools on Richard Duckett's whole-class demonstrations that Peter Davies decided to use this as a model for what he called the Birmingham Brass Chorale – a group of brass teachers, led by Head of Brass John Lewis, who started making visits to primary schools to deliver presentations. Davies then extended this model, introducing it to the Woodwind and Strings departments, and it became known as Centre Sounds (Figure 3.1) – a project that continued to thrive until the closing years of the twentieth century when funding was no longer available to support it. Duckett later observed, however, that in setting up the Birmingham Brass Chorale and then Centre Sounds, Davies was missing the main point of his demonstrations. 'I was trying to break down the elitism associated with instrumental music,' said Duckett, 'by broadening the access and by integrating music more into the life of a school.' But, according to Duckett, Peter Davies saw Centre Sounds merely as a way of getting professional musicians to perform to children and explain to them how the instruments worked. 'So we often found ourselves delivering Centre Sounds in schools where there was no instrumental teaching taking place,' said Duckett, 'so there was no opportunity for the children to take up the instruments afterwards.' My own feeling, upon joining the Music Service in the mid-1980s, was that there was a strong element of tokenism in the Centre Sounds project: at a time when instrumental teaching was still concentrated mainly in the middle-class suburbs of Birmingham, we were sending the message to schools in less advantaged areas that, although their children did not qualify for the experience of learning to play musical instruments, at least they were lucky enough to hear the instruments being played by professional musicians. It was actually a return to the model of performance visits to schools by CBSO players, which Desmond MacMahon had established in the 1940s and was subsequently brought to an end by Stanley Adams.

In the early 1970s violinist Denyse Hyett, specialist music teacher at Ley Hill County First School in Sutton Coldfield, had been reading about the groundbreaking work of Japanese violin teacher Shinichi Suzuki, which was based on the principle of teaching children to play music by ear rather than from written notation. Inspired by this idea, Hyett went to watch Suzuki giving demonstration lessons during a visit to Britain and then set about teaching the violin at Ley Hill, basing her teaching on this approach. So Hyett's violin pupils attended their lessons in small groups, with their parents present in the room, and they learnt to play by ear, without any reference to musical notation. For a teacher to work in this way at a state school in England during the 1970s was hugely innovative. And crucial to Hyett's work was the great encouragement she received from Peter Davies who presented her with a book on Suzuki teaching, as a gift, to support her in her project. One example of the great success of Hyett's Suzuki teaching at Ley Hill was her violin pupil Helen Feltrup who, as well as playing in the BSSO, went on to become the leader of Britain's National Youth Orchestra.

In 1979 Peter Davies appointed the young, newly qualified Heather Doust as a full-time violin teacher for the Music Service. Shortly after starting her new post, Doust visited Ley Hill in order to watch Denyse Hyett's Suzuki teaching. So inspired was Doust by what she saw that she soon started to undertake training herself as a Suzuki teacher, attending the British Suzuki Institute's weekend and holiday courses in Hitchin, Hertfordshire, during the early 1980s, and going on to become a fully qualified Suzuki violin teacher. Peter Davies was quick to acknowledge the value of Doust's work by including groups of her Suzuki pupils in the Junior Schools Music Festival concerts at Birmingham Town Hall. And very soon, her outstanding work in this area was to be recognized not only within the Birmingham Music Service but also at a national level.

As with Richard Duckett's innovative work on playing by ear and improvising, Doust's Suzuki teaching had a huge impact on the culture of the Music Service. Although it was not until much later that large numbers of teachers started to follow her example in undertaking Suzuki training, her work very quickly began to have the effect of legitimizing approaches to instrumental teaching that were not centred on the reading of musical notation. It was seen that, although her pupils were being taught in a manner considered to be unorthodox at the time, they were developing into high-level players, occupying places in the top Central Ensembles, and some of them going on to become successful professional musicians.

Denyse Hyett, who had introduced Suzuki teaching in Birmingham schools, went on to become one of the city's Consortium Music Teachers – a role that will be explained later in this chapter. And then, in the late 1980s, she moved to North Yorkshire to take on the post of Head of Harrogate Music Centre (which, as we have seen, had been established some thirty years earlier by Stanley Adams while he was Music Adviser in the West Riding). When I met up with Hyett many years later, she contrasted the response to Suzuki teaching in Birmingham with the response she met with when supporting the same teaching methods in Harrogate. 'Although there were some committed Suzuki teachers in North Yorkshire,' she said, 'the work was much less successful than it had been in Birmingham because many teachers were sceptical about any approach which was not centred on the teaching of musical notation. There wasn't the same open-mindedness that I'd found in Birmingham.' And, according to Hyett, this scepticism was shared by many parents too. 'Typically,' she said, 'a parent might ask, "Why hasn't my child done her Grade 3 exam on the violin yet?" It was sometimes hard to get over to them that it didn't really matter what grade they were on – it was how well they played the violin that mattered!'

As we have seen earlier in this chapter, there was still a strong element of elitism associated with instrumental music teaching in Birmingham during the 1970s – demonstrated, for example, by the concentration of teaching in the city's middle-class areas. I believe it is also important to acknowledge, however, the extraordinarily high quality of musical experiences that Music Service teachers were providing for young people in many Birmingham schools at that time. As part of my research for this book, I met up with Alan Davis who, as well as being one of the country's leading recorder players, was Head of Music at Kings Norton Girls' School from 1971 to 1981. Davis described the 'terrific contribution' made by the seven Music Service teachers who made weekly visits to that school during the 1970s. 'They taught large numbers of pupils,' he said, 'many of whom achieved high standards of playing and over half of whom played in Music Service ensembles. And the school had a thriving orchestra and choir which were regularly involved in ambitious public performances for parents. We did an abridged version of Handel's *Messiah* and musicals such as *The Boyfriend*, where the school orchestra was augmented by members of Music Service staff, including Keith Allen on saxophone, Bob Vivian on trumpet and violinist Chris Bull leading the orchestra.' Davis also recalled concerts held at the school for pupils and parents that were presented entirely by Music Service staff, and which included performances of Mozart's Quintet for Piano and Winds and William Walton's *Façade*. And Davis spoke about the fantastic opportunities the Music Service had provided for his own children. His daughter Ruth, having received double bass lessons at Shenley Court School and progressed through the Music Service ensembles, became a professional freelance bass player whose work included playing with the London Symphony Orchestra, the Philharmonia Orchestra and the CBSO.

Breadth and diversity

During the 1960s and 1970s the work of English music services was almost exclusively concerned with the teaching of classical orchestral instruments. This was because the main purpose of instrumental music teaching, arguably, was to develop enough players to the right standard to fill places in music service youth orchestras. The year 1979, however, marked a turning point for children's music in Birmingham. Notwithstanding Peter Davies's over-riding preoccupation with the BSSO, in that year he began to broaden the work of the Music Service in ways that were unique to Birmingham and which were to lead the service in new and exciting directions.

First of all, Alan Davis from Kings Norton Girls' School approached Peter Davies to suggest the idea of forming a new Central Ensemble for recorder players. 'Peter was a bit dubious at first,' said Alan Davis, 'because music services didn't have recorder ensembles at that time. But I really wanted to do it because I was keen to put recorder on the map a bit more, and eventually Peter Davies agreed to try out the idea.' So the Birmingham Schools' Recorder Sinfonia (BSRS) was created under the direction of Alan Davis, who continued to conduct the group until his retirement 31 years later. Over that period of time, the BSRS made many appearances in the National Festival of Music for Youth at London's Southbank Centre, took part in foreign concert tours and performed a huge variety of repertoire, including first performances of many of Davis's own arrangements and compositions, which later went on to be published. In 1980, shortly after establishing the BSRS, Davis was threatened with redeployment from his post at Kings Norton Girls' School, so he approached Peter Davies to ask if he could work for the Music Service as a recorder teacher. Typically, Davies agreed to this innovative suggestion so, in 1981, Alan Davis became the Music Service's first salaried recorder teacher, mainly teaching small groups of pupils in primary schools.

Shortly after his arrival in Birmingham Peter Davies appointed jazz musician Adrian Ingram to work as a part-time, hourly-paid guitar teacher in schools – probably the first non-classical musician and the first player of a non-orchestral instrument to work for the Music Service. And in 1979, building on the success of Ingram's work, Davies took on Evan Crawford and Bryan Lester as the Music Service's first full-time, salaried guitar teachers – probably among the first guitar teachers to be employed on this basis anywhere in the country. Bryan Lester already had a well-established career as a professional musician having, for example, performed the guitar part in Mahler's Symphony No. 7 with the Hallé Orchestra under the baton of Sir John Barbirolli at Manchester's Free Trade Hall. Lester was to go on to make a huge contribution to the development of guitar teaching in Birmingham, as well as authoring some very important publications of educational guitar music. In 1982, following the successful start of his career with the Music Service, he decided to follow the example of Alan Davis and made the suggestion to Peter Davies that an advanced-level guitar group be established as one of the city's Central Ensembles. Once again, Peter Davies gave the go-ahead for this suggestion and thus was formed the Birmingham Schools' Guitar Ensemble (BSGE), which Bryan Lester continued to direct until his retirement in 1994. The BSGE was, possibly, the first music service guitar ensemble anywhere in the country and, soon after its formation, it went on to perform in high-profile concerts at Birmingham Town Hall as well as playing in the National Festival of Music for Youth at London's Royal Festival Hall. And during the 1990s the BSGE was to take part in concert tours in Hungary, as well as performing in broadcasts on BBC Radio 3 and Radio 4.

Around the same time that Bryan Lester was appointed, Peter Davies found out about Trinidadian-born Roy Jacob who was teaching steel pans and running the highly successful Maestros steel band at the Midlands Arts Centre (MAC). Since the MAC was located just around the corner from the Martineau Teachers' Centre, Davies walked over there one day to introduce himself to Jacob and, typically, signed him up there and then to take on some hourly-paid teaching for the Music Service. So Jacob started teaching steel pans at Broadway School, Calthorpe Special School and, most notably, Aston Manor School, which was soon to become Birmingham's leading school in this area of work, with a steel band in each of the school's five year-groups for young people to play in. In May 1981, an up-and-coming 16-year-old steel pans player from Wolverhampton, Norman Stewart, started assisting Jacob in his teaching work in Birmingham. Tragically, in October of that year Jacob died suddenly at the age of 50, while travelling home from a musical engagement, whereupon the young Norman Stewart immediately took over all of his teaching – at the MAC and in Birmingham schools. When I asked Stewart what it felt like to be working in schools as a teacher at the age of 16, he told me, 'My age didn't come into it. Sometimes I was teaching sixth-formers who were a year or two older than me, but I was there for a reason – to teach steel pans – and they wanted to learn.' Soon after taking over Jacob's teaching, Stewart took the Joseph Chamberlain Sixth Form College Steel Band on a concert tour in Germany, and he put together some of his strongest pupils to form the Birmingham Schools' Steel Band, to take part in the 1982 National Steel Band Festival at the Warwick Arts Centre. This was a one-off event but, by putting such a group together, Stewart was paving the way for the Birmingham Schools' Steel Band that would be created as one of the Music Service Central Ensembles a few years later. In addition to developing these opportunities for steel pans playing for Birmingham children, Peter Davies also gave great support to African-Caribbean choral music that was taking place within individual schools, such as the outstanding Handsworth Wood Girls' School Gospel Choir directed by Don Gwinnett, which was given regular opportunities to perform in high-profile Music Service concerts.

In 1962 sitar player Sneh Lata, having gained a master's degree in Indian classical instrumental music in India, moved from the Punjab to take up residence in Birmingham. From 1966 to 1974 she worked as a classroom teacher at Springfield Junior School and, from 1978, she started to teach adult-education classes at Holyhead School in Handsworth, organized through the city council's Community Education and Recreation Department. Initially this work involved teaching English as a second language, but soon Lata started to include the teaching of sitar as part of her work. In 1980 the headteacher at Holyhead School was so impressed by the results of Lata's sitar teaching that he fixed up a meeting for Lata with Peter Davies. As a result of this meeting, Davies immediately created a post for Lata as a full-time, salaried sitar teacher with the Music Service – almost certainly the first post of its kind anywhere in the country – and Lata was to remain in this post until her retirement in 1994. Initially, Lata taught sitar in primary and secondary schools – mainly in the Handsworth area where there was a large Asian population. From the outset, however, she considered it important to work with children from different communities, so her pupils included African-Caribbean and white children as well as children from Asian backgrounds. Davies attached such importance to this new area of teaching that he immediately established the Birmingham Schools' Indian Music Ensemble under Lata's direction, and this new Central Ensemble gave its debut performance in the Music Service Christmas Concert at the Town Hall in December 1980, only a few months after Lata had started her Music Service teaching. Sneh Lata had a strong commitment to the idea of fusing music from different cultural traditions, so at King Edward VI Handsworth School her sitar pupils played in the school orchestra alongside children playing Western instruments. And at a Schools' Gala Concert in the late 1980s I recall hearing the Birmingham Schools' Indian Music Ensemble performing an arrangement of 'Morning Has Broken' alongside the Birmingham Schools' Concert Orchestra.

Bernard Herrmann started his musical career playing flute and piccolo with the renowned Geraldo Orchestra in the early 1950s. From 1961 onwards he became well known through his work as Director of the BBC Northern Dance Orchestra (NDO), which broadcast daily on the radio, and Musical Director of the BBC television series *The Good Old Days*. In 1973 Herrmann moved from Manchester to Birmingham to work as a flautist with the BBC Midland Radio Orchestra, although he continued to travel back to Manchester every Sunday for live broadcasts of *The Good Old Days* until the show came to an end in 1986. Never one to miss an opportunity for spotting great talent, shortly after Herrmann arrived in Birmingham, Peter Davies took him on as an hourly-paid woodwind teacher for the Music Service. And in 1981, when Antony le Fleming left his post in Birmingham, Davies appointed Bernard Herrmann to replace him as conductor of the Birmingham Schools' Training Orchestra (BSTO). When Herrmann took over the BSTO, however, he was determined that the ensemble should establish an identity of its own and be valued in its own right, rather than being seen merely as a training ground for the BSSO. (As we have seen, it was exactly this issue that had led Peter Bridle to resign as the BSTO's conductor eight years earlier.) So Herrmann persuaded a slightly reluctant Peter Davies that the orchestra's name should be changed to Birmingham Schools' Concert Orchestra (BSCO) and that the orchestra should now include a drum kit in order to facilitate the performance of popular, as well as classical, music. Around the same time, Herrmann also persuaded Davies to allow him to establish a jazz big band as one of the Central Ensembles. Davies was insistent, however, that neither the term 'jazz' nor 'big band' should appear in the title of this new ensemble – perhaps because this would suggest a style of music of which he did not, wholeheartedly, approve. So the group became known as the Birmingham Schools' Dance Orchestra (BSDO) – probably a very appropriate choice of name since it echoed the title Northern Dance Orchestra, the band with which Herrmann was still very much associated in the public mind. Not surprisingly, given Herrmann's prestigious experience as a musical director, both the newly named BSCO and the newly formed BSDO quickly developed into highly successful ensembles that were soon to give their first performances at London's Southbank Centre as part of the National Festival of Music for Youth.

In 1980 Jeffrey Skidmore was appointed as Head of Music at John Willmott School, just as the school was opening its new, purpose-built music block, which was the first of its kind in Birmingham. 'I felt I'd landed on my feet,' said Skidmore. 'It was one of the leading secondary schools in Birmingham at the time, with an inspirational headteacher who was passionate about music.' Skidmore told me that John Willmott was seen as a flagship school at that time and it was for this reason, he believed, that the Music Service sent some of their strongest instrumental teachers to work there, including Keith Allen and Bob Vivian. 'There was wonderful collaboration between the Music Service teachers and the school,' said Skidmore. 'They always came along to our concerts to help out, and one of the highlights was when Consortium Music Teacher Paul Slater composed a pop cantata for the school choir, working alongside our Head of English who wrote the lyrics.'

Shortly after his arrival at John Willmott, Skidmore set up a school choir to complement the orchestra and wind band that were already well established at the school. So impressed was Peter Davies upon hearing John Willmott's newly formed choir, and knowing about Skidmore's extremely successful work with the Ex Cathedra choir, which he had founded over ten years earlier, in 1982 Davies asked Skidmore to set up a new, high-level, children's choir as one of the Music Service Central Ensembles. Thus was born the Birmingham Schools' Chorale, which Skidmore continued to direct until 1994 when he left his post at John Willmott in order to focus more fully on his work with Ex Cathedra.

In addition to Davies's work in increasing the number and breadth of the service's Central Ensembles, another hugely important initiative of his was the introduction of open-access Consortium Orchestras for beginner and elementary pupils. These were groups that met weekly, at the end of the school day – each one catering for pupils in one of the city's Consortia. (The Consortia, of which there were over 30, were small geographic areas into which the city was divided at the time for purposes of administration and collaborative support between schools and colleges.) If, however, the intention had been to create an ensemble in each of these Consortia, then this was certainly not achieved, because there were Consortia in the inner-city areas and some of the poorer outer suburbs that did not have sufficient instrumental teaching to populate musical ensembles. Consortium Music Teacher Paul Slater recalled running two of these ensembles – one in Hall Green, in the south of the city, and one in Sheldon, in the east of the city. 'These were great experiences for the kids,' said Slater, 'because it meant that, not only were they playing in ensembles as soon as they started having instrumental lessons, but also they were getting the chance to play in a bigger ensemble than any individual school could provide.'

Classroom music

The team of Consortium Music Teachers – of which Paul Slater was a member – was another of Peter Davies's important innovations. Very soon after his appointment in 1975 Davies created this team of 13 highly effective music teachers whose role was to support the teaching of classroom music in schools – some specializing in primary and others in secondary work. This showed that, even though Davies's chief priority was the BSSO and the structure of teaching and ensembles that supported it, he also had a commitment to developing classroom music teaching. His creation of the Consortium Music Teachers anticipated by several years the creation of the ten Divisional Music Co-ordinators in the Inner London Education

Authority (ILEA) in 1979, who had a similar role in London schools. Following her work as a music specialist teacher at Ley Hill School, and before being appointed Head of the Harrogate Music Centre, Denyse Hyett spent 12 years as one of Birmingham's Consortium Music Teachers, specializing in primary school support. When I spoke to Hyett many years later, she described this work as 'the most rewarding part of my career'. 'Typically,' she said, 'we would start off by delivering a series of workshops for non-specialist primary school teachers. Then we would go into schools, putting this into practice with the children, and working alongside those classroom teachers. We would then leave them to it for a few weeks before making a return visit, to see how things were going and offer more support, if necessary.'

It appears, however, that the situations in which the secondary specialist Consortium Music Teachers found themselves were often very different to this. One of those teachers described the method of their deployment to me in very negative terms. 'We were just like glorified supply teachers,' he said, 'teaching in some of the most challenging schools in the city, which didn't even have a music department.' But Richard Worth, who left his post at John Willmott School in 1975 in order to become a Consortium Music Teacher, was more positive in his reflections: 'We went into secondary schools where music was failing, spending one or two days per week in each school, trying to improve things. And we went and taught in schools which did not have a music teacher at all.' According to Worth, 'This reflected Davies's vision of providing continuity and excellence in music teaching for all children, even in the most difficult of situations.'

Towards the end of the 1970s, Neil Scrimshaw, Chair of Birmingham City Council's Education Committee, flew out to Birmingham's twin city Frankfurt in order to attend the final concert of a BSSO tour. He was so impressed that following the concert, in a taxi on the way back to the airport, he said to Peter Davies, 'If there was one thing I could do to help the Music Service right now, what would it be?' Immediately, Davies replied that he would like to have a new post created within the Music Service – someone who could act as an assistant to Davies, particularly in co-ordinating the work of the Consortium Music Teachers. Accordingly, the post of Advisory Teacher for Music was created, demonstrating that the culture of patronage, at every level of the local authority, was as strong as ever. Once Davies had received the go-ahead to appoint someone in this new role, he went and made what was, possibly, one of the worst decisions of his career. Davies simply asked Richard Worth if he would like the job, and then appointed him without even an interview. 'Looking back,' said

Worth, 'this was entirely inappropriate and, understandably, it caused disruption because there were 12 other Consortium Music Teachers who weren't even given the opportunity to be considered for it.' Such was the disruption, according to one of Richard Worth's colleagues, that the city's Chief Inspector for Schools, Arnold Ingoldsby, felt the need to come and address the team, 'in order to calm the waters'.

The appointment of Worth as Advisory Teacher meant that Peter Davies now had an assistant with whom he got on well, and with whom he could work effectively, in contrast to the Assistant Music Inspector, Antony le Fleming, with whom he clearly did not get on. In 1981, shortly after Worth's appointment, le Fleming left Birmingham in order to become County Music Adviser in Devon, and to continue to develop his extremely successful career as a composer. He was not replaced, and the post of Assistant Music Inspector ceased to exist.

Worth explained to me that his main responsibility as Advisory Teacher was to look after the classroom teaching element of the Music Service's work. So, as well as co-ordinating the work of the Consortium Music Teachers, he oversaw, for example, a panel of secondary music teachers who came together for regular meetings. 'However,' said Worth, 'Peter Davies relinquished responsibility for jobs as though they were stuck to his fingertips. He was not a trusting person so he might, for example, ask for my view on someone's deployment, then he'd say to me, "I don't think we'll do it in quite that way." One area which Davies did properly delegate to me, however, was the Enrichment Centre – one of his most brilliant innovations.' The Enrichment Centre was a programme of teaching sessions that took place on Wednesday afternoons at the Birmingham School of Music for A-level music students from schools across the city. The sessions were led by Consortium Music Teachers and secondary-school music teachers, with contributions from established professional musicians including CBSO players and composers – each dealing with an area of their specialist expertise that related to the A-level music curriculum. Worth explained that 'Jeff Skidmore, for example, might lead a session on a piece of choral music, Alan Davis might talk about baroque music and, on some occasions, we had visits from well-known composers including Nicholas Maw and Oliver Knussen. The students were transported to and from the School of Music by taxi,' said Worth, 'and all of this was paid for by the city council. For those students to be brought together from different parts of the city gave them a fantastic experience and it was just one example of Peter Davies's amazing innovations, demonstrating how phenomenal his contribution to music in Birmingham was.'

There can be no doubt that the Enrichment Centre was an imaginative and extremely successful initiative in terms of bringing sixth-form pupils together, from different areas of Birmingham, to learn collaboratively alongside some of the city's – and the country's – finest musicians. Notwithstanding the huge value of this enterprise, however, it seems that Peter Davies's general view of classroom music teaching, like that of his predecessor Stanley Adams, was very firmly stuck in the past. Martin Fautley began his career in music education in 1978 as a teacher at Sheldon Heath School in Birmingham. He later went on to develop a prestigious academic career and, at the time of writing, is Director of Research at Birmingham City University's School of Education and Social Work, and is regarded as one of the country's leading academics in the fields of creativity and assessment in music education. When I visited Fautley in his office at Birmingham City University, as part of my research for this book, he told me that, when he was training as a teacher, he had been 'thoroughly ingrained in John Paynter's philosophy of creative music-making in the classroom. My view then, and ever since,' he said, 'has been that composing should be central to classroom pedagogy.' But, according to Fautley, this was clearly not the view of Peter Davies, nor was it a view reflected in the Music Service support provided to him as a newly qualified teacher. Fautley recalled attending training sessions for classroom music teachers at the Martineau Teachers' Centre in the late 1970s. 'I found these quite irrelevant,' he said, 'including a session led by Peter Davies on Mozart's Piano Concertos – I didn't see how this was going to enthuse my pupils at Sheldon Heath!' Fautley spoke highly, however, of Consortium Music Teacher Paul Slater's commitment to engaging pupils through pop and rock music. 'But I felt that this reflected Slater's own, personal interest,' he said, 'rather than the ethos of the Music Service as a whole.'

Music therapy

One day in 1970, a young musician named Angela Fenwick knocked at the door of Rubery Hill Mental Health Hospital in the south of Birmingham and said that she would like to work there as a music therapist. The Hospital Director asked, 'What's a music therapist?' to which Fenwick replied, 'I don't know yet, but what I do know is that music can have a good effect on people with mental health problems.' So persuasive was Fenwick in the ensuing conversation that a new post was created, and Angela Fenwick was duly appointed as the hospital's music therapist. When I met up with Fenwick nearly fifty years later, she explained to me that, at that time, music therapy was barely established as a profession in England, and no official training courses in music therapy had yet been established. 'But,' said Fenwick, 'for a long time, people had been going into hospitals to do music with psychiatric patients. For example, Edward Elgar's first paid musical employment was as a bandmaster at Powick Asylum in Worcestershire in the 1880s.'

After several years of working at Rubery Hill, Angela Fenwick decided that she would like to gain some experience of working with children, so in 1976 she arranged a meeting with Peter Davies to ask if he would consider her for a job with the Birmingham Music Service. Typically, Davies agreed to this proposal and immediately created a full-time, salaried post for Fenwick, meaning that Birmingham was among the first music services in the country to employ a music therapist. In addition to making regular visits to Birmingham's 36 special schools, Fenwick established the Special Schools Music Festival, which took place annually – first of all at the Methodist Central Hall and then at Carrs Lane Church Centre. The great success of Angela Fenwick's work led to a considerable increase in demand for music therapy in Birmingham schools, such that, by the time of her retirement in 1993, the service had taken on two additional full-time music therapists. I believe that the appointment of Angela Fenwick, along with that of Sneh Lata, Jeffrey Skidmore, Bernard Herrmann, and others referred to in this chapter, demonstrates what Richard Worth described as 'Peter Davies's incredible ability for spotting people with talent and drawing them into the Music Service'.

Foundations for the future

We have seen that, in the course of Peter Davies's eight-year tenure, a new philosophy was beginning to emerge within the Birmingham Music Service that was to remain central to the organization's ethos for decades to come. One aspect of this new philosophy was a development in pedagogical thinking – a move away from what Richard Duckett described as the 'stultified' method of one-to-one, notation-based teaching, towards more collaborative, creative approaches. This development was definitely the result of teachers like Richard Duckett, Denyse Hyett and Heather Doust trying out and sharing new ideas within schools. And it appears that it was a development that Peter Davies responded to with ambivalence – on the one hand, it seems that throughout his career he articulated his belief that one-to-one, notation-based teaching was the ideal; on the other hand, he gave crucial support to the Suzuki teaching of Hyett and Doust, which contravened both of those principles. Another aspect of the emerging philosophy within the Music Service at that time concerned diversity – in terms of celebrating a wider range of musical styles, including those associated with Birmingham's African-Caribbean and Asian communities, and in terms of providing musical opportunities for children with special educational needs. In these areas, as we have seen, the developments often took place through Peter Davies listening to and responding positively to suggestions made by staff, even when those suggestions seemed to go against Davies's more traditional instincts.

The content of Davies's last two Schools' Prom concerts – at Birmingham Town Hall in July 1983 – demonstrated his enormous contribution to children's music-making in the city, as well as encapsulating the complexities of the man and his career. To close the second of these concerts, and to close his career in Birmingham, Peter Davies directed the Birmingham Schools' Chorale and a massed Combined Schools' Choir, accompanied by the BSSO, in a selection of music by Gilbert and Sullivan, followed by performances of 'Jerusalem' and 'Land of Hope and Glory'. This choice of repertoire, echoing the patriotic character of the BBC Last Night of the Proms, showed the very traditional side of Davies's personality. On the other hand, performances given by the Suzuki Violin Group, the Birmingham Schools' Indian Music Ensemble and the Broadway School Steel Band demonstrated the great innovation in terms of pedagogy and diversity that had taken place during Davies's tenure in Birmingham – innovation that would form the foundations of the Music Service's philosophy for decades to come.

Chapter 4

Music for all

From the mid-1980s onwards, following the period of great expansion and innovation that had taken place under Peter Davies, the Birmingham Music Service began to modernize itself in a variety of ways. First of all, there was an official recognition and active encouragement of the 'bottom-up' influence of certain members of staff in developing more creative approaches to instrumental teaching. Second, real attempts were made to offer musical opportunities in the inner-city areas of Birmingham that, historically, had been neglected. And third, there was a drive towards developing the classroom music experience for all children, with a focus on the more creative approaches that had been developing in England since the 1970s.

Key to these developments was the appointment of Linda Gilbert as Advisory Teacher for Music in April 1983, taking over from Richard Worth upon his promotion to General Inspector for Music in the Borough of Sandwell. The appointment of Gilbert was an inspired one – showing that Davies continued to make brave, creative decisions right up to the end of his career – because she was unlike anyone who had preceded her in Birmingham. Gilbert moved to Birmingham from being a Divisional Music Co-ordinator with the ILEA. This meant that, because of the pioneering work that had been taking place in London schools, she brought to her new post a strong commitment to celebrating diversity, promoting equality of opportunity and encouraging innovation in classroom music teaching. Also, this was the first time that a woman had been appointed to such a senior position within the Birmingham Music Service.

Shortly after Gilbert's appointment Peter Davies, at the age of 55, retired as Senior Inspector for Music. Just as Davies had done a few months earlier, the local authority now showed great imagination and bravery in appointing Linda Gilbert as his successor from September 1983, but now with the new title, General Inspector for Music. This meant that the person now responsible for Birmingham's music education was a young woman whose main passion was providing high-quality musical experiences for all children, rather than being the conductor of the BSSO. As well as being one of the first women to be appointed as a Music Adviser in England, Gilbert was probably the first Music Adviser in the country to come from a background in primary rather than secondary education. And, unlike her predecessors, Gilbert's approach to leadership was collaborative rather than dictatorial.

Linda Gilbert then appointed Richard Howlett to replace her as Advisory Teacher for Music with effect from September 1984. Howlett came from a background as a classroom music teacher in the Lake District and, again, brought to the Music Service a commitment to creative music-making in the classroom. And, at the same time as Howlett's appointment, I was appointed as the service's new Head of Woodwind, taking over from Val Allen, who had moved to a post with the Wirral Music Service. It was early in my career to gain such a senior position – I was 28 years old and had been working as an instrumental teacher in the London area for only four years. I found myself, with one exception, to be the youngest member of the Woodwind Department for which I was now responsible. And I recall that on my first day in the job, one of my new colleagues enquired as to how long I had been teaching, and then emitted a gasp of horror upon hearing my response.

I believe that I was appointed to the post in Birmingham because of my passion for innovation in instrumental music teaching: encouraging pupils to compose, to improvise and to play by ear, and to do these things in group rather than one-to-one situations. And, as Gilbert explained to me many years later, she believed that, because of my experience with the ILEA, I would support her in trying to broaden access to instrumental music, and increase the provision for children in the inner city and from ethnic minorities. It was reported back to me many years later by one of the Consortium Music Teachers that when Gilbert came out of the interview room, having just offered me the job, she said, 'I hope I've done the right thing – I've just appointed a new Head of Woodwind, but he's a bit controversial!'

These three appointments in 1983/84 meant that, for the one and only time in its history, the Music Service was subject to the influence of a group of external candidates who were appointed to senior posts at more or less the same time. Following these appointments, the Music Service would have to wait a further 30 years before any other external candidate would be appointed to a senior position within the organization. Perhaps part of the reason for this series of external appointments was that the local authority was determined to avoid the débâcle that had followed Worth's internal promotion, without an interview, a few years earlier. And maybe the local authority believed that the Music Service could be brought more up to date through the influence of people who had worked outside

Birmingham – particularly in the capital. When I interviewed Gilbert she reflected that, upon starting her new post, she received great support from the local authority's Chief Inspector for Schools, Arnold Ingoldsby, and the West Midlands Music HMI, Tess Stiles – with both of whom she shared the same educational values.

Gilbert went on to explain that the situation she found upon her arrival in Birmingham was very different from what she had experienced in London. 'At that time,' she said, 'classroom music in Birmingham didn't have the status that it had in the ILEA, so there was a real challenge to take on: how to raise the status of classroom music, and thereby raise the awareness that there was an entitlement to high-quality music education for all children.' Gilbert told me that her predecessors in Birmingham had worked hard to develop the instrumental team so, by the time she arrived, it was a well-established, high-status group of teachers. According to Gilbert, this allowed her to devote her energy to trying to develop classroom teaching, which hadn't enjoyed a similar status or level of support. 'There were a lot of exciting initiatives influencing music education nationally at the time,' said Gilbert, 'such as the publication of the Gulbenkian Report, *The Arts in Schools* (Robinson, 1982), which emphasized the importance of the creative arts in the curriculum, but these didn't seem to have impacted yet in Birmingham. These national developments needed to take root in Birmingham, and needed nurturing and developing widely across the city.'

So, although Gilbert was to exert a positive, forward-looking influence on aspects of the instrumental team's work, particularly in relation to broadening of access, her main focus, unlike that of her predecessors, was on developing classroom music teaching. This meant that, for the first time, the day-to-day management of instrumental teaching was now fully delegated to the Head of Instrumental Staff, Keith Allen. 'The instrumental teachers must have been aware that my main focus was not on their work,' said Gilbert. 'I was a young woman from the ILEA with a background in classroom music, whereas my male predecessors had a rather traditional background and an important part of their role was to conduct the BSSO, which I did not do. So I think I may have been viewed with some suspicion within the instrumental team.' My own recollection is that the perception of Gilbert within the team was mixed: some teachers thought that they should not be answerable to someone who did not have the skills necessary to conduct the BSSO; others were excited by the new direction in which the service was moving. Many years later Peter Bridle told me that he respected Gilbert because 'she was the first music adviser in Birmingham whose main concern was the quality of music in schools, whereas her predecessors had been mainly concerned with the BSSO'. It is particularly interesting that this observation was made by someone whose main connection with the Music Service, as we shall see in future chapters, was as the BSSO's longest-serving conductor.

'Best person for the job'

Because Gilbert had no intention of conducting the BSSO – thus breaking the 20-year tradition established by her predecessors – the post of BSSO Conductor was advertised and, following an interview process, Hilary Davan Wetton was appointed to the role in 1983. Davan Wetton, who was based in Milton Keynes, Buckinghamshire, was already a well-established professional conductor as well as being Director of Music at the prestigious St Paul's Girls' School in London. His appointment as conductor of the BSSO represented a huge turning point because it meant that, for the first time in its history, the orchestra was now conducted by the best person for the job, rather than by whoever happened to be the city's Music Adviser at the time. And the fact that Gilbert did not conduct the BSSO represented a major shift in the culture of the Music Service – a move away from the traditional role of the English local authority music adviser as the charismatic, male boss, whose main job was conducting the top-level children's orchestra. We saw in Chapter 1 how the position of local authority music adviser was first created in the 1930s in order to provide someone who would conduct high-profile musical events for children. Even as the role of music adviser broadened towards the end of the twentieth century, however, it was still often assumed that either that person, or the head of the music service, would conduct the youth orchestra – regardless of whether or not they were the best-qualified person to do so. I was made very aware of this assumption when, in 1991, I was interviewed for the post of Head of the Wiltshire Music Service. My first task in the interview process was to conduct the Wiltshire Youth Orchestra in a rehearsal of Brahms's *Academic Festival Overture*. So it was clear that conducting the youth orchestra was seen as an essential feature of that post and, since orchestral conducting was not an area in which I was experienced, I was, unsurprisingly, not offered the job. And in many music services this was a model that remained unchanged well into the twenty-first century.

This break with tradition in Birmingham, signalled by the appointment of Hilary Davan Wetton, meant that, from the mid-1980s onwards, the BSSO was always directed by professional-standard conductors, and this resulted in a dramatic improvement in the orchestra's standard of performance. One of the highlights of Davan Wetton's tenure with the BSSO was the occasion when he brought the orchestra to St Paul's Girls' School in London, to give the first-ever performance there of *The Planets* suite by Gustav Holst (who was one of Davan Wetton's predecessors as Director of Music at the school). On that visit the BSSO were joined by the Birmingham Schools' Dance Orchestra and the Birmingham Schools' Indian Music Ensemble, thus sharing the Birmingham Music Service's commitment to breadth and diversity with one of the country's oldest independent schools.

In 1985 Davan Wetton stepped down as conductor of the BSSO, possibly because the weekly journey from Buckinghamshire was proving too onerous, and Stephen Block was appointed to take over for one year in a caretaker capacity. Towards the end of that year a petition was organized by members of the instrumental team calling for Peter Bridle to be appointed as the orchestra's conductor. (Many of the signatories were familiar with Bridle's prodigious conducting talent through being members of Wednesday Band – a rehearsal orchestra he directed on Wednesday evenings at King Edward's School.) The petition was handed to Keith Allen, following which Bridle was appointed to the post in 1986, commencing his 20-year tenure as conductor of the BSSO, making him, by far, the longest-serving conductor of the orchestra to date. In 1987, shortly after Bridle's appointment, he took the orchestra on a visit to Frankfurt, along with the Birmingham Schools' Chorale under the direction of Jeffrey Skidmore, where the combined groups gave the first performance outside the UK of Rutter's Requiem – much to the delight of John Rutter. During his time with the BSSO, Bridle was to bring the young musicians to levels of performance and introduce them to a range of challenging repertoire that previously would have been unimaginable, as will be explained more fully later.

Inequalities to be challenged

In acknowledgement of Birmingham's cultural diversity, Linda Gilbert renamed the Music Service's annual Christmas Concert at Birmingham Town Hall. From 1983 it became known as the Winter Celebration and began to draw on a greater breadth of musical styles. In 1985, for example, the concert included performances of pupil compositions based on themes related to festivals and celebrations of different cultures at that time of year. And Gilbert changed the name of the end-of-year Town Hall performances from Birmingham Schools' Prom Concerts to Summer Gala Concerts, and these events no longer concluded with 'Land of Hope and Glory'. (In 2018 the Birmingham Music Service re-adopted the word 'Prom' for this series of concerts, renaming them the Birmingham Youth Proms. But I was assured by then Head of Service, Ciaran O'Donnell, that the service would not revert to closing the final concert with 'Land of Hope and Glory'. 'That wouldn't be the right thing for multicultural Birmingham,' he told me.)

According to Gilbert, one of the main difficulties she faced upon starting her new post in Birmingham was the response she received from some Music Service managers when she began to challenge the lack of instrumental teaching in inner-city schools, and the predominantly white, middle-class make-up of the city's ensembles. These inequalities in provision were, by then, well established and, up to that point, had remained unchallenged. And, although some instrumental teaching did take place in less advantaged areas of the city, the strongest teachers tended to teach in the grammar schools and in the more affluent areas, while the weaker teachers often worked in the more challenged schools. The result of this was that pupils from middle-class backgrounds tended to have the best possible support in their music-making, enabling them to gain access to, and make progress through, the Central Ensembles, whereas the highest quality of teaching was often not available to those children who probably needed it the most. There were, however, some notable exceptions to this, such as Glynis Squires – an oboe pupil of Alison Lancaster at Tilton Road Girls' School in Small Heath during the late 1970s. Glynis, whose parents were from the West Indies and who was brought up in one of the poorer areas of Birmingham, progressed through the Central Ensembles up to the BSSO and then went on to study oboe at the Royal Academy of Music – a rare achievement then for someone from an inner-city, ethnic-minority background. Although Glynis did not pursue a career as a professional musician she continues, at the time of writing, to play the oboe in various settings including the Redditch Choral Society Orchestra where she sits next to her first oboe teacher, now known as Alison Whatley.

As soon as I arrived in Birmingham, I was aware of the gross underfunding of instrumental music teaching, notwithstanding the strong culture of local-authority patronage that has already been described. While working for music services in the London area, I had found that nearly all local-authority schools received instrumental music provision and that funds were normally available to replace old or damaged musical instruments as necessary. In Birmingham, however, a large number of schools – mainly in the poorer areas of the city – had no instrumental teaching at all, and when instruments needed to be replaced, this often happened by moving instruments from one school to another, rather than purchasing new instruments. One of the first tasks I was given, following my appointment as Head of Woodwind, was to move instruments in this way from one school to another. I was asked to visit two secondary schools in challenged areas of the city to meet with headteachers and explain that, because woodwind teaching was not succeeding in their schools, we would be withdrawing the teaching, along with the musical instruments that were on loan, with immediate effect. Although I felt nervous about these meetings, neither headteacher offered any resistance to what I was saying – one merely responded by saying, 'You're right – this isn't the thing for our kids.' So I filled my car with flutes and clarinets and drove to Sutton Coldfield where I redistributed them to schools where, it was assumed, they would be put to better use. While feeling uneasy about this, as a young teacher in my first few weeks in a management post, I had not yet developed the clarity of philosophy, nor the confidence to challenge those higher up in the organization.

I also recall that in April 1985, at the start of the new financial year, I was allowed to purchase just two clarinets and two flutes for the entire city of Birmingham – such was the paucity of funding available for musical instrument purchase at that time. Predictably, two of these instruments were allocated to a school in Sutton Coldfield and two of them to a school in Hall Green. These stories exemplify the largely unchallenged assumption in Birmingham at that time that it was acceptable to concentrate the Music Service's limited resources in the middle-class areas of the city. Although Linda Gilbert certainly did begin to challenge this assumption, it would not be until the mid-1990s that there would be a real shift towards greater equality of provision – resulting from changes in the structure of local authority funding, which will be explained in the next chapter.

In June 1985 a huge controversy erupted, hitting the headlines of the Birmingham press: in the week that pupil auditions for Music Service Central Ensembles were due to take place, letters were sent out to parents of 25 children from independent schools, cancelling their auditions. This was because Birmingham's Labour-controlled council had decided to hold a review of the Central Ensembles, examining the percentages of children in the ensembles who were from the inner city and from ethnic minority groups, and considering whether or not children from independent schools should continue to be eligible for places. Within a week, however, following an outcry from headteachers of independent schools, and following extremely unfavourable press coverage, the council stated that any policy change should not affect the make-up of the ensembles until the following year, so the cancellation of auditions was lifted. As part of its coverage of this issue, the *Birmingham Evening Mail* published a cartoon that would now be considered highly inappropriate (Whittock, 1985). Headed

'City of Birmingham Schools Orchestra', the cartoon showed a group of caricatures including black children playing steel pans, someone wearing Native American headdress playing a drum, a girl in Welsh costume playing the harp and a girl in Swiss costume playing the alpine horn. The cartoon showed a distraught-looking conductor, with two Education Department officials looking on, and the caption underneath read, 'We've got the social and racial mix right – now if only they could play the instruments ...!' According to Linda Gilbert, 'This implied that, if you increased diversity, you would lose quality.' Gilbert also told me that, following the cartoon's publication, she visited a school to assist with the appointment of a new music teacher and saw that very same cartoon pinned to the wall behind the headteacher's desk. 'To me,' said Gilbert, 'that summed up the huge challenge we were facing at the time.'

Flourishing ensembles

In the summer of 1984, shortly before my arrival in Birmingham, the Birmingham Schools' Dance Orchestra (BSDO) had been scheduled to perform at a concert in London. Bernard Herrmann, the BSDO's director, travelled by coach with the young musicians while a senior member of Music Service staff, whose job was to assist Herrmann with the ensemble, drove to London in a van, transporting the band's equipment. Unfortunately, the van arrived in London later than scheduled, causing disruption to the planned performance and, according to Herrmann, this was because the van driver had 'stopped at every pub on the way'. Herrmann then demanded that his assistant be immediately dismissed from his role whereupon, within a few weeks of my arrival in Birmingham, I was invited to take his place – probably because it was known that I had some experience as a jazz musician. This job involved some administrative work, coaching of the saxophone section, and occasionally deputizing for Herrmann as director of the group when he was unavailable. I learnt an enormous amount from working alongside Bernard Herrmann at the weekly rehearsals of the BSDO, which, under his direction, achieved remarkable standards of performance. The huge success of the ensemble was rooted partly, I believe, in the fact that Herrmann treated the young musicians very much as though they were professional musicians – having extremely high expectations and conducting rehearsals with a calm efficiency and jocularity that, I understand, had also characterized his work with the Northern Dance Orchestra. A particular factor in the BSDO's extraordinary success, in my view, was that Herrmann took great care in balancing the dynamic levels of the band's different sections – giving the

BSDO an almost orchestral quality of sound that set the band apart from many other amateur and youth big bands at the time and since.

In the summer of 1985 the Birmingham Schools' Concert Orchestra (BSCO) performed under Bernard Herrmann's direction in the National Festival of Music for Youth at the Royal Festival Hall in London. Following this performance, an adjudicator at the festival made seriously disparaging comments about Herrmann's choice of pop-orientated repertoire for the orchestra. So offended was Herrmann that, on the homeward-bound coach journey back from London that evening, he scribbled on the back of an envelope his letter of resignation – from both the BSCO and the BSDO – with immediate effect. When Keith Allen walked into his office first thing the following morning, he found the letter of resignation on his desk, throwing the Music Service management into a state of panic, given the huge esteem in which Herrmann's work with the two ensembles was held. Allen immediately telephoned me to ask if I would meet with Herrmann as a matter of urgency, to ask him to reconsider his decision – probably because Allen knew that I had developed a close relationship with Herrmann over the preceding months while assisting him with the BSDO. So that evening Herrmann and I duly arranged to meet at the Martineau Teachers' Club. I bought Herrmann his favourite drink – a pint of mild – and a long conversation ensued, the outcome of which was that Herrmann withdrew his resignation from the BSDO but stood by his resignation from the BSCO.

To cover for Herrmann's immediate absence from the BSCO, it was decided that three of the orchestra's sectional coaches, who were members of the instrumental teaching team, would take turns on a weekly basis at conducting the orchestra. One of these coaches was brass teacher Bob Vivian who, to his surprise, found that he greatly enjoyed the experience of conducting a full orchestra, so it was soon agreed that he would take on the job as BSCO's conductor on an interim basis, until a permanent replacement for Herrmann could be found. After a few months, however, it was evident that Vivian was doing such a brilliant job with the orchestra that he was appointed as their regular conductor, a role that he continues to occupy at the time of writing, over thirty years later.

In 1986, two years after I had started assisting Bernard Herrmann with BSDO rehearsals, I began to feel that there was a need for a second big band in the Music Service, in order to accommodate the increasing number of talented young jazz musicians emerging within the city's schools. So I suggested to Keith Allen that we start a new band, which could act as a feeder ensemble to the BSDO. In just the same way as Peter Davies would have done, Allen gave the go-ahead to this new idea, and thus was formed the Birmingham Schools' Jazz Orchestra (BSJO), directed by myself.

Around this time, I was developing a strong interest in strategies for teaching jazz improvisation, having been inspired by a summer course I attended at the Guildhall School of Music and Drama in London. The course included teaching sessions led by Scott Stroman, Eddie Harvey and Richard Michael – leading lights at that time in developing new approaches to the teaching of improvisation. These new approaches were based, first and foremost, on listening, on rhythmic feel, and on the belief that, in the right environment, anyone can learn to become a jazz improviser. These principles contrasted sharply with the more theoretical, notation-based and less inclusive approaches that had tended to prevail up until that time. I recall, for example, hearing a professional jazz musician saying that he expected his students to be fluent in all their scales (including whole tone, diminished and Greek modes) before he would allow them to start improvising, and another saying, 'There's no point trying to teach someone to improvise – you can either do it or you can't!' So, inspired by the work of Stroman, Harvey and Michael, I decided to place jazz improvisation and playing by ear at the heart of my work with the BSJO – often building up whole musical arrangements in this way, without any use of musical notation.

I also placed a strong emphasis on inviting established, well-known jazz musicians to appear with the BSJO as guest soloists. So in 1988, Don Rendell, my old saxophone teacher, and veteran of the Ted Heath and John Dankworth bands, appeared with the BSJO in a concert tour in London, culminating in a memorable Sunday lunchtime session in the crowded Watermans Arts Centre bar, overlooking the River Thames, where the BSJO alternated sets with Rendell's own quartet. I remember the great feeling of support I felt upon seeing my boss Keith Allen walking unexpectedly through the door of the Arts Centre, just as we were about to start our first set. He had driven all the way from Sutton Coldfield with his family that morning in order to hear our performance. In 1989, the BSJO won first prize in the Midlands section of the Daily Telegraph Young Jazz Competition, for which we were rewarded with an inspiring masterclass on jazz improvisation led by pianist Stan Barker and Director of the Royal Northern College of Music Big Band, Clark Rundell. Later that year the BSJO performed at the Four Oaks Schools' Summer Fair in Birmingham, with trad jazz icon Kenny Ball as a featured trumpet soloist, and then the band embarked on its first foreign tour – to Normandy in France – again, with Don Rendell as a soloist. Although the BSJO was originally seen as a training band for younger, less experienced players, who would then progress into the BSDO, by the end of the 1980s its status had risen to the point where the two bands were considered to be on the same level and differentiated not so much by playing ability as by musical style – the newer band focusing on more contemporary jazz arrangements and with a stronger emphasis on improvisation.

In the mid-1980s, sitar teacher Sneh Lata suggested to Keith Allen the idea of appointing to the Music Service a teacher of tabla. According to Lata, this would be a way of providing the Birmingham Schools' Indian Music Ensemble with tabla players, which was an essential requirement for authentic performance of Indian classical music. Again, just as Peter Davies would have done, Allen took on board this advice and one of Birmingham's leading tabla performers, Harjinder Matharu, was duly appointed as a part-time, salaried teacher for the Music Service. Matharu's contract was later increased to full-time, with his work expanding to include the teaching of dhol as well as tabla, and at the time of writing, over thirty years later, Matharu continues his inspiring work in schools all over Birmingham.

We have seen that, during the 1970s, Peter Davies established Consortium Orchestras for beginner and intermediate pupils, but that these served predominantly the middle-class suburbs of the city. Determined to redress this imbalance, Linda Gilbert suggested that such an orchestra should be established in the inner city. So she and I set about organizing a beginner ensemble that would meet for weekly rehearsals, at the end of the school day, at Lea Mason School in the economically disadvantaged area of Ladywood – very close to the city centre. I assisted with running the ensemble's weekly rehearsals, working alongside the school's Head of Music, Tony Eno. Sadly, however, although the ensemble got off to a good start, it was short-lived, due to the underlying problem that only a limited number of children in that area were receiving instrumental tuition, so there were insufficient pupils to sustain the group's existence.

In the spring of 1985, in another attempt to open up opportunities for children in less advantaged areas of the city, and with the support of Linda Gilbert and Keith Allen, I organized a Woodwind Festival – a series of six after-school rehearsals in different areas of the city for a large group of woodwind pupils, culminating in a performance at Queensbridge School in Kings Heath. The seven salaried members of the woodwind team took turns at rehearsing different items of repertoire. After the event one of the teachers, Fiona Biddulph, writing in the Music Service newsletter *Keynotes*, described the impact of the Woodwind Festival on her pupils, and on her own professional development:

> Not only have I seen a marvellous increase in confidence and technical ability as the weeks progressed but opening their eyes to what goes on behind their normal routine has led to enquiries about Saturday orchestras and any other opportunities to play together again ... I too have learnt a lot by watching six other conductors in action and hearing the difference in response to our styles and personalities showed us quite clearly what did and did not work. (Biddulph, 1985: 16)

In 1987 woodwind teacher Philip Leah, working alongside Richard Duckett, established the South-West Area Wind Band – an open-access ensemble for beginner-level pupils that met on Friday evenings at Dame Elizabeth Cadbury School in Bournville. The South-West Area Wind Band continued very successfully for a number of years and became the prototype for the huge structure of Area Ensembles for pupils throughout the city that was to develop from the early 1990s and which, at the time of writing, consists of no fewer than 43 ensembles.

One of the founder members of the South-West Area Wind Band in 1987 was 9-year-old Bournville Junior School pupil and tenor horn player, Anneke Scott. In November 2016, I visited Birmingham's Symphony Hall to hear a stunning performance of Bach's Mass in B Minor, given by Ex Cathedra under the direction of Jeffrey Skidmore. The obbligato horn solos in the 'Quoniam' movement were performed with virtuosity and beautiful sensitivity by Anneke Scott (Figures 4.1 and 4.2) who, by then, had established an international reputation as one of the leading exponents of natural horn playing. When I met up with Scott after the concert, I reminded her of my first meeting with her in the South-West Area Wind Band, nearly thirty years earlier. 'I'd just started having lessons when I joined that band,' she told me. 'I could only play a few notes, so I just watched the fingering of the girl playing next to me and copied her.' Soon Anneke transferred from tenor horn to French horn and, while still at primary school, passed an audition to gain a place in the Birmingham Schools' Training Wind Orchestra (BSTWO), directed by myself. Upon transferring to secondary school Anneke started having lessons with French horn specialist Richard Duckett and then began to progress through the Music Service Central Ensembles. She moved to the BSCO and then the BSSO, as well as playing in the Birmingham Schools' Brass Ensemble directed by Bob Vivian and the Birmingham Schools' Baroque Orchestra directed by Alan Davis, and singing with the Birmingham Schools' Chorale directed by Jeffrey Skidmore (with whom, as we have seen, she was to work again many years later in a professional capacity). Some of the highlights that Scott recalled from her experiences with these ensembles included playing Joe Zawinul's 'Birdland' with the BSTWO at the Midlands Arts Centre (on the front cover of this book), playing Gershwin's *An American in Paris* with the BSCO in rehearsal under the direction of Simon Rattle, and playing *The Rite of Spring* and Mahler's Symphony No. 4 with the BSSO. It would be difficult to imagine a greater wealth and variety of experience for a young musician. 'The beauty of the system,' said Scott, 'was that, soon after starting lessons, you were playing in a non-auditioned ensemble and then there was a pathway through the Central Ensembles. And, unless you get that ensemble experience, what's the point of learning to play a musical instrument? Playing music is to do with being part of a community of musicians and that's how we learn. I remember so many times on this journey when I felt I was out of my depth, so I would watch and listen to my peers – very often I learnt more from them than I did from my instrumental lessons. And there is no doubt that I would not be doing what I'm doing today, had it not been for my experiences with the Birmingham Music Service.'

Figure 4.1: Anneke Scott performing with the Birmingham Schools' Training Wind Orchestra outside Birmingham Town Hall, *c.*1989 (Photo: Michael Bates, Birmingham Music Service)

Figure 4.2: Anneke Scott performing with the Australian Romantic and Classical Orchestra, Sydney, 2018 (Photo: Nick Gilbert)

Creativity and disorder

I will now describe my own personal reflections on two important characteristics of the Birmingham Music Service at this stage of its history. I believe that the first of these – an openness to new ideas – set Birmingham apart from many, if not most, other English music services at that time. The second characteristic – a serious laxness in regard to management and accountability – was, I believe, entirely consistent with the culture in many other music services.

My first impression of the Birmingham Music Service's instrumental team upon my arrival in 1984 was that, although some teachers were very traditional in their approach – favouring one-to-one teaching and the exclusive use of classical repertoire played from musical notation – there was an openness, at all levels of the organization, to more creative approaches, and there was often vibrant discussion on such matters. So I felt, straight away, that there was huge potential for the organization to move forward, in a way that I had not seen in other music services up to that stage in my career.

One of the first instrumental teachers I got to know in Birmingham was brass teacher Richard Duckett. We have already seen that in the late 1970s Duckett was pioneering small-group instrumental teaching at

Greenmeadow Primary School. By the mid-1980s he had moved on to teaching instrumental music to whole classes of 30 children at that school – anticipating by some 20 years the introduction of Wider Opportunities teaching in English schools, which will be dealt with in Chapter 7. Working alongside the school's specialist music teacher, Molly Wicks, Duckett established each class in the school as an orchestra, with pupils performing on a range of instruments. When Head of Instrumental Staff, Keith Allen, visited the school, he was so impressed that he doubled Duckett's teaching time there from half a day to one whole day per week. According to Duckett, such a response was typical of Allen: 'He was a good listener – he would allow people to do new things and to blossom, and he encouraged the sharing of new ideas amongst the staff.' Allen gave further acknowledgement to Duckett's work when, in July 1985, he gave the young musicians of Greenmeadow the opportunity to take part in one of the Summer Gala Concerts at Birmingham Town Hall – the classes of 10 and 11 year olds performed as an orchestra, accompanying the younger pupils singing Paul McCartney's 'We All Stand Together' and Elvis Presley's 'Love Me Tender'. Another area of innovative work being developed by Duckett at Greenmeadow was the encouragement of pupil composition – culminating in an opera, composed and performed by the children, based on the story of *Alice in Wonderland.* One of the pupils who benefited from Duckett's whole-class instrumental activities at Greenmeadow was Chris Egan who went on to become one of Britain's leading film music composers and whose story will be told in the next chapter.

At the end of my third week with the Music Service in 1984, I attended a national meeting for local-authority Suzuki teachers, held at the Martineau Teachers' Centre. The choice of Birmingham for the location of this meeting suggests that, by this time, the Birmingham Music Service was established as one of the leading music services, if not *the* leading music service, in pioneering Suzuki teaching in state schools. This was chiefly the result of the enthusiastic work of Heather Doust whose passion for Suzuki teaching had been ignited only a few years earlier. By 1985 the status of Suzuki teaching within the Music Service had grown to the extent that both Heather Doust and Head of Upper Strings, Jeremy Blunt, were supported in making a three-month visit to Matsumoto in Japan, in order to research the Suzuki teaching method and to study with Shinichi Suzuki himself. During my research for this book, Doust explained to me that Blunt and herself were probably the first Suzuki-trained teachers to adopt this method of teaching in state schools in England. At that time, Suzuki teaching was taking place almost exclusively in the private sector but, since then, it has grown enormously within local authorities, undoubtedly due, in part at least, to Doust's influence. The growth of interest in Suzuki teaching in Birmingham led, in 2007, to the British Suzuki Institute establishing a teacher training course in the city. The Birmingham Music Service provided funding for teachers to attend this course and, as a result, the new millennium saw a huge increase in the number of Suzuki-trained teachers within the organization. At the time of writing, the service has 12 Suzuki-trained violin teachers, a Suzuki-trained cello teacher and a group of guitar teachers involved in a new Suzuki guitar-teaching course, set up by the Music Service in conjunction with the British Suzuki Institute.

Perhaps one of the reasons for the hugely successful growth of Suzuki teaching within the Music Service was that, for much of the period during which this was developing, Doust was simply a rank-and-file teacher, influencing other teachers through her inspirational work that included regular public performances given by her pupils. Had she been a manager at the time, instructing other teachers to adopt the Suzuki method, I feel sure that she would not have had the same impact. It was also seen that, although her pupils learnt through a method that did not involve the reading of musical notation, once they found themselves in Music Service ensembles, they very quickly learnt the skills of reading music, and many of her pupils progressed to becoming highly valued members of the BSSO. Through her influence as a teacher, Doust not only inspired other Suzuki teachers but she also helped to nurture a culture in the Music Service whereby it was accepted that young people could be involved in worthwhile musical activities without necessarily reading from musical notation.

As mentioned in the Introduction, from the day I joined the Birmingham Music Service in 1984 I was aware of a rather casual approach to management and accountability within the organization. And this impression was not inconsistent with what I had experienced working with music services in the London area at the start of my career in the early 1980s. Halfway through my probationary year in 1980, for example, while working for the Hertfordshire Music Service on a full-time, salaried contract, I received a telephone call from the office, asking if I had time available to fit an additional school visit into my weekly schedule. Clearly the office did not know how many hours per week I was working and, since I was reluctant to cut back on my leisurely one-hour lunch breaks, I replied that my timetable was full, and that was the end of the conversation. During the whole of that probationary year I did not receive a single visit or hold a single conversation with anyone else in the organization about how my work was going. I passed my probationary year, even though nobody, apart from my pupils, had seen any of my teaching during that year. Looking back, I believe I would have benefited enormously – and so would my pupils – if I had received some feedback and had opportunities for sharing ideas with more experienced colleagues. I also think that the organization would have benefited from knowing whether or not I was doing a good enough job!

Upon completion of that year in Hertfordshire I was keen to move back to London, where I had lived as a student. So I secured part-time, hourly-paid teaching posts with three different music services: the ILEA, the London Borough of Richmond upon Thames and the London Borough of Havering, the last of which appointed me without an interview or even a telephone conversation. I was working two days per week for the ILEA and was keen to change my contract to a salaried one. I was told this might be possible, but that a manager from the ILEA Music Service would need to observe my teaching first, to make sure my work was up to the required standard. The manager duly arrived at Haggerston School in Hackney to watch me teach a group of beginner clarinet pupils, followed by an advanced, individual pupil working at the slow movement of Mozart's Clarinet Concerto. Half-way through the pupil's performance of that piece, I turned around to see our visitor seated in the corner of the room – fast asleep. By the end of the lesson he had woken up again and said to me, 'Everything seems to be going OK.' So I was awarded a salaried contract, finding myself to be one of only a very small number of ILEA instrumental music teachers to enjoy such terms of employment at that time.

These stories, from the start of my teaching career in the early 1980s, paint a picture of disorder and lack of rigour that, I believe, characterized much instrumental music teaching in England at the time, and which would be unimaginable in a music service, or in any educational institution, at the time of writing. And, in many respects, I found the culture of the Birmingham Music Service during the 1980s to be consistent with these initial impressions. For example, a senior member of staff at the time was reputed to have a blank timetable on Friday afternoons, in order to facilitate visits to the supermarket to stock up on provisions for the weekend. And it was well known that members of staff, including a senior manager, would often visit the Sir Harry public house at lunchtimes and then arrive at their afternoon schools slightly late and 'under the influence', or stroll further down the road to spend the afternoon at Edgbaston Cricket Ground.

Professional development

When I arrived in Birmingham in 1984, there were no formal structures in place for supporting the professional development of instrumental teachers, other than occasional staff meetings at the end of the school day, and training days on the first or last day of a term. Linda Gilbert, however, was keen to establish more forward-looking approaches to professional development, based on collaboration and sharing of ideas between teachers. I saw an example of this on my very first day with the Music Service, as described in the Introduction, when Gilbert arranged for different teachers to take it in turns to talk about their work.

And in 1986 Gilbert initiated thought-provoking discussion within the service when she asked me to set up and chair a working party of instrumental teachers – to hold discussions with a view to agreeing some core principles of good practice in instrumental teaching. The working party consisted of ten teachers including Suzuki violin teacher Heather Doust, keyboard teacher Bill Hunt, guitar teacher Bryan Lester and sitar teacher Sneh Lata. And, in line with Gilbert's 'bottom-up', inclusive approach to leadership and professional development, none of these teachers, apart from myself, was a manager. In 1987, after a series of meetings had taken place, the working party produced a document, *Instrumental Music Teaching – A forward look* (City of Birmingham Education Department, 1987), summarizing the group's discussions, and this was supported by a video showing examples of effective teaching by Music Service staff. Although the document was, I believe, soon forgotten, its publication served to highlight the importance of more progressive approaches to instrumental teaching, developing within the Music Service since the 1970s but not officially recognized or valued before. I would suggest that it explores issues that are as relevant and challenging today as they were in 1987: collaboration between instrumental music teachers and classroom teachers, group teaching, composing, improvising, playing by ear, diversity of musical styles.

Notwithstanding these examples of Linda Gilbert's collaborative approach to professional development, the main approach within the 1980s Music Service continued to reflect the dominant view within educational institutions at that time – that teachers' work would improve through one-off training sessions delivered by visiting experts. This top-down method reached its peak a few years later and was epitomized in a process known as 'cascading', whereby a senior manager would attend a course to hear a presentation by an expert; the manager would then return to the workplace to deliver that message to the middle managers who would then, in turn, deliver it to the rest of the workforce.

Clive Kempton, Advisory Music Teacher from the Shropshire Music Service, exemplified the 'visiting expert' approach when he spent two days leading training for Birmingham Music Service teachers towards the end of the 1980s – introducing us to the new GCSE Music syllabus. (In 2001 Kempton was to visit the Birmingham Music Service once again – this time in his role as HMI, to undertake the service's one and only Ofsted inspection.) These two days of training included a strong emphasis on pupil composition, since this was a key element of the new GCSE curriculum, and an area that most instrumental teachers at the time did not consider to be part of their work. I can remember being sent off to a small room with a group of instrumental teachers, having been given a series of three chords upon which we were asked to base our group composition. And I remember the mood of cynicism within that room, and the feeling among some teachers that their time was being wasted. To this day, however, I recall a suggestion made by Kempton during the training that inspired me at the time and has remained a regular feature of my teaching ever since. Kempton's suggestion was that, at the crossover point between two instrumental lessons – when one group was finishing off and the next group had just arrived – all the musicians present in the room could spend a few minutes making music together. This meant that pupils might find themselves in unexpected musical situations – perhaps joining in with others who were at different levels, or who played different musical instruments – acknowledging the huge potential for learning that can arise from unplanned and unpredicted situations.

Around the same time as Kempton's visit, and encouraged by my new-found passion for teaching jazz improvisation, I led a practical session on improvising for the whole team of Music Service staff. In the course of the session, the teachers were taking turns at improvising two-bar phrases on a major scale over a Latin-American rhythmic background. When it came to the turn of one of the teachers, who was clearly not taking the activity seriously, he simply chose to play the opening two bars of 'On Ilkley Moor Bar t'At'. A few months later, an even more cynical attitude was shown by the instrumental staff when Advisory Teachers Joyce Rothschild and Patricia Scott were leading a session, introducing the team to strategies being developed in primary school classroom music at the time. Again, it was a practical session and this time staff were asked to join in with songs and clapping games. I was seated in the front row and I remember turning around at one point to see a row of instrumental teachers sitting with their arms folded, looking at the floor. One of them muttered, 'I'm not joining in with this – I'm a violin teacher!' And I can remember the look of frustration on the presenters' faces at the end of the session.

So there was still a long way to go before the mass of instrumental teachers in Birmingham would understand the broader context of their work. But, I would suggest, there was also a long way to go before we, as managers, would understand what kind of experiences would engage teachers and move them forward in their professional learning. Based on my conversations with teachers, and on my observation of their work at the time, I do not believe that the 'visiting expert' model of training had a significant impact on their work – apart from the fact that it brought a disparate workforce together as a team and I am sure that teachers learnt from one another's experiences through conversations during coffee breaks. It would not be until well into the twenty-first century that the seeds for meaningful professional development, sown by Linda Gilbert in the 1980s, would eventually come to fruition – as we shall see in a later chapter.

Despite the limited value of the training day model described above, I do believe that extremely effective professional learning was taking place within the Music Service during the 1980s, but that this was happening in ways that were informal, unplanned and not fully understood at the time. Many years later, Richard Duckett shared with me his reflections on this. 'In some music services,' he said, 'initiatives were dictated from above which the teachers did not believe in, and this had a corrosive effect on morale. But in the Birmingham Music Service, nobody at the top ever said, "This is the way we're all going to do things from now on."' Duckett explained that, partly because Birmingham was such a large authority, there was scope for different teachers to try out different approaches in different schools, and this often resulted in colleagues being inspired by one another to try out new ideas. 'Everything was mixed up,' said Duckett, 'with different things going on in different places, and different teachers learning from one another. It was like balls being juggled in the air, or like a living organism – nobody was in charge, but somehow the whole thing worked. And people were given freedom – although within limits, because you always had to be able to justify what you were doing.'

I believe that two teachers, in particular, were responsible for this positive influence within the Music Service. One was Richard Duckett himself – he was not part of the management team and rarely gave presentations at training days, but he had a profound impact on other staff in relation to group teaching, creativity, repertoire and working with pupils at the highest levels. The other teacher was Heather Doust who, as we have already seen, had a huge influence through her Suzuki violin teaching.

Through the unintended occasions for professional development described above, the Music Service was, I believe, unknowingly modelling an approach to leadership that was to become well understood and highly valued some 20 years later. When leadership expert Roy Leighton led a training session for Music Service teachers in 2010, he likened professional development to the unpredictable, yet coherent, nature of jazz improvisation – not unlike Duckett's description above. And Margaret Wheatley, in her book, *Leadership and the New Science,* suggests that effective leadership works in the same way as chaos theory:

> In this chaotic world, we need leaders. But we don't need bosses ... We need leaders to understand that we are best controlled by concepts that invite our participation, not policies and procedures that curtail our contribution ... In chaos theory it is true that you can never tell where the system is headed until you've observed it over time. Order emerges, but it doesn't materialize instantly. This is also true for organizations, and this is a great challenge in our speed-crazed world. It takes time to see that a well-centred organization really has enough visible structure to work well. (Wheatley, 1999: 131–2)

Although in the last chapter I indicated my reservations about the value of the Centre Sounds programme of musical performances in schools, one very positive aspect of this project, in my opinion, was that it provided a unique opportunity for staff to work alongside each other in teams – to socialize and to share ideas. So teachers learnt from one another about different ways of writing musical arrangements, different ways to talk to children and different methods of involving pupils in musical performances – perhaps through singing or joining in on percussion instruments. It was a rare opportunity at that time for groups of instrumental teachers to come together to work as a team over a period of time.

In the 1980s there was still no tradition in the Music Service of instrumental teachers being visited in schools by their managers. Soon after my arrival, however, I began to undertake such visits to members of the Woodwind Department, because I saw this as an essential way of supporting their work. I used to give notice to a teacher that I would visit them at a particular time at a particular school. I would then go and watch two or three lessons, following which we would both sit down and talk about the lessons I had seen, discuss any ideas for future development and, finally,

I would give a handwritten report to the teacher. I developed this approach as a result of conversations with my brother Brian Loane in which he shared with me the methods he was adopting as a Divisional Music Co-ordinator for the ILEA. Not only were such visits unusual in the Birmingham Music Service, but I do not believe they were the norm in many music services at that time.

Towards the end of the 1980s, however, Keith Allen made the decision to break with tradition and organize visits by Heads of Department to instrumental teachers in schools. But unfortunately these visits were organized in a way that, far from appearing supportive, looked forward instead to the style adopted by Ofsted many years later. Heads of Department were advised at a meeting that during a particular week – referred to as 'Blitz Week' – each member of staff would receive a surprise, unannounced observation visit from their Head of Department. Given that the word 'blitz' is commonly used in Britain to refer to the bombing of British cities during the Second World War, when this information eventually leaked out, through conversations in the Sir Harry public house, it did not create a positive feeling among the staff. I cannot now remember whether or not the visits actually took place but, if they did, the exercise was certainly not repeated. At the start of the 1990s, however, the Music Service was to establish a structure of professional support visits (PSVs) that were truly supportive in nature, and which would continue right up until the time of writing. This important innovation will be fully described in the next chapter.

Classroom music

Linda Gilbert explained that, when she arrived in Birmingham, she considered that the Consortium Music Teachers were being used as 'peripatetic classroom music teachers, making short visits to schools which did not have permanent music staff, in order to teach music' – very similar to Richard Worth's description in the previous chapter. Gilbert's aim, however, was to encourage schools to employ their own full-time music teachers, so that the Consortium Music Teachers could spend their time supporting the work of those teachers in schools instead of working themselves as visiting music teachers. This would bring the Consortium Music Teachers' role in line with the work of the ILEA Divisional Music Co-ordinators, as described by John Stephens, Staff Inspector for Music in the ILEA during the 1980s:

> Their conditions of service indicate that they are to spend half their time in schools, teaching for the purpose of improving

> the pedagogical skills of teachers, rather than acting as highly paid supply teachers. They only teach when a teacher is present. (Stephens, 1982: 50)

So one of the first things Gilbert did upon starting her post as General Inspector was to take the whole team of Consortium Music Teachers to London to meet John Stephens and the Divisional Music Co-ordinators, in order to share ideas and find out about how things worked in the ILEA. 'I wanted to get them fired up and to understand what I was trying to do,' said Gilbert.

In 1987, however, it was decided that Birmingham's team of Consortium Music Teachers, which numbered ten at the time, should be replaced by a much smaller team of four Advisory Teachers. The reasons for this restructure are unclear – some of those involved have suggested that it was merely a cost-cutting measure; others have suggested that the purpose was to retain those staff who had the skills necessary to support the introduction of the Music National Curriculum one year later. So all the Consortium Music Teachers went through an interview process following which four of them were appointed as Advisory Teachers and the other six had to look for other employment. Since Paul Slater was not appointed to one of the new roles, Keith Allen seized on this opportunity to take him on as the Music Service's first full-time keyboard teacher and thus cater for the increasing interest in this area of work within schools. Over the preceding few years, brass teacher Bill Hunt had gradually been reducing the amount of brass teaching on his timetable to enable him to take on more keyboard teaching. But the appointment of Slater signalled the start of a huge expansion in this area that would lead to the keyboard team – when eventually it joined up with the guitar team – becoming one of the largest departments in the Music Service. And in 1988, in order to manage this expanding team, Slater was promoted to the newly created post of Head of Keyboards. Shortly after that, as other areas of the Music Service were also expanding, his job title was changed to Head of Percussion and Allied Studies, meaning that he was now responsible for the teaching of percussion, keyboard, guitar, voice, Asian instruments and steel pans.

One of Linda Gilbert's key priorities towards the end of the 1980s was to establish the three principles of the new National Curriculum for Music – composing, performing and listening – as the basis for classroom music teaching. 'This was already happening in a small way,' said Gilbert, 'with new teachers coming into schools having been trained in this approach, but there was still a lot of support needed for this way of working.' An important innovation of Gilbert's, designed to facilitate this support, and consistent with her collaborative approach to professional development, was the setting up of networks of music teachers in different areas of the city for regular meetings and sharing of ideas. 'Because that's how teachers develop,' said Gilbert. 'They learn from each other because they do not threaten one another.'

A crucial way in which Gilbert raised the status of classroom music teaching in Birmingham primary schools was through re-establishing the partnership that had existed between the local education authority and the CBSO, but which had been brought to an end by Stanley Adams during the 1960s. When Gilbert was appointed as General Inspector, she was aware that the CBSO's new Principal Conductor, Simon Rattle, had an interest in educational work, so she approached him to suggest re-establishing those links. Accordingly, the groundbreaking Adopt a Player scheme was created whereby a CBSO player would make regular visits to a primary school, working with small groups of pupils on creative music-making, supported by one of the primary Consortium Music Teachers. Initially six CBSO musicians were involved, including Simon Rattle himself (Figure 4.3) who modelled huge enthusiasm for the project and who, apparently, used to arrive secretly at Victoria Special School, in order to avoid the likely media attention. Many of the schools involved were in challenged inner-city areas such as Handsworth that, historically, had been under-represented in terms of Music Service provision. 'We were doing the kind of work that is very familiar today,' said Gilbert, 'but which, at that time, was quite innovative. We would take a piece of musical repertoire, draw out some key features and then improvise around these alongside the CBSO musician.' After a series of visits from the CBSO player, the children would then attend the Town Hall for a CBSO concert. Before the concert, they would meet up with the player they had been working with, and they would then have the excitement of seeing that person on stage as part of the orchestra. According to Gilbert, the contentious part, as far as Birmingham Town Hall audiences were concerned, was that the parties of schoolchildren were often seen to be occupying the best seats in the house. Gilbert recalled one of these occasions when a group of inner-city children, with whom trombonist Alwyn Green had been working, made a banner saying, 'Hello Alwyn'. 'And when Alwyn walked on stage that evening,' said Gilbert, 'the children unfurled their banner over the side of the balcony, to the surprise of the audience and the orchestra. When Alwyn saw this, he gave the children a wave – breaking through the barrier that had traditionally existed between Town Hall audiences and the CBSO.' During the run-up to Christmas

2018, I bumped into Alwyn Green in Birmingham city centre where, well into his retirement from the CBSO, he was performing Christmas carols with a Salvation Army brass band. When we spoke, he recalled with great fondness his work with Birmingham schoolchildren during the 1980s and, in particular, that welcome he was given as he walked onto the Town Hall stage 30 years earlier.

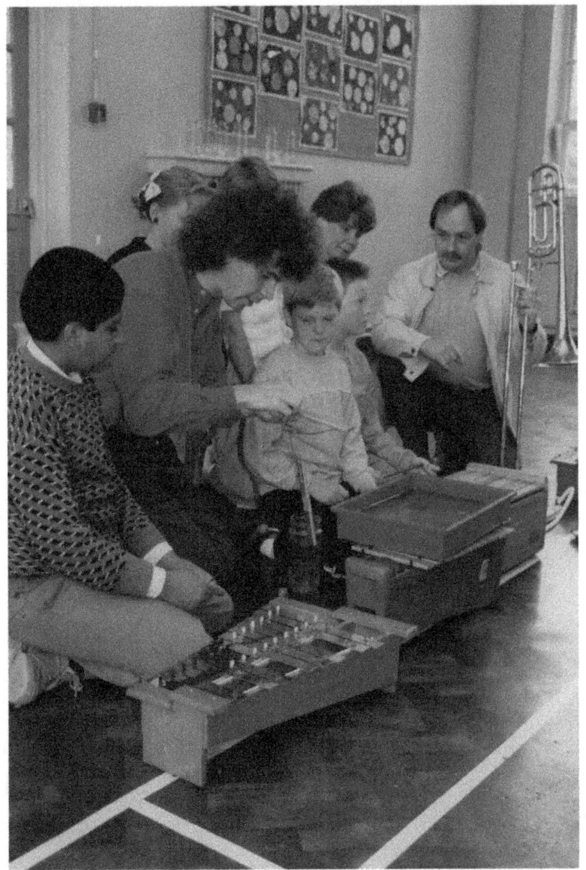

Figure 4.3: Conductor Simon Rattle and CBSO trombone player Danny Longstaff working alongside pupils in a Birmingham junior school as part of the Adopt a Player scheme, *c.*1985 (Photo: Michael Bates, Birmingham Music Service)

This rebirth of the collaboration between the Birmingham Music Service and the CBSO represented something very different from the CBSO's visits to schools in the time of Desmond MacMahon and Stanley Adams. Children were now involved in meaningful experiences where they were getting to know professional musicians and creating their own music alongside them, rather than merely being performed to by those musicians. This practice of giving schoolchildren the opportunity to work alongside professional musicians was to become a hallmark of the Music Service's philosophy from this time onwards, as we shall see in future chapters. Linda Gilbert told me that her inspiration for the creative partnership with the CBSO had been the work of Peter Renshaw, who had been Principal at the Yehudi Menuhin School before being appointed in 1984 as Head of Research and Development at the Guildhall School of Music and Drama. And I remember, shortly after my arrival in Birmingham, attending a discussion session at the Birmingham School of Music that was organized by Linda Gilbert and led by Peter Renshaw. The session was attended by groups of CBSO players, Birmingham Conservatoire students and Birmingham Music Service teachers and the main area for discussion was the predicted diversification of the role of the orchestral musician in the years ahead – bringing the work of professional musicians into the wider community, including schools.

A new home

In July 1989 the city council moved out of the Martineau Teachers' Centre in Edgbaston and the Birmingham Music Service now found itself based in new, much more spacious accommodation at the newly named Martineau Education Centre, a former approved school on Balden Road in Harborne. The building had closed its doors as a school in 1984 and, by the time the Music Service moved there in 1989, it was also home to other centrally based teams within the Education Department such as the advisers and the educational psychologists. In many ways, the new Martineau Education Centre was a great improvement on its predecessor building on the Bristol Road. Because it had been a large school, there were two halls, two gyms and numerous classroom-sized rooms – all providing excellent accommodation for staff training, rehearsals of Music Service ensembles and adult education classes for the local community. The centre had a pleasant restaurant and a comfortable bar where Music Service staff would often meet at the end of the day and mingle with members of the advisory team and schoolteachers from around the city. There was also a fully operational swimming pool, which was used by local schools and was open to the centre's staff – I often made use of this facility myself, during lunch breaks on my days at the office, and during the school holidays. I believe that these greatly improved facilities at the Martineau Education Centre helped to reinforce the feeling of professionalization and confidence that was to develop within the Music Service during the 1990s, as well as contributing to improvement in the quality of professional development for staff.

Shortly after the Music Service's move to its new accommodation, Linda Gilbert saw the opportunity for another innovation to support classroom music teaching in the city. In one of the rooms of the Martineau Education Centre, Gilbert established the Birmingham Music Education Resource Centre – a place that school music teachers could visit in order to talk to one another and to the Advisory Teachers. The Resource Centre had examples of pupils' work on display and it housed a wide range of classroom instruments that teachers could try out. According to Linda Gilbert, 'It was a place where music education in Birmingham became visible. And, to raise awareness as much as possible, we were able to get Simon Rattle to come along and open the Centre.'

Area Sounds

In 1989, Richard Duckett approached me to ask if I would collaborate with him in writing a series of tutor books for woodwind instruments to complement his *Team Brass* series that had been published a year earlier. Duckett's *Team Brass* books were unlike anything that had preceded them because they were based on ensemble pieces combining the different brass instruments (reflecting Duckett's commitment to group instrumental teaching), and they included contemporary film-music themes as well as suggestions for pupil composition and improvisation. The series therefore fulfilled a need among brass teachers for material that reflected some of the newer approaches being developed within instrumental teaching. Since sales of the books were high from the moment of publication, the publisher very quickly asked Duckett if he would write a similar series of books for woodwind instruments. So, when Duckett invited me to work with him in writing the *Team Woodwind* series of books (Loane and Duckett, 1991), I leapt at the opportunity, and from then, up to the publication of the books in 1991, I spent many hours working alongside him at his home in Halesowen in the Black Country.

Very often, at the end of a long evening's work, Duckett and I would retire to his local pub, The Fairfield, to enjoy a pint of Banks's Bitter and a leisurely chat. It was during one of these pub visits that Richard Duckett said to me, 'I've got an idea about something new we could try out in the Music Service – it would be called Area Sounds.' Duckett's vision was that Area Sounds would represent a more educational version of Centre Sounds – the programme of Music Service performance visits to schools described in the last chapter. In Area Sounds, Duckett suggested, a small group of instrumental teachers would be formed in each of the local authority's three areas – North, Central and South – and each group would spend one afternoon per week presenting music workshops to primary schools in their area. But unlike Centre Sounds, which was essentially a musical performance given to children, Area Sounds would be an occasion for pupils to be actively involved in the music-making. After my enthusiastic endorsement, the suggestion was duly presented to Keith Allen who, typically, gave the go-ahead and the new project was launched. As far as possible, the staff involved were already established as teachers in the areas where they were delivering the workshops, so they often already knew the schools they would be visiting. This meant that they were building on existing relationships within schools, and that the content of workshops could be geared to the needs of particular schools. Also, the model was forward-looking in terms of leadership because, unlike Centre Sounds, the groups were led by rank-and-file teachers rather than by Heads of Departments. The most important feature of Area Sounds, however, was that children were now participating fully in the music-making, rather than merely having music played to them. So, the Area Sounds team in the South Area, for example, which was led by Richard Duckett, developed complete shows for the children to take part in, including a musical based on the *Jack and the Beanstalk* story. And preparatory visits were often made to schools, with materials being delivered for the children to work on in advance of the main visit. Whereas Centre Sounds was, arguably, a project that was done *to* schools, Area Sounds was certainly something that was done *with* schools. Richard Duckett worked for the Birmingham Music Service up until his retirement in 1997, but his influence on the organization continued to be felt a long time thereafter.

25th Anniversary Concert

On 11 February 1990 the BSSO celebrated the first quarter-of-a-century of its existence with a 25th Anniversary Concert at Birmingham Town Hall. The BSSO, conducted by Peter Bridle, opened the concert with *An Orkney Wedding, with Sunrise* by Peter Maxwell Davies, showing how far the orchestra had developed in terms of tackling challenging, contemporary repertoire. The concert continued with Arutiunian's Trumpet Concerto, with BSSO trumpet player Paul Sharman playing the solo part (Figure 4.4), and the *Valse* from Tchaikovsky's *Swan Lake*. After the interval, Bridle conducted a performance of Stravinsky's *Firebird Suite* given by the Golden Oldies Orchestra, made up of musicians who had been members of the BSSO over the preceding 25 years. Many of these were now well-established professional musicians, such as double bass player Roderick Dunk, clarinettist Joy Farrell, oboist Karen O'Connor and the leader of the orchestra Margaret Faultless. The orchestra also included violinist Lizo Mzimba who had been leader of the BSSO in the early 1980s and, at the time of writing, is well known for his television appearances as the BBC News Entertainment Correspondent. The Golden Oldies Orchestra then closed the concert with a rousing performance of William Walton's *Crown Imperial* conducted by the BSSO's founder, 80-year-old Stanley Adams. Peter Davies was also present at the concert and I remember both him and Adams mingling with former BSSO members and Music Service staff at a social event for all concerned at the Martineau Education Centre the evening before the concert.

Figure 4.4: The Birmingham Schools' Symphony Orchestra performing at their 25th Anniversary Concert at Birmingham Town Hall in 1990, with conductor Peter Bridle and trumpet soloist Paul Sharman (Photo: Robert Nagle)

Impending uncertainty

In August 1990 Linda Gilbert resigned her post as General Inspector for Music in order to return to London – not long after Richard Howlett had resigned his post as Advisory Teacher in order to take up the position of Head of Music Service in Hampshire. No immediate attempt was made by the authority to appoint replacements for either Gilbert or Howlett. Upon Gilbert's departure, however, Lewis Coley, who had been working as Schools Adviser in the North Area of the city (and whose work as a schoolteacher was mentioned in Chapter 2), took over responsibility for music. 'My main responsibility continued to be general advisory work in my 34 schools in the North Area,' said Coley, 'but, when Linda left, I also started to undertake reviews of music in schools right across the city.' This meant that Linda Gilbert was replaced by someone whose main responsibility was not music and who had not previously occupied a senior position in music education. This, combined with the fact that Howlett was not replaced at all, meant that Keith Allen was now seen as having sole responsibility for the Music Service, as well as being by far the most senior musician within the Education Department. It was within this context in the early 1990s that the Music Service had to start addressing the implications of the 1988 Education Reform Act, signalling the most far-reaching changes to take place in English state education since the Second World War. As far as schools were concerned, the most significant of these changes was the introduction, for the first time in this country, of a National Curriculum. But for music services the most important change was the introduction of Local Management of Schools (LMS), meaning that local authorities would now be required to delegate much of their funding directly to schools. This was a potential threat to music services since, if a local authority decided to delegate its funding for instrumental teaching, it would then be up to individual schools to decide whether or not they wished to continue buying in that teaching from music services. I recall a Music Service staff meeting that took place around that time at which Keith Allen outlined these challenges and updated staff on conversations he was having with Education Department officers on the matter. At the end of the meeting, one of the instrumental teachers stood up and, on behalf of those present, expressed confidence in everything Allen was doing to get the Music Service through difficult times, and thanked him. Such deference towards Allen seemed to hark back to the days of MacMahon, Adams and Davies, when complete trust was placed in one individual at the top of the organization, who was seen as being single-handedly in charge.

Visit to the USSR

Notwithstanding the impending uncertainty described above, I was extremely fortunate that, in November 1990, the Birmingham Music Service supported me in making a visit to the Soviet Union, in order to undertake research for the British Council into instrumental music teaching in that country. In the course of my two-week stay I visited the Moscow State Conservatoire, the Leningrad State Conservatoire and a number of children's music schools in both cities where I had fascinating conversations with teachers and students, observed inspirational teaching and heard wonderful musical performances. The most memorable of these experiences was my visit to the Vesna [Spring] Children's Music School in Moscow. Following my journey from the city centre in the incredibly beautiful and efficient Moscow Metro, I found myself walking through a rather poor, bleak-looking north-Moscow suburb dominated by high-rise flats. But when I walked through the doors of the Vesna Music School I felt that I had entered an oasis of palatial luxury – with its 12 grand pianos, state-of-the-art computer technology and a majestic, acoustically superb concert hall. And most inspiring of all was the fact that the music school was attended at the end of the school day by young people from the local area – without any form of selection or payment of fees – to receive music lessons and take part in the Vesna Children's Choir. At the time of my visit the choir had acquired a reputation throughout the Soviet Union, where it had toured extensively but, at the time of writing, the choir is regarded as one of the best children's choirs in the world, having won many awards at international choral competitions. When I sat down alongside my interpreter to interview the Vesna Music School Director, Aleksandr Ponomaryov, we were treated to plates of delicious Azerbaijani halva to accompany our cups of tea – seeming to symbolize the privileged status of the music school at a time of extreme food shortages for ordinary Soviet citizens. According to an English-speaking piano teacher I interviewed at the school, this position of privilege, exemplified by the plates of halva and the 12 grand pianos, was the result of Ponomaryov's position within the Soviet Communist Party. 'He's got *blat*!' said the piano teacher. (*Blat* was a colloquial term used in Russia at the time to describe the corrupt practice of acquiring limited resources through informal personal networks – not unlike the patronage associated with English music services, described elsewhere in this book.)

My affable meeting with Aleksandr Ponomaryov, however, resulted in a very positive outcome: a reciprocal invitation whereby the Birmingham Schools' Jazz Orchestra would visit Moscow for a concert tour in 1991 and the Vesna Children's Choir would visit Birmingham in 1992. During the summer of 1991 arrangements were going ahead for the BSJO visit, with saxophonist Don Rendell having agreed to join the tour as a guest soloist. But, while walking along Birmingham's New Street on 19 August 1991, I was shocked to read on a newspaper hoarding that an attempted coup d'état had just taken place in the Soviet Union, resulting in President Mikhail Gorbachev being deposed from office and held captive in Crimea. Although the coup was unsuccessful and Gorbachev returned to power two days later, a period of instability in the country was to follow, leading to parents of BSJO members expressing concerns regarding the safety of the proposed trip. Sadly, therefore, what would have been an extremely exciting exchange visit for our young musicians never took place.

Approaching the end of an era

In 1991 Birmingham Education Department advertised the post of Schools Adviser for Music because, according to Lewis Coley, 'We needed someone who would have special responsibility for music since I could no longer do justice to the subject on my own.' Among the candidates interviewed for this post were two senior teachers from the ILEA Music Service, who were looking for jobs following the recent government decision to abolish the ILEA. These candidates were the ILEA's Head of Instrumental Teaching, Mark Wyatt, and my brother Terry Loane who, like my brother Brian, was one of the ILEA's Divisional Music Co-ordinators. In the course of the interview, however, Terry withdrew his application because he felt that, although the post had been advertised as focusing mainly on music, it was becoming apparent during the interview that music would only be a small part of the job. Mark Wyatt was duly appointed, becoming Birmingham Education Department's sixth, and penultimate, Music Adviser. When Wyatt started his new post in April 1991, he took over responsibility for music across the whole city, but Coley continued to retain some limited involvement with the subject. 'I continued to attend meetings on the music curriculum,' said Coley, 'alongside Mark and the Advisory Teachers.'

Also in April 1991 a new management structure was introduced within the Music Service meaning that, overnight, the team of Music Service managers increased from six people to fourteen. So the management team, which up to then had comprised a Head of Service and five Heads of Departments, now consisted of a Head of Service, Head of Strings, Deputy Head of Strings, Head of Wind, Deputy Head of Wind, Head of Percussion and Allied Studies, Deputy Head of Percussion and Allied Studies, three Area Co-ordinators (North, Central and South), three Assistant Area Co-ordinators and a GCSE Co-ordinator. The main role of the Area Co-ordinators was to manage and administrate the newly established Area Sounds workshops in their respective areas and the role of the GCSE Co-ordinator was to liaise with secondary schools regarding Music Service support with the performance component of the new GCSE music examination. These new management appointments were all made internally, and I found myself being promoted to the post of Head of Wind, meaning that I was now responsible for brass as well as woodwind teaching, and my newly appointed Deputy Head of Wind was brass teacher and Conductor of the Birmingham Schools' Concert Orchestra, Bob Vivian.

This creation of eight additional management posts was extremely costly, not only in higher salaries but also in the increase in office-based, non-teaching time. I have no recollection of any explanation being given at the time regarding the purpose of this restructure, and looking back now it seems astonishing that it took place just as the Music Service was facing serious, unprecedented threats to its financial security through the imminent introduction of LMS. Furthermore, it is difficult to understand why, within the new structure, almost everyone in the management team now had a deputy or an assistant, apart from the person who probably needed this most of all – the Head of Service. I recall, however, that at the time, the restructure was very much welcomed by Music Service staff, including myself, as it gave many of us the opportunity for promotion and increased salary. Perhaps this could be considered to be the Birmingham Music Service's final example of patronage, which as we have seen was such a strong feature of local authority music provision in the city during the twentieth century – the bestowing of favours and rewards by those who were in positions of power and influence. One outcome of the restructure, which was to play a crucial role in the Music Service's future development, was that it provided the first rung on the ladder of promotion for cello teacher John Clemson who was now the service's Assistant Area Co-ordinator – South Area. Reflecting on this promotion, Clemson later told me, 'I found myself part of a large, expensive management structure – a lot of people on salary allowances, with non-contact time, but without very much work to do! And creating all those new posts was a move in exactly the wrong direction – just a short time before LMS.'

On 15 April 1991, four thousand people flocked to Birmingham's wonderful new Symphony Hall to hear Simon Rattle conduct the CBSO in the hall's opening concert, a performance that included Ravel's *Daphnis et Chloé*. During the 1920s Adrian Boult, then conductor of the City of Birmingham Orchestra, had been promised a new concert hall by the city council, because of the limitations of the Town Hall. It would not be until 70 years later, however – as a result of the international reputation achieved for the CBSO under Simon Rattle – that this new home for the orchestra was finally built, as part of Birmingham's International Convention Centre.

The audience at the Symphony Hall's inaugural concert included parties of children from Birmingham schools, demonstrating the ongoing partnership between the CBSO and the local authority that had been rekindled by Linda Gilbert. And the city's commitment to young people's music-making was demonstrated by the fact that, within a week of its opening concert, the Symphony Hall hosted the British Gas Flame of Youth Music Festival – two complete days of musical performances by young people from music services all over the West Midlands. The Birmingham Music Service was represented at this occasion by the Birmingham Schools' Indian Music Ensemble directed by Sneh Lata, the Birmingham Schools' Symphony Orchestra directed by Peter Bridle and the Birmingham Schools' Brass Ensemble directed by Bob Vivian, which performed an opening fanfare for the Saturday night Gala Concert. I remember being part of a group of Music Service representatives who welcomed Prince Edward to this concert as he arrived at the Symphony Hall, having crossed the newly constructed pedestrian bridge over Broad Street, accompanied by Festival Director, Jeremy Patterson.

Two months later, on 12 June, the BSSO again performed at the Symphony Hall in the company of royalty. This time the orchestra was taking part in the Royal Gala Performance that marked the official opening of the International Convention Centre by HM Queen Elizabeth II. And, on 15 and 16 July, the Music Service's Young Sounds concerts (as the Summer Gala Concerts were now known) took place for the first time in the Symphony Hall. These concerts included guest appearances by two internationally known musicians – percussionist Evelyn Glennie, who performed as a soloist with the Birmingham Schools' Wind Orchestra directed by Keith Allen, and jazz trumpeter Humphrey Lyttelton, who performed as a soloist with the Birmingham Schools' Jazz Orchestra (BSJO), directed by myself. It had been a particularly exciting week for the BSJO because, only a few days earlier, they had accompanied another renowned jazz trumpet player, Digby Fairweather, in a performance at the Midlands Arts Centre, as part of the Birmingham International Jazz Festival. (Twenty-six years later, following my retirement from the Birmingham Music Service, I was privileged to appear once again alongside Fairweather in another Birmingham Jazz Festival performance – this time in my role as clarinettist with the Chase Jazzmen, a West Midlands traditional jazz band.)

So the summer term of 1991 had been, perhaps, the most exciting time ever for the Birmingham Music Service, culminating in two Young Sounds concerts at the recently opened Symphony Hall involving the service's 16 Central Ensembles and five groups of musicians from individual Birmingham schools. A few days later, the whole team of Music Service teachers was invited to attend a quiz night at the Martineau Education Centre bar, in order to celebrate the end of the academic year. The occasion was well attended and I recall the warm, friendly atmosphere, and the great feeling of relaxation as teachers looked forward to their well-earned six-week break. Little did we know then the huge shock that was in store for us – involving theft on a massive scale at the highest level of the organization – which was to rock the Music Service to its foundations only a few days later.

Chapter 5

From crisis to confidence

It was the second day of the school holidays when I drove to the Martineau Education Centre in order to undertake some interviews, alongside Keith Allen, for part-time, hourly-paid woodwind teaching staff. To my surprise, I was met in the car park at 9.00 a.m. by Music Adviser Mark Wyatt who asked me the purpose of my visit. 'I'm here to do some interviews with Keith,' I said. Wyatt looked very serious. 'I'm afraid the interviews will have to go ahead without Keith,' he said, 'because he's just been suspended from his job while an audit investigation is taking place.' Hearing this information out of the blue left me speechless, whereupon Wyatt added, 'This is a lot more than just sloppy accounting.' He went on to say that the room normally used for interviews, Allen's office, would not be available that morning. So, at the last minute, I managed to find another member of staff to assist with the interviews and we installed ourselves in another room, directly opposite Allen's office. I then became aware, while the interviews were in progress, why I had been asked to find a different room – Allen had now arrived and, under the supervision of Wyatt, was removing personal possessions from his office to his car, parked outside, including a new, state-of-the-art Roland electric piano. Apparently Allen had arrived much earlier in the morning to do this, but had been refused admission to the building until Wyatt arrived. I recall being in a state of shock, to the extent that I was in tears as I related these events to a relative in a telephone conversation that evening. This feeling of shock and disbelief was shared by other Music Service colleagues at the time and was rooted, I believe, in the fact that we had placed all our trust in one individual, who had neither a deputy nor an assistant. It now appeared that this trust may have been misplaced, leaving the Music Service without a leader at a time when leadership was needed more than ever.

The next day, Birmingham City Council accountant Michael Channell moved into Allen's office, which now became the base for an audit investigation that would last several months, and would entail, in that predigital age, sifting through huge piles of paperwork. From the moment of Allen's suspension, Rod Evans, Schools Support Manager (South Area), took over the day-to-day management of the Music Service, working closely alongside Mark Wyatt. Evans immediately delegated to Bob Vivian and myself the responsibility for opening all incoming mail to the Music Service, so that we could alert Evans to anything that appeared sensitive, including all invoices. Vivian and I duly took turns at coming into the Martineau Education Centre on alternate days throughout the summer holiday, forgoing the six-week break that we had both been looking forward to.

Through conversations with other Music Service managers during the summer holiday period, I learnt something about the events that had taken place during the summer term that had led to Allen's suspension. Apparently some senior managers had begun to notice certain financial irregularities (including, for example, invoices addressed to the Music Service that were not related to Music Service purchases), seemingly pointing a finger of suspicion towards Keith Allen. The managers addressed Allen about these issues, but no satisfactory explanations were given, and more irregularities came to light as the term progressed. Further meetings took place between these managers and the Head of Service, but still there was no resolution. One of the managers then raised the matter informally with a senior officer in the local authority, whom he happened to know socially, but was advised not to do anything that might 'rock the boat'. Ignoring this advice, the group of managers then went to Mark Wyatt to express their concerns and this resulted in Allen being suspended from his duties. It has been suggested that the authority may have deliberately delayed his suspension until after the conclusion of the Young Sounds concerts in the Symphony Hall, and until the end of term, in order to minimize disruption and adverse publicity.

When this pattern of events leading to Allen's suspension was explained to me, I then recalled seeing the group of managers going into Allen's office for long meetings during the summer term. And I also recalled, on at least one of these occasions, seeing them leave his office – all looking extremely upset, and one of them in tears.

On the first day back at work after the summer holidays, all Music Service staff met at the Martineau Education Centre, where Mark Wyatt introduced us to Rod Evans – our new, temporary boss. Evans came across to the staff as a rather formal and stern figure, and gave a brief, official update on the Music Service's situation. He spoke about the need for extreme regularity in all financial matters, including the prompt submission of teachers' monthly travel expenses claims. Evans then looked slightly perturbed when brass teacher Roger Rae stood up and asked for reassurance that his backlog of nearly 12 months of unsubmitted claims would still be paid.

On the second day of term, it suddenly occurred to me that nobody had yet been lined up to take the place of Keith Allen as conductor of the

Birmingham Schools' Wind Orchestra (BSWO), whose first rehearsal of the school year was scheduled to take place that coming Saturday. So I immediately walked over to Bob Vivian's desk in our office and shared the problem with him – it was something that neither of us had foreseen, even though we had known six weeks earlier about Allen's suspension. Vivian and I agreed that it would be a good idea to approach a colleague named David Perkins to ask if he would consider stepping in to conduct the BSWO for a few weeks. Perkins had been a very successful Head of Music in two Birmingham secondary schools, Bishop Walsh RC School and Cockshut Hill School. In the second of these he had directed an accomplished wind band that, only a year earlier, had performed at the closing night of the Music Service Gala Concerts at Birmingham Town Hall. Perkins had only recently left his job at Cockshut Hill in order to work as one of the Music Advisory Teachers based at the Martineau Education Centre. So I phoned Perkins and put the question to him. To my disappointment he declined the invitation, explaining that he had recently been asked to take on a very big new project that would take up all of his time and energy. He said that he was not yet allowed to reveal what that project was, but that I would find out about it very soon. I then telephoned Tony Veal, Head of Solihull Music Service, and conductor of the Solihull Music Service Wind Orchestra. He also declined the invitation but recommended that I contact Colin Touchin, Director of Music at the University of Warwick. Touchin immediately accepted the job offer and remained as the highly successful conductor of the Birmingham Schools' Wind Orchestra for a number of years.

A new beginning

Later on during that first week of term, Mark Wyatt called a meeting of Music Service managers in Keith Allen's office at the Martineau Education Centre. When I walked into the room, I was taken aback to see that David Perkins, whom I had recently spoken to on the phone, was also present at the meeting. All became clear, however, when Wyatt introduced Perkins as 'our new, interim Acting Head of Service' – this was obviously the 'very big, new project' that Perkins had referred to in our telephone conversation. Wyatt then quickly left the room in order to leave us in no doubt that Perkins was now the one who was in charge. The main thing I remember Perkins saying in this, his first address to us as our new boss, was that he was not going to be 'a mere puppet of Margaret Street'. ('Margaret Street' was the city centre location of the Education Department headquarters, and was the term used colloquially by teachers, referring to the local authority.) In saying this – and he said it twice – I believe Perkins was making the point that his intention in this new job was not merely to manage the fall-out from the Keith Allen débâcle, but to move the Music Service forward as an organization – even though there was no expectation at the time that he was going to be Acting Head of Service for more than a few weeks. In the end, his tenure lasted for nine years and during that period he led a huge improvement in the quality of the service's work, which will be the main focus of this chapter.

During that very first management meeting chaired by Perkins at the start of September 1991, he did something that had never happened before in the Music Service – he delegated tasks to all his senior staff, in such a way that each of us became responsible for overseeing an important area of the service's work. I recall, for example, that I was given the responsibility for looking after the Central Ensembles. Initially there was a feeling of resentment among some of the managers that they were suddenly being given substantial extra work to do by someone who was a newcomer to the organization. Very soon, however, the management team's response became a positive one because there was a feeling that we were being trusted and involved in decision-making in a way that had not happened before.

When I interviewed David Perkins he described his recollections from that period. 'I took over the Music Service at an unusual and difficult time,' he said. 'I'd been away on holiday during August and when I got back, right at the start of the autumn term, Mark Wyatt asked me if I would look after the Music Service for two or three weeks because Keith Allen had been suspended, pending an audit enquiry. In fact, I continued in the role of Acting Head of Service for a lot longer than three weeks, and eventually, in 1992, the job was advertised, and I was appointed on a permanent basis. Luckily for me, Mark Wyatt had been appointed as Music Adviser a few months before I arrived. He was a great support because, of course, he understood our work, having been Head of the ILEA's instrumental team.' Perkins went on to explain that he believed Wyatt was influential in securing his appointment with the Music Service. 'I think one of the reasons Mark wanted me to take over the job was the fact that I was a musician, and he believed that would give me credibility within the team.' (Before starting his career in education, Perkins had worked as a professional trumpet player, performing in West End shows and on cruise liners.) Perkins added that his enthusiasm for working with the Music Service was rooted in his passionate commitment to instrumental music teaching, which stemmed from the fact that his own life had been transformed through access to free instrumental lessons while a school pupil in Hertfordshire. 'And I wanted to help extend those opportunities to others,' said Perkins, 'especially those from "the wrong side of the tracks".'

One of the first issues that Perkins tackled in his new position was unprofessional behaviour within the service, which has been referred to earlier in this book. So the leisurely lunch breaks enjoyed by senior managers at the Court Oak public house, across the road from the Martineau Education Centre, soon came to an end – partly because this was no longer seen to be professional, but also because there was now much more work to get done, due to the delegation of responsibilities. And the senior member of staff who reputedly spent Friday afternoons at the supermarket could now be found teaching in schools at that time of the week. According to Perkins, 'One effect of the climate created by the audit report was that some management issues, which could have proved tiresome, were able to be sorted out quite quickly. So I could say, for example, "Sorry folks, but this has just got to stop – we're going to do it this way from now on."'

I believe that Perkins's style of management, from his early days as Acting Head of Service onwards, was complex. As we have already seen, he immediately delegated tasks to senior managers in a way that had not happened before and, on at least two occasions, I recall him changing his view on important matters having listened to the opinions of others – something that was certainly not the norm in the days of Stanley Adams, for example. From the day he became Acting Head of Service, Perkins paid great attention to detail, taking extremely tight control of every aspect of the Music Service's work – he was very clearly the boss. I remember, for example, that he insisted on every letter written by a senior manager being checked by him before it left the office. And every Friday he would spend several hours alone in his office, totalling the week's expenditure by hand, making sure that the books balanced. I recall that, shortly after he took over, two school pupils came to the Music Service for a work experience placement and Perkins took responsibility for every detail of their placement, including giving a severe reprimand to one of them for arriving several minutes late at the office one morning.

When I asked Perkins to reflect on the quality of the Music Service's work at the time he became Acting Head of Service, he said, 'The standard of some of the pupils we taught was very high indeed. For example, I can remember Bob Vivian's ten-piece brass ensemble playing at the Town Hall and it was as good as anything I'd heard as a student at the Royal College of Music. And I think that, across the board, the teaching was mostly good and sometimes outstanding.' (It is interesting that Perkins chose to use the words 'good' and 'outstanding' – part of the vocabulary of categorization adopted by Ofsted, for whom he was to work as an inspector later in his career.) Perkins went on to say, 'The service included some leading lights nationally, such as Richard Duckett and yourself, who were doing important pioneering work in the area of group teaching. So, despite the awful things that had happened, there was a vibrant atmosphere and exciting things were going on both within the service and beyond.' Perkins reflected that, although the reputation of the Music Service had been damaged by the news of Allen's suspension, the reputation of individual teachers was still largely intact, because headteachers and music teachers in schools were able to separate the two matters. 'The crucial thing,' said Perkins, 'was that we had a critical mass of good, open-minded teachers – they were the majority and they were in the ascendancy. They weren't necessarily people who had carefully thought through the pedagogy, but they were good people whose heart was in the right place and who wanted to do the best for the kids. Had I inherited staff with poor morale or low expectations – and there were music services like that in some other parts of the country – then I think the things we achieved in those years would either never have happened or it would have been much harder.'

Perkins went on to say, however, that he soon became aware of some isolated pockets of poor practice, indicating complacency and low expectations. 'These were matters,' he said, 'which clearly had not been addressed under the previous regime. And, of course, there was the huge problem that we were only teaching in about 50 per cent of the city's schools. So you were alright if you lived in middle-class areas like Sutton Coldfield, or if you attended one of the grammar schools, but otherwise, you didn't get a look in – and that was unacceptable.'

As Music Service teachers were beginning not only to accept, but also to take pride in, their organization's new and long-overdue professionalization, the council auditors were completing their report on the service's financial irregularities. This was passed on to the police, who confirmed in November 1991 that they were investigating the disappearance of funds. In March 1994 Keith Allen was found guilty of 11 charges of theft from Birmingham Education Department over a period of four years, amounting to almost £56,000, and he was given a jail sentence of 18 months. He spent most of this sentence at Hewell Grange open prison in Worcestershire. Never one to shy away from the limelight of publicity, Allen appeared in a television broadcast during the course of his sentence, being interviewed as an inmate of the prison and talking eloquently about the neo-Gothic architecture of the fine nineteenth-century building, described in

The Telegraph as 'Britain's poshest prison' (Preston, 2003). While in prison, Keith Allen took every opportunity to share his musical talents with others – playing the organ for weekly services in the chapel and directing a choir of inmates that performed at the local parish church.

A senior manager from the Music Service, who knew Allen well, later told me: 'The city council's checks and balances were, clearly, grossly inadequate. It's often the case that when people get it into their heads that they are impregnable – they hold the purse strings and the cheque book and so on – unless there are rigorous checks and balances, then there is the potential for things to go wrong, which they did.' And a senior officer within the local authority at the time suggested to me that there had been cases where headteachers found to have misappropriated funds were dismissed but not prosecuted. These reflections throw some light on the climate that prevailed in the local authority at that time, which perhaps made it easier for Allen's crime to take place.

'Improving on previous best'

Notwithstanding the shock and continued media coverage of Keith Allen's suspension, trial and imprisonment, the Birmingham Music Service continued to grow stronger during the 1990s through its confident and successful responses to a range of challenges. In addition to the professionalization of behaviour and the raising of teaching standards within the service, another area that Perkins set his mind to, right from the start, was changing the management structure – gradually decreasing the number of management posts and creating a deputy post. So in 1992, John Clemson was promoted to the newly created post of Senior Tutor – meaning that he was, in effect, Perkins's deputy. Three years later, this post was re-named Deputy Head of Service and, following a further interview, Clemson continued to occupy the role.

In the autumn of 1993 four developments took place within Birmingham Education Authority that were to have a transformative effect on the city's schools and on the work of the Music Service: the publication of Ted Wragg's report on the city's education provision; the appointment of Tim Brighouse as Chief Education Officer; the delegation of local authority funding to schools through LMS; and the departure from the local authority of a large number of schools as they moved to grant-maintained status (which, like LMS, was a provision of the 1988 Education Reform Act).

At the start of the 1990s Birmingham Education Authority had recognized that its education system needed improvement: morale in schools was low, it was hard to attract good teaching staff and school buildings were in a poor state of repair. I recall, for example, that when I was directing Saturday morning rehearsals of the Birmingham Schools' Training Wind Orchestra at George Dixon School, buckets had to be positioned at various positions in the school hall, in order to collect rainwater that was dripping through the ceiling – an image that perhaps symbolizes the way in which Birmingham's education was perceived at that time. All of these problems were widely considered to result from underfunding of schools and poor support from the local authority and, as a result, many Birmingham schools in the early 1990s were considering applying for grant-maintained status in order to escape local-authority management.

So in 1993, under the leadership of Dick Knowles, Birmingham City Council took action to improve the quality of their schools, as described by Wendy Berliner in *The Guardian*:

> The local authority accepted it had to do something to stop the rot in education and did two very brave things. It set up an independent commission of inquiry chaired by the outspoken progressive education academic, Professor Ted Wragg of Exeter University, and it appointed Tim Brighouse, another man unlikely to pull his punches, to be the new chief education officer. (Berliner, 2002)

The Wragg Commission pointed to ways in which Birmingham could improve its education provision, involving increased allocation of funding and collaborative work between schools and the local authority. And, according to Tim Brighouse himself, his appointment as Chief Education Officer in 1993 was probably due, at least in part, to him being recommended to the city by Wragg as the ideal person to implement the commission's recommendations. In the words of David Perkins, 'Tim Brighouse was about to embark on leading and inspiring the most prolonged and successful era of school improvement in any local authority ever – the atmosphere in the city was buzzing when he was appointed!'

There can be no doubt that during his tenure of almost ten years in Birmingham Brighouse transformed the city's education – from being seen as one of the weakest education services in England, Birmingham came to be seen as a model for the rest of the country. My first impression of Brighouse concerned how visible he was, especially when compared with some of his predecessors who, rightly or wrongly, were sometimes regarded as bureaucrats, rarely seen in schools or at public events. Within the first few weeks of Brighouse's appointment, he held a number of question-and-answer sessions for teachers at schools in different areas of the city. When

I attended one such event at Stockland Green School in Erdington, I found the school hall packed with teachers at the end of the school day – all keen to hear what Brighouse had to say, and to ask searching questions about the future of education in Birmingham. To this day I recall vividly my reaction to what Brighouse said on that occasion, which was the first time I heard him speak. I was inspired by the way he talked in detail about the day-to-day situation in Birmingham schools, and yet framed this within a clear educational philosophy, and within a broad historical and geographical context (not unlike the way he has constructed the Foreword to this book). And he spoke in an informal and straightforward manner that seemed far removed from the kind of language expected from education authority officials at the time.

In his first few months in Birmingham, Brighouse appeared at many a secondary school prize-giving, in order to hand out prizes to pupils. I remember attending one such occasion at Shenley Court School, where I was directing the school Jazz Band in a performance, as a warm-up to Brighouse's appearance. I recall that the evening finished later than scheduled because, typically, Brighouse had a short conversation with each prize recipient, rather than merely handing over a book to each of them in turn. Colleagues said that Brighouse was hardly seen at his Margaret Street office during the first few weeks in his new post. This is because he was spending much of his time in schools, making contact with the people he was going to be working with – headteachers, classroom teachers, parents and students. Brighouse soon acquired the reputation for making unscheduled, unannounced visits to schools. Apparently, when he found himself with a few minutes to spare in a particular area of the city, he would pop into a school and visit one or two classrooms to see for himself what was going on. Far from being viewed as threatening or inspectorial, however, such visits were welcomed by teachers, since Brighouse was seen as being warm, approachable and, above all, supportive. Classroom teachers commented to me that, in their conversations with the new Chief Education Officer, what came across most strongly was his passion for, and fascination with, children's learning. Brighouse soon established himself as a regular attender at Music Service concerts – the first occasion I met him was when he and I were the first to arrive at the interval reception of one of these concerts in the Adrian Boult Hall. Pointing out of the window towards the Central Library and the Birmingham Conservatoire, Brighouse said to me jokingly, 'Do you know that they're planning to knock all this down soon – because it's looking a bit scruffy!' That was the first I had heard of the huge building development that was to take place in that area of the city in the twenty-first century. Around the same time, I was one of many hundreds of teachers in Birmingham to receive a Christmas card from Brighouse, with a personal, handwritten message. Such gestures made teachers in Birmingham feel valued and trusted in a way that they had not done in the preceding years.

In all these ways, I believe that Brighouse was demonstrating one of the core principles of his leadership philosophy – the essential importance of establishing good personal relationships with colleagues, based on conversation, respect and trust. In no way, however, did his approach signify any lack of rigour. On the contrary, it was well known that he did not shy away from difficult conversations, particularly with headteachers, when this was necessary.

In her article in *The Guardian,* Wendy Berliner went on to give her description of the way in which Brighouse worked at the start of his tenure in Birmingham:

> Brighouse went visiting schools and held workshops – 11 of them in his first year – in which all the city's head teachers participated. The aim? School improvement. He wanted to examine the processes and practices that made the huge differences in schools with teachers and share what worked with everyone ... Target setting was introduced, but the way it was done was the polar opposite of the way it's done by the current Labour government and the Thatcher and John Major Conservative ones. Instead of imposing targets from outside, teachers were asked whether they could improve on their previous best. The usual reply was yes, then targets were agreed between the school and the Authority. (ibid.)

The term 'improving on previous best' was to become a mantra that summed up the local authority's approach to supporting schools under Brighouse's leadership – emphasizing the principle of moving every school forward, rather than measuring and rank ordering schools in accordance with externally imposed criteria, which was increasingly becoming the hallmark of central-government policy from that time onwards.

In his conversation with me, as part of my research for this book, Brighouse explained his priorities as Chief Education Officer in Birmingham: 'While we had to improve in what the world would measure us by – GCSE outcomes and SATs [Standard Attainment Tests] – I was very keen that we shouldn't lose sight of the wider curriculum, so that all children would get access to the kind of opportunities you and I would want for our kids – and hence the guarantees.' The guarantees were published statements from the education authority setting out proposed expectations for what every early years, primary and secondary pupil should experience in terms of the wider curriculum while at school. For primary pupils, for example, the guarantee included the following:

- Every primary child will have a residential experience.
- Every six-year-old and nine-year-old takes part in a 'public performance'.
- All ten-year-olds carry out an environmental project.
- All parents of six- and eight-year-olds will be told what their child is particularly good at in the expressive arts and be encouraged to provide support.

(Brighouse and Woods, 1999: 165)

When I asked Tim Brighouse to describe his first impressions of the Music Service upon arriving in the city, he said, 'I couldn't believe my luck when I walked into Birmingham and found out how good the music was. Now, I think Brummies have got an underlying degree of self-doubt and tend not to shout about their achievements. Having worked in both London and Oxford, I know the same doesn't apply in those cities – both London and Oxford were incredibly proud of their music and yet, when I went to Birmingham, I discovered that their music was better than either place!'

Brighouse went on to say that one concern he did have upon arriving in Birmingham was the lack of non-white faces in the Music Service ensembles. 'But during the time I was in Birmingham,' he said, 'I saw that the Music Service really did start to embrace diversity.' I believe, however, that the point raised by Brighouse here is a complex one – it certainly appeared that, by the start of the twenty-first century, there were more non-white faces to be seen in the Central Ensembles. My own recollection, however, is that although there were increased numbers of pupils from Asian background joining the ensembles over this period of time, these young people were, very often, from professional, middle-class families. So, while there may have been a wider ethnic representation, it could be argued that there was little increase in the numbers from the city's under-privileged working class.

Tim Brighouse made very interesting comments on the style of leadership within the Music Service. 'David Perkins and Mark Wyatt were always talking about the amazing people within the team,' he said, 'and I thought that was an incredibly good sign. There was no sense in which the people leading the service were hogging the limelight, which is what you find in some music services. It struck me as unusual in a music service that there wasn't one person who shone so brightly that they put the others in the shade. There was a feeling, organizationally, that this was like an improvised jazz performance where everyone made their contribution, making the whole thing spin really effectively. I was thanking my lucky stars that the music was so good but, like the residential centres, for example, I was anxious that it should get stronger and stronger.'

Towards the end of my conversation with Tim Brighouse, he summed up where he believed the City of Birmingham fitted into the development of education in modern Britain:

> The flourishing of music and the other arts in post-war British education was entirely due to the influence of Alec Clegg in the West Riding, to local education authorities having the power to do things, and competing with each other in relation to their residential centres, youth services, music services, etc., and everyone believing that education was a good thing and that it should be left to the professionals to decide what is taught and how it should be taught. These good times lasted until the early 1970s when things began to move backwards again, due to Margaret Thatcher's involvement as Education Secretary. But I think that in the 1990s in Birmingham we were lucky to be able to hold on to a small pocket of possibility. When I arrived in Birmingham, I think the local politicians had been seriously thinking of giving up on education and allowing all schools to go grant-maintained. But, by commissioning the Wragg report and appointing me, they were giving it one last chance.

In October 1993, only weeks after Brighouse's arrival in Birmingham, Secretary of State for Education, John Patten, speaking at a Conservative Party Conference fringe meeting said, 'Birmingham have put this nutter in as its director of education – Brighouse ... I fear for Birmingham with this madman let loose, wandering round the streets, frightening the children.' Brighouse sued Patten for libel, winning substantial damages that he used to fund the setting up of the University of the First Age, a national education charity that continues to thrive. Brighouse told me that, in the wake of the Patten fracas, he heard Birmingham Council Leader Dick Knowles saying to Education Committee members, 'Don't tangle with Brighouse – he's not afraid to take people on.' Implicit in Brighouse's comment was the suggestion that, at the start of his tenure in Birmingham, his successful legal action against Patten had, perhaps, strengthened his position in relation to the city's Education Committee.

From the moment of Brighouse's appointment, the city council began to allocate more funding to education and from 1997 the new Labour Government greatly increased education expenditure. 'So we had a magical opportunity in Birmingham,' said Brighouse. 'I always thought how lucky I was to be in the right place at the right time – you really couldn't fail in supporting things like the Music Service at that time.'

Local management of schools

In the months leading up to the introduction of LMS in 1993, David Perkins, as Head of Service, was part of the working party of headteachers and local authority officers set up to agree arrangements for the delegation of funding to schools. In that forum, Perkins argued strongly that the entire instrumental teaching budget should be delegated to schools, while the budget that supported Music Service ensembles should continue to be held centrally. This was because he believed that full delegation of the teaching budget would open up the potential for expanding the provision of teaching, whereas the ensembles would need central funding if they were to continue operating without charges being made to parents. Others argued that, in the interests of the Music Service's survival, as much of the teaching budget as possible should be held centrally. I remember, for example, attending a meeting organized by the National Union of Teachers (NUT) for all Music Service teachers at which Bill Anderson, General Secretary of the Birmingham NUT branch, argued that we should be fighting for just that. Looking back, I presume this was because the NUT saw LMS as a first stage in the disempowering of local education authorities, thus paving the way for the marketization of education that we have witnessed in the twenty-first century. Birmingham Education Authority finally made the decision to delegate the whole of the budget for instrumental teaching to schools, but to retain centrally the budget that supported the Music Service ensembles. This is exactly what David Perkins had argued for and the decision facilitated a huge growth in Music Service provision for schools in the course of the 1990s.

'Many people saw LMS as a threat,' said Perkins, 'but I always viewed it as a potential vehicle for achieving what I wanted in terms of breadth – getting out to more kids in more schools, and making sure that all kids were getting good quality teaching and making great progress, no matter which part of the city they lived in. When Tim Brighouse arrived, he created a culture of "improving on previous best" and I wanted the Music Service to be part of that.'

In the summer of 1993, once the local authority had made the decision to delegate the Music Service's teaching budget to schools, David Perkins set about visiting every secondary-school headteacher in the city and he established a task force of Music Service managers who, between them, visited every primary-school headteacher. As a member of that task force it was my job to visit schools in the Sheldon area of East Birmingham – quite a disadvantaged area that, historically, had not been well-served by the Music Service. So I often found myself having conversations with headteachers whose schools had never received any provision from the service and yet, I picked up no feelings of resentment towards the organization, but only an eagerness to make the most of the new opportunities that were now on offer.

When LMS finally came into effect in September 1993 there was, exactly as predicted by David Perkins, a considerable increase in demand for instrumental teaching, leading to an expansion in the size of the Music Service. Schools that had been ignored since the service's inception decided to establish instrumental music as part of their curriculum for the first time, and many schools that had already benefited from this provision decided to buy in additional teaching. Furthermore, the conversations with headteachers leading up to LMS, and the fact that the service now needed to respond to what schools wanted, led to a great broadening of provision. So, for example, we saw a significant increase in electric keyboard and drum-kit teaching, and electric-guitar teaching was introduced into schools for the first time. Also, the fact that several hundred headteachers rather than a single Music Adviser now held the purse strings meant that the tradition of patronage, which had played such an important part in the earlier development of Birmingham's music education, was now dead.

Following the introduction of LMS, most English education authorities – unlike Birmingham – continued to hold centrally a portion of their budget to support instrumental music teaching. Music services in those authorities were, therefore, able to set their charges to schools at hourly rates that did not reflect the real cost, and that were considerably lower than Birmingham's rate of £26 per hour (a rate that has remained unchanged in real terms over the intervening years). The Birmingham Music Service was exceptional in that it ran its instrumental teaching for six years – from the introduction of LMS in 1993 up to the introduction of central government funding in 1999 – supported solely by revenue from schools. And the Birmingham Music Service has also been unusual in that, throughout its history, it has continued to increase the number and range of its pupil ensembles and has achieved this without making any charges to parents for ensemble membership.

Grant-maintained status

In September 1993, along with the introduction of LMS, a large number of Birmingham secondary schools (including all five of the King Edward VI grammar schools) adopted grant-maintained status (GMS), meaning that they were now funded directly by central government and were no longer part of the local authority. The local authority would not allow the Music Service to teach in grant-maintained schools so, overnight, the service lost 15 per cent of its work, including many of its most advanced pupils. Also, it was deemed that, once a school opted out of local-authority control, it would take over the ownership of resources that had been on loan from the council. This meant that the Music Service suddenly lost all of the musical instruments that had been on loan to those schools. (The service had some success in mitigating the effects of this, however, by asking their teachers, in the months leading up to GMS, to remove from these schools any instruments that were not currently in use.) Yet another consequence of the move to GMS was that some Music Service teachers, who had been teaching predominantly in the King Edward VI grammar schools, resigned from the service, in order to continue teaching in those schools on a privately employed basis.

The loss of schools to GMS had been a major worry for the Music Service, but the fact that LMS was introduced at the same time, leading to an increased demand for instrumental teaching, more than compensated for the loss of those schools. I have very fond memories of an evening concert at Fairfax School in Sutton Coldfield, just before the school left the local authority to adopt GMS. Fairfax was a secondary school that had enjoyed a very strong musical tradition, with instrumental teaching provided by a large number of visiting Music Service teachers, including myself, over many years. Not only did all of the school's visiting teachers attend this concert to give their support, but so too did David Perkins, along with the full team of Music Service managers, in order to celebrate the long and successful collaboration between Fairfax and the Music Service, and to communicate the message that the service hoped to return to the school at some time in the future – which indeed it did.

In 1994 the one-form-entry St Francis C of E Primary School in Bournville adopted grant-maintained status. As well as being the smallest school in the country to have become grant-maintained up to that point, St Francis School was also the last school in Birmingham to do so because, by

1994, the transformative effect of Tim Brighouse's presence in Birmingham was such that schools no longer wanted to leave the local authority – headteachers and school governors who had been planning for GMS were now changing their minds. The story of the Music Service's relationship with St Francis School is an interesting one. When John Croghan was appointed as headteacher in 1988, he was surprised to find that only a very small number of pupils were receiving instrumental music lessons and that these lessons were taking place on a one-to-one basis. 'I couldn't understand why the children weren't being taught in groups,' said Croghan, 'because, first of all, more children would have been involved and also, children learn better in that way.' In 1990 this concern was partly resolved when Richard Duckett started teaching brass instruments at the school. Not only was Duckett committed to teaching pupils in groups, but he soon started a school wind band that, straight away, began to give regular performances, both in school and at the local church. 'Through the wind band,' said John Croghan, 'children started to achieve excellence together, while inspiring their peers, their parents and the local community. We were so lucky to have Richard, because he had such a talent and passion for teaching music.' When the school became grant-maintained in 1994, however, Duckett, like other Music Service teachers, had to discontinue his visits and was replaced by privately employed brass teacher, John Saunders. Saunders continued to develop brass playing at St Francis up to 1998 when the school returned to the local authority, whereupon Duckett and other Music Service teachers resumed their visits and the school's music-making grew from strength to strength. Nowhere was the school's musical achievement more evident than at the 'Happy Retirement Concert for John Croghan', organized by the Music Service at the Adrian Boult Hall in 2010. The concert featured superb performances by the Birmingham Schools' Wind Orchestra and the St Francis School Wind Band, both of which were directed by Music Service teacher Adrian Taylor, who had taken over as St Francis School's brass teacher following Richard Duckett's retirement. Another sign of the huge development in St Francis School's music-making over the 22 years of Croghan's tenure was the fact that, in his retirement concert, the school's wind band numbered fifty children – nearly a quarter of the school's pupil population.

Professional development

Along with rescuing the Music Service from potential disaster following Keith Allen's suspension, and expertly managing the service's responses to LMS and GMS, David Perkins's greatest contribution to the organization, in my view, was his overseeing of an increased professionalism and confidence among the staff. And an important aspect of this was his groundbreaking approach to professional development. Prior to the 1990s there was no established pattern of visits to observe the work of Music Service teachers. But Perkins, within the first few months of his appointment, established professional support visits – regular, one-hour visits by Heads of Departments to all staff, to observe lessons, give verbal feedback, and then send written reports to teachers. According to Perkins, 'Our PSVs were unique – I don't know any other music service that had such a big programme of staff visits at that time. And they were, genuinely, support visits – they weren't inspectorial or judgemental in any way. I believe they were a real means of stimulating teachers and moving them forward.' And in the words of Richard Duckett: 'The PSVs were very good because they challenged people in a way that was unthreatening.'

Such was the success of the PSVs that, by the mid-1990s, they had been extended to include the work of directors of Central Ensembles, as well as instrumental teachers – sometimes involving visits from experts outside the service, such as highly esteemed music educators Jeremy Patterson and William Salaman. This meant that all aspects of the Music Service's work were now benefiting from the approach being encouraged in the city at the time by Tim Brighouse: the supportive, but challenging, professional conversation with a 'critical friend'. Also, by establishing this approach to supporting teachers, David Perkins was sowing the seeds for the exciting developments in professional development that were to take place within the Music Service in the new millennium.

Breadth and quality

Another important area of development at this time was the way in which David Perkins built on the work of Peter Davies and Linda Gilbert in broadening the Music Service's provision, especially in relation to celebrating Birmingham's multicultural diversity. From the late 1980s, Coventry musician Stephon Phillip had begun to establish himself as the Music Service's new steel-pans teacher, having initially taken over from Norman Stewart at the steel-band flagship school, Aston Manor, in 1988. So impressed was David Perkins with Phillip's work that he greatly increased his steel-pan teaching in schools during the early 1990s, moving him onto a three-day-per-week, salaried contract and establishing the Birmingham Schools' Steel Band (BSSB) as a new Central Ensemble under Phillip's direction. Such was the success of the BSSB that, by the end of the 1990s, they had appeared on BBC television's *Blue Peter* and performed at

London's Southbank Centre in the National Festival of Music for Youth. And, due to the huge success of Phillip's work in schools, not only was his contract increased to full-time, but the service had to start employing additional steel-pans teachers in order to meet increased demand. Like Sneh Lata, from the start of her career as a sitar teacher, Stephon Phillip was committed to the principle that his teaching should be available to all children, regardless of ethnic background. So white children, Asian children and African-Caribbean children were all to be seen working alongside one another in his steel bands – just as they did in Sneh Lata's Asian music ensembles.

In the early 1990s Robert Bunting, Head of Wolverhampton Music Service, arranged for a local bhangra band to lead a workshop for schoolchildren. 'Following the workshop,' said Bunting, 'the tabla player, Harjit Singh, got the bug for teaching and started coming along to Saturday morning classes at the Wolverhampton Music Centre, teaching tabla and harmonium. And I worked alongside him, helping him to learn how to manage groups in a classroom-type situation.' But because there was only a limited amount of teaching work available in Wolverhampton, Bunting suggested to Singh that, if he would like to teach full-time, he should contact the Birmingham Music Service to see if they had any vacancies. Accordingly, in the summer of 1994, Singh met up with David Perkins who suggested to him that, although there was no work available at that time, Singh could make contact with schools in Birmingham in order to try and generate work. So, in September and October 1994, Harjit Singh spent his time presenting free workshops in schools, as a result of which several schools decided to buy in his work, through the Music Service, as a tabla teacher. This teaching soon built up to the point where he was working full-time on an hourly-paid basis and then, one year later, he was appointed on a salaried contract. 'At that time,' said Singh, 'there were just three of us teaching Asian instruments – Harjinder and myself teaching tabla and Ranjit Singh [who had taken over from Sneh Lata upon her retirement] teaching sitar. But, from the mid-1990s onwards, other schools began to see what was going on, so the demand for Asian music teaching began to expand further, and the service had to take on more teachers.' In 1998, both Harjit Singh and Harjinder Matharu started to teach the dhol as well as tabla, and this proved very successful because the dhol was very popular as a bhangra instrument.

In 1995, shortly after commencing his work with the Birmingham Music Service, Harjit Singh, working alongside Ranjit Singh, established the Birmingham Schools' Asian Music Ensemble (replacing the Birmingham

Schools' Indian Music Ensemble, which had been suspended upon Sneh Lata's retirement the previous year). The ensemble continued the tradition, established by Lata, of fusing the ensemble's work with Western musical styles. So Harjit Singh recalled a very successful performance given at Birmingham Town Hall where the Asian Music Ensemble performed a raga, alongside a string ensemble directed by Head of Strings, Chris Rogers. Other highlights included a number of performances at London's Southbank Centre and at the Royal Albert Hall as part of the National Festival of Music for Youth and an appearance on BBC television's *Songs of Praise* in 2000. In my conversation with Harjit Singh he described to me what he considered to be the key factors determining the success of Asian music teaching in Birmingham. 'There was a lot going on,' he said. 'There was teaching in schools during the day and Music Service ensembles rehearsing in the evenings. And the children were always performing in public – every school I ever taught in had its own ensemble which gave regular performances in school, whether I was present or not.'

Because of the huge expansion described above, the Music Service's world music teachers were established as a department in their own right in 1998, and Harjit Singh was appointed Head of World Music. At the time of writing, Harjit heads what is now the Department of World Music and Percussion, which consists of six Asian music teachers, five steel-pans teachers, three djembe teachers and fifteen orchestral percussion and drum-kit teachers.

In April 1999, in order to celebrate the culture of Birmingham's largest ethnic minority group, David Perkins organized the Birmingham Schools Irish Music Festival at the city's Irish Centre, which featured performances of traditional Irish music and dance given by schoolchildren from all over the city. At around the same time, Perkins appointed one of Birmingham's leading Irish traditional musicians, Pat Brennan, to start teaching for the Music Service. To begin with, Brennan visited a small number of primary schools, teaching the tin whistle to pupils in small groups. Very soon, however, following the example of Harjit Singh a few years earlier, Brennan started to tour the city's primary schools, giving free live performances, and this resulted in a huge increase in the demand for his work. So, by 2003, Brennan was teaching 13 hours per week for the Music Service and the number of pupils he was teaching per week had increased to 500 – partly because he was then teaching whole classes instead of small groups. Brennan had made the decision to switch to whole-class teaching because he considered this to be a much more effective and inclusive approach and, in so doing, he was anticipating by several years the Music Service's adoption of Wider Opportunities teaching. Brennan was regularly assembling large groups of his pupils to perform Irish music and dance at high-profile Music Service events such as the Summer Gala Concerts. In keeping with the Music Service's philosophy of inclusivity, and echoing the comments of Sneh Lata and Stephon Phillip quoted earlier, Brennan told me that he considered it important to involve all children in playing Irish music – not just those of Irish background. 'So, at Wyndcliffe Primary School,' said Brennan, 'the great majority of children were from Asian background, but they loved their tin whistle playing and did brilliantly at it.' One of Pat Brennan's most memorable contributions to children's music in Birmingham was the Primary Schools Folk Festival – a one-day event organized by Brennan through the Music Service, which took place annually over six consecutive years at Newman College of Higher Education in Bartley Green. Following preparatory visits by musicians to primary schools across the city, over 200 children from those schools would attend the festival, joining in with some of Birmingham's top professional musicians representing a range of world music styles: Irish music, English country dancing, banghra, Arabic music, African drumming, Chinese music, Korean music and Andean music.

In addition to the Birmingham Schools' Steel Band, the 1990s saw the creation of a number of new Central Ensembles reflecting an increasingly broad range of musical styles: the open-access, gospel-inspired Young Voices choir directed by Clyde Forde, the Birmingham Schools' Azaad Dhol Group directed by Harjit Singh, the Birmingham Schools' Percussion Ensemble directed by Steven Lloyd and the Birmingham Schools' Baroque Orchestra (BSBO) directed by Alan Davis. The BSBO was made up of some of the most advanced young players in the city, playing entirely baroque repertoire in baroque style – an area in which Davis was, of course, an expert. Over the five years of the BSBO's existence, the ensemble performed all six of Bach's *Brandenburg Concertos*, with the solo trumpet part in Concerto No. 2 being played by leading baroque trumpet player Crispian Steele-Perkins. And in 1995, one of the great collaborations between different Music Service ensembles took place: to mark the 300th anniversary of the death of Henry Purcell, the BSBO, along with the Birmingham Schools' Chorale (BSC) and the Birmingham Schools' Brass Ensemble, performed Jeremiah Clarke's *Ode on the Death of Purcell* at St Paul's Church in Birmingham's Jewellery Quarter. And, around the same time, a memorable visit was made by the BSBO and the BSC to Birmingham's twin city, Lyon, where the combined groups gave a performance of Vivaldi's Gloria. Reflecting on this visit, Jeffrey Skidmore commented to me, 'Those foreign trips bound people together and developed the ethos of the groups in a unique way.'

In addition to the creation of these new Central Ensembles, the 1990s also saw a significant increase in the number of Area Ensembles for beginner and intermediate players. This was because the value of ensemble experience for pupils from the earliest stages of their learning was increasingly being recognized, as was the vital role played by the Area Ensembles in preparing young musicians for the higher-level Central Ensembles. Very often at this time, a new Area Ensemble would be created by holding a one-day workshop at a school, for instrumentalists in a particular area of the city, and the pupils who attended would then be invited to come back to the same venue for weekly, after-school rehearsals.

At the other end of the scale, the ensemble that had signalled the start of the Birmingham Music Service 30 years earlier – the BSSO – continued to grow from strength to strength. In 1996 the orchestra performed Sibelius's Violin Concerto in the Symphony Hall, with Tasmin Little as the soloist, and in 1998 the orchestra undertook a highly successful concert tour in Hungary. In 1999 the BSSO concluded the decade with a concert in the Symphony Hall that, for me, was their most memorable ever – a performance of Brahms's Violin Concerto, with soloist Natsuko Yoshimoto, followed by that most seminal work of the twentieth century, Stravinsky's *The Rite of Spring*. Conductor Peter Bridle later explained to me how the decision came about to perform *The Rite of Spring*. 'I was talking to Simon Rattle,' he said, 'and told him that the BSSO had already performed Stravinsky's *Firebird* and *Petrushka*. So Simon said, 'Well, why don't you do *The Rite of Spring* – it's easier!' Then, in 1999, I saw that we had exactly the right line-up – two phenomenal tympanists, a brilliant trumpeter and bassoonist – so we went ahead.' Of course, repertoire such as *The Rite of Spring* would have been well out of reach of the BSSO and probably most other English youth orchestras only a few years earlier – indeed, it was a piece that continued to challenge professional orchestras well into the twentieth century. Such had been the amazing development of the BSSO in the first 35 years of its existence, however, that the orchestra was now able to deliver a powerful performance of this work under the direction of Peter Bridle.

The 1990s was also a decade when the BSCO continued to flourish. When I asked the BSCO's conductor Bob Vivian to describe some of the orchestra's highlights during those years, he spoke about the occasion when Simon Rattle came to a rehearsal to conduct Gershwin's *An American in Paris*. 'It was absolutely astonishing,' said Vivian. 'I couldn't understand how he got such amazing results from the kids so quickly!' Vivian also spoke about the long association the orchestra enjoyed with film music composer Ron Goodwin during those years. Goodwin made a number of visits to Birmingham to conduct the BSCO in performances of some of his most well-known film themes. Most notably, in the last night of the Gala Concerts at the Symphony Hall in 1993, Goodwin directed stunning renditions of 'Where Eagles Dare' and 'Those Magnificent Men in their Flying Machines'. Under Vivian's direction the BSCO continued to be a regular participant in the National Festival of Music for Youth and on several occasions had the great honour of closing the final concert of the festival at the Royal Albert Hall.

Figure 5.1: Georgie Fame rehearsing with the Birmingham Schools' Jazz Orchestra at Birmingham Town Hall, 1994 (Photo: Mirrorpix)

During the 1990s, the Birmingham Schools' Jazz Orchestra went on to develop its collaboration with leading British jazz musicians. In the annual Summer Gala Concerts at Birmingham Town Hall from 1992 to 1994, the ensemble performed, respectively, with trombonist Don Lusher, trumpeter Kenny Baker, and singer Georgie Fame (Figure 5.1). And in 1995, having changed its name to the Birmingham Schools' Jazz Ensemble (BSJE), the band performed at Birmingham's Ronnie Scott's Club as part of the Birmingham International Jazz Festival and appeared in the Summer Gala Concert at the Town Hall with saxophonist John Dankworth as a featured soloist. In 1996 I stepped down as director of the BSJE in order to spend more time with my young family, handing over to John Ruddick who had directed the Midland Youth Jazz Orchestra with huge success since the 1980s. When I reflect on the achievement of the BSJE over the eight-year period that I directed it, I believe that this was in no small part due to the strength of the band's rhythm-section players. One of the country's leading jazz and rock drummers at the time of writing, Ian Palmer, was a member of the BSJE as a young teenager in the late 1980s, and he returned to perform with the band once again in their 1994 Birmingham Town Hall concert with Georgie Fame. (The next time I was to see Ian Palmer was in 2008. Again, this was a performance at Birmingham Town Hall with Georgie Fame, but on this occasion Palmer was a member of Fame's own, professional backing band.) The keyboard players who played with the BSJE during the time I was director all went on to become highly successful musicians: Tim Amann was to become one of the top handful of jazz pianists in the West Midlands, playing in bands led by legendary saxophone players Andy Hamilton and Steve Ajao; Nick Finlow was to become one of the top musical directors in London's West End theatreland; and I shall now tell the story of the musical journey of Chris Egan, who was mentioned earlier.

Nurturing world-class talent

Following my appointment with the Birmingham Music Service in 1984, I spent over ten years as a woodwind teacher at Shenley Court School in the south of Birmingham. It was a very successful secondary school – one of the purpose-built comprehensive schools of the 1960s – and at one stage in its history it was, reputedly, the largest school in the country. Shenley Court provided a rich educational experience, with a strong emphasis on music and the performing arts, for children from the neighbouring council estate, as well as the middle-class offspring of staff at the University of Birmingham, situated nearby. In the mid-1990s I became aware of a 14-year-old boy at the school named Chris Egan, who was often to be found in the Music Department at lunchtimes playing boogie-woogie on the piano – with great flair and fluency. From chatting to Chris I learnt that he could also play classical music, could read from staff notation and chord symbols, and had perfect pitch (the rare ability to immediately identify the letter-name of a note upon hearing it). At the time, I was looking for a keyboard player for the BSJE, so I invited Chris to come along to rehearse with the band on a trial basis, and I then immediately offered him the place.

Twenty-two years later I met up again with Chris Egan at Abbey Road Studios in London. By that time, at the age of 36, he was now established as one of the country's leading film-music composers and musical directors – based at Abbey Road Studios where he undertook much of his recording work. This was my first-ever visit to the world's most iconic recording studio so, after taking a photograph of the famous zebra crossing featured on the cover of the Beatles album, I went inside and met up with Egan who gave me a guided tour of the building. This included a visit to the famous Studio One, which opened in 1931 with Edward Elgar conducting the London Symphony Orchestra in recordings of his own music. Egan told me that he believed this room had the best acoustics of any recording studio in the world – and he should know because he has worked in many of them.

Following our tour of the studios, Egan and I went outside and, within a few seconds, he had hailed a taxi and I was being whisked off to The Ivy Club in the heart of London's West End – a private club that includes many celebrities among its members. In the course of our leisurely dinner, Egan gave a fascinating account of his career and current projects, interrupted only by the occasional email from composer and conductor Carl Davis with suggestions for the following day's recording session – the soundtrack for the movie *Napoleon*, which Egan and Carl Davis were working on together. In addition to his recording work, Egan explained that he had worked as musical director for Elaine Paige, written arrangements for Shirley Bassey and Lionel Richie, and had just completed the recording of his arrangements for the stage musical *The Bodyguard*.

According to Egan, his journey as a musician started at the age of 4 when the family's local pub was trying to get rid of their piano, which was no longer required. His dad accepted the piano into the family home, on the basis that he was going to arrange lessons for himself. Egan told me that 32 years later, his dad had still not got around to arranging those piano lessons, but 4-year-old Chris started having lessons with a teacher who lived around the corner, and that is how it all started.

Egan told me that, right through his childhood and teenage years, he was exposed to fantastic musical opportunities through the Birmingham Music Service. First of all, as a pupil at Greenmeadow Primary School, he studied the cello with Birmingham Music Service teacher and former CBSO player, Colin Humphreys. He then took part in whole-class music-making activities at Greenmeadow, led by Richard Duckett. Egan then told me about the musical opportunities he received when he transferred to Shenley Court School in 1992. 'Nobody in that school knew how lucky they were,' he said. 'We just took it for granted that, if you wanted to learn an instrument, you got free lessons and the free loan of an instrument. It's only now, in hindsight, that I appreciate what an amazing opportunity that was – at the time, we just assumed it was the norm!' First of all, he started having guitar lessons with Bryan Lester, and then, a while later, saxophone lessons with me. He took his Grade 6 examination on the soprano saxophone, following the classical syllabus, and then Grade 8 on the alto saxophone following the jazz syllabus. And all this time he was continuing with his private piano lessons.

'When I was 14,' said Egan, 'I started playing piano in the school Jazz Band and the Birmingham Schools' Jazz Ensemble, both of which were directed by yourself. I remember we played 'Watermelon Man', as well as arrangements by Sammy Nestico and Lennie Niehaus. Nestico later became a great inspiration to me as an arranger, and I was privileged to meet him recently at a recording session in Los Angeles.' Egan went on to say, 'The big thing I learnt from you was about phrasing. One thing you always did was that you sang phrases to us and got us to sing them back before playing them on our instruments – and then the whole thing made sense. And that's stayed with me ever since. Even now, when I'm writing, I sing the phrases, just like you used to do, and that's become an important part of the way I work. I use that technique every day of my working life.'

Egan reminded me that it was through the BSJE that he gained his first experience of arranging music. In 1996 he made an arrangement of Duke Ellington's 'Don't Get Around Much Anymore' for a BBC Radio 3 programme on jazz arranging – the aim of which was to give an opportunity for young musicians to write for a big band. So Egan's arrangement was performed and broadcast by the BBC Radio Big Band, directed by Richard Niles, at the BBC Pebble Mill Studios in Birmingham. 'I consider that to have been my first proper arrangement,' said Egan, 'and certainly my first arrangement to be performed by professional musicians. My handwritten score is framed and still hangs on the wall of my studio at home.' Egan went on to do more writing for the BSJE, including an arrangement of 'The Christmas Song (Chestnuts Roasting on an Open Fire)' that was performed by a choir of 300 primary schoolchildren accompanied by the BSJE and directed by Jeffrey Skidmore in the 1995 Winter Celebration concert at the Symphony Hall.

When I asked Egan how he learnt as a teenager to write musical arrangements, given that he had received no formal lessons in arranging, he told me, 'I learnt in two ways – first of all, from sitting in the BSJE and listening to what was going on. And secondly, you used to lend me scores of the arrangements which I used to take home and study. And that's also how I learnt to do orchestral writing – by looking at John Williams's scores for his big films. I never had lessons in arranging or composing. I learnt by writing an arrangement and then listening to a band playing it – then I'd know what things I was going to do differently the next time.' Egan went on to say, 'There was a big emphasis in the Birmingham Music Service on getting people to learn not by being taught, but by actually getting involved and doing it. So how did I learn to play jazz? You didn't talk to me about it – you put me in a jazz group!'

Speaking about the main projects he was currently involved with, Egan told me, 'Although I do concerts from time to time, I'm essentially a studio musician now and I split my work between Abbey Road Studios, AIR Studios, Angel Studios and some of the studios in Los Angeles. I might be conducting at a recording session or I might be composing or orchestrating music for recording – it might be a TV advert, a film score, a video game or an album.'

Finally, Chris Egan summed up what he considered to be the impact of the Birmingham Music Service on his life as a musician, as well as on the lives of people who had not become professional musicians. 'I wouldn't be doing what I'm doing now,' he said, 'without the experiences I had as a teenager through the Music Service. But the value of the Music Service was much more than just that – it was to do with making more rounded people. So there are many people who were taught by the Music Service who didn't become professional musicians but whose lives were enriched forever through the experience of making music when they were young.'

'Freedom, creativity and friendship'

Coincidentally, on my train journey back to Birmingham that evening, following my meeting with Chris Egan, I bumped into somebody who perfectly demonstrated this last point. I saw a woman in her forties, seated a few rows away from me in the same carriage. She looked slightly familiar, but I could not recollect where I knew her from. When the train was slowing down to pull into Birmingham New Street Station, she came up to me, shook me by the hand and said, 'I just want to thank you for everything you did for me when I was doing music at school.' This was Lesa Kingham whom I then remembered as a 13-year-old percussion player in the Birmingham Schools' Training Wind Orchestra, which I directed when I first moved to Birmingham in 1984. A few weeks after our chance meeting on the train, Kingham and I arranged to meet up again, this time in the café of the new Library of Birmingham, in order to catch up on the intervening 32 years. Kingham explained to me that her involvement with music started when her clarinet teacher at George Dixon School invited her to attend a rehearsal of the Birmingham Schools' Training Wind Orchestra at the school, to have a go at playing percussion instruments. 'I was absolutely terrified the first time I went along,' she said. 'I was a shy person. I'd never played with such a big group of musicians before and the instruments I had to play made such a loud noise! But I really enjoyed the experience, so I carried on going to those Saturday morning rehearsals. Particularly for me, coming from a less wealthy background,' said Kingham, 'it was a fabulous experience: getting out of bed on Saturday mornings to do something productive, making new friends, doing concerts in schools in different areas of the city, and having this great sense of achievement. It really helped to develop my confidence.'

Lesa Kingham remained in the Birmingham Schools' Training Wind Orchestra for two years and then auditioned successfully for a place in the Birmingham Schools' Concert Orchestra (BSCO), which she stayed with until leaving school, ending up as the orchestra's principal percussionist. As a member of the BSCO, she performed in Birmingham's Town Hall and Symphony Hall, as well as in the Royal Festival Hall and the Royal Albert Hall as part of the National Festival of Music for Youth. 'Whenever I see the film *Where Eagles Dare* on the television,' said Kingham, 'it reminds me of the time we performed the theme music at the Royal Festival Hall. I was one of the two side-drum players standing at opposite sides of the stage, starting the piece off with that dramatic introduction.' But Kingham's most memorable experience with the BSCO, she told me, was when she took part in the orchestra's first-ever foreign trip, which was to Switzerland. Summarizing the impact of the Birmingham Music Service upon her as a young person, Lesa Kingham said:

> I found the culture of the Music Service ensembles quite different to the culture at school – it was all to do with freedom, creativity and friendship. And it was to do with giving young people the opportunity to learn through having great musical experiences. We didn't see yourself or Bob Vivian as teachers, but rather as people we were working alongside. It felt that we were being treated like professional musicians and that everybody respected one another. I'll never forget the energy that was there as we were about to go on stage for a performance and the feeling of 'we're all in this together'. I think the whole thing was inspirational and that if more young people felt supported in that kind of a way, we'd be a lot further forward as a society. It's to do with recognizing people as individuals, treating them with respect and giving them the guiding hand they need in order to go and achieve something. And I just stumbled into that whole world by accident!

Echoing the story of Robert Heeks, told in Chapter 2, Lesa Kingham went on to say that, although she stopped playing percussion instruments when she left school, she had recently bought herself a bodhrán (a traditional

Irish frame drum), which she was now learning to play – building on those musical foundations laid in her teenage years.

New arrivals

In 1998 Mark Wyatt left Birmingham in order to take up a senior appointment with the Telford and Wrekin Education Department, whereupon Robert Bunting was appointed to replace him as Adviser for Music. Bunting had already enjoyed a wide-ranging, high-profile career in music education. He worked alongside John Paynter in York during the 1970s as part of the Schools Council Music Project, which was concerned with developing creativity in secondary-school music teaching. And he played a significant role nationally in establishing composing as a key element of the GCSE music syllabus that was introduced in 1988. From the 1980s onwards, Bunting worked in Wolverhampton – first of all as a secondary-school Head of Music, then as an Advisory Teacher and, finally, as Head of Wolverhampton Music Service. When I asked Bunting to describe his first impressions of the Birmingham Music Service upon starting his new post in 1998, he told me:

> It was great coming into a service which had, alongside the traditional orchestral and band instruments, electric guitar, drum kit, steel pans and Asian instruments – we couldn't have got to that stage in Wolverhampton – because the city wasn't big enough and the funding wasn't there. And in Birmingham there was a solid body of teachers who were used to getting their pupils to improvise and play by ear. All of this created a very liberal atmosphere where teachers weren't just obsessed with notation or the teaching of technique – there was a much wider vision of what music was about. And the cohesion of the instrumental team was excellent, especially when you consider that it was so huge, and a large proportion of the staff were neither full-time nor qualified teachers. And, whenever I worked with the Music Service teachers, I found them to be positive, friendly, and always open to new ideas – there was none of the scepticism that I'd met with in some other music services.

Also in 1998, Birmingham Education Authority appointed Mick Waters to the post of Chief Adviser for Schools – a role in which he was to work closely alongside Tim Brighouse and in which he was, effectively, the head of BASS (Birmingham Advisory and Support Service). Waters had been headteacher at two primary schools in Cumbria, as well as lecturer in education at

Charlotte Mason Teacher Training College in Ambleside – renowned for its forward-looking approach in regard to child-centred learning and its strong emphasis on the creative arts. As soon as he started his post in Birmingham, it was clear that Waters was going to be an extremely strong supporter of the Music Service – like Brighouse, he was often to be seen in the audience at the service's concerts. Waters remained in Birmingham until 2002 when he was appointed Chief Education Officer for the City of Manchester and, in 2005, he was appointed Director of Curriculum for the QCA (Qualifications and Curriculum Authority). In 2009 he returned to the West Midlands to take on the role of Professor of Education at Wolverhampton University, where I met up with him to hear his recollections about his time in Birmingham and, in particular, the Birmingham Music Service.

Mick Waters explained to me that, when he arrived in Birmingham, the new Labour Government had been in power for only a year, so his main job was the implementation of their new education policies: Excellence in Cities, Education Action Zones and Specialist Schools. 'But the really big one,' said Waters, 'was Fair Funding. This was to do with giving more money directly to schools instead of to local authorities. So, many areas of the local authority's provision were now being questioned by headteachers and school governors.' Waters said that he often attended meetings where headteachers talked about local authority provision, saying, 'Why does that need to be run by the local authority? If we want it, we'll sort it out ourselves. But there was never a conversation like that about the Music Service,' said Waters, 'which spoke volumes to me about the service's work – obviously the schools that used the Music Service were very happy with what they were getting.' Waters said that he believed this was because the Music Service's leadership had continued to develop the organization over the years, unlike some other areas of the country where music service provision in the 1990s was the same as it had been in the 1970s. 'So, when Fair Funding started to take hold,' said Waters, 'the Birmingham Music Service was built on strong foundations and was secure.' Waters also spoke about the breadth of provision in Birmingham – in terms of the range of instruments being taught, the range of musical styles covered, and the range of ensemble and performance opportunities for young people at every level of their learning. Commenting on the Music Service's professional development, he said, 'The teachers were brought together for training, not just in music, but in the latest educational thinking. So people in the service knew the bigger picture – it wasn't simply the nomadic trombone player going in and out of schools without any understanding of what else was going on.' Another reason for the success of the Music Service, according to Waters, was that music education was extremely highly valued by the Chief Education Officer Tim Brighouse, by the advisory service and by a significant number of the city's councillors. 'And the other factor,' said Waters, 'was that diversity had driven innovation – Birmingham's changing population from the 1970s onwards meant that teachers had to adapt and think afresh, and the Birmingham Music Service had been part of that.'

Around the turn of the millennium, momentous changes were to take place in English music education at a national level, and in the leadership of the Birmingham Music Service. These changes were to usher in, I believe, the most exciting developments yet for young musicians in Birmingham and an examination of these will form the main focus of the next two chapters.

Chapter 6

Wider leadership in the new millennium

In 1999 the Labour Government introduced the Music Standards Fund, which was to have a transformative effect on music services throughout England, including Birmingham. The Music Standards Fund provided £59.6 million per year in order 'to protect, support and expand' England's 150 local authority music services. So, for the first time since I joined the Birmingham Music Service 15 years earlier, and thanks to Tony Blair's Labour Government, it suddenly felt within the service that we had plenty of money to spend. Gone were the days when, as Head of Woodwind, my annual allocation of funding would allow me to purchase just two clarinets and two flutes for the whole city. And gone were the days when I had to use my own money to purchase reams of paper to feed the office photocopying machine. So, upon receipt of this new funding, the first thing the service set its mind to was replacing its stock of old, rather dilapidated musical instruments with brand-new, high-quality instruments. This resulted in an immediate and noticeable improvement in the quality of performance of Birmingham's young musicians including, for example, a new warmth of sound within the ensembles' clarinet sections, due to the use of wooden rather than plastic instruments. I also recall the purchase of many sets of new, high-quality steel pans, facilitating a further huge expansion in that area of teaching.

In March 2000, David Perkins suddenly and unexpectedly left the Music Service in order to take up a new, more senior role within the local authority. 'My departure from the Music Service was similar to the way I arrived,' said Perkins. 'A crisis had developed because the authority had put in a major bid to the New Opportunities Fund which had gone badly wrong, so they asked me at very short notice to go and sort it out. They thought this would take about three weeks, but I actually never returned to the Music Service after that.' So, at that point, John Clemson immediately stepped up to become Acting Head of Service, and I was appointed Acting Deputy Head of Service. Only a few weeks later, in May of that year, Clemson was rushed into hospital for a major operation and was then absent from work for three months while recuperating. So, very soon after being promoted to

Acting Deputy Head of Service, I found myself being promoted again – this time to Acting Head of Service – a role that I occupied until Clemson's return to work in September 2000. Those few months provided an interesting and valuable experience for me, partly because I learnt that I had absolutely no desire to be the head of a music service on a permanent basis – even though I had been applying for such posts in the preceding few years. The amount of time I had to spend in my office, and the colossal number of emails I had to read each day, meant that I missed my direct involvement with children's music-making, which, of course, was the reason I had become an instrumental music teacher in the first place.

Initially the Music Standards Fund, which was distributed to music services in response to bids, had been allocated on an annual basis, but from 2001 it started to be allocated in three-year batches. The increased financial security resulting from this led John Clemson to make the momentous decision to introduce some free instrumental teaching for schools: one free hour per week for all primary schools and two free hours per week for secondary schools. 'The reason for this,' said Clemson, 'was that, in 1992, we had been teaching in 40 per cent of the city's primary schools, and the introduction of LMS in 1993 enabled us to increase this to 50 per cent. My belief, however, was that the only way we could increase this still further was by offering some free teaching to schools – so that schools which had never had instrumental teaching could experience what it was like.' To deliver this additional teaching the Music Service appointed 12 new, full-time, salaried teachers in 2001. Since this increase in staffing was paid for by the Standards Fund, which was only guaranteed for three years, these teachers were initially appointed on three-year contracts, but after a few years these were extended to permanent contracts. For the remaining years of the Labour Government, up to 2010, the Music Service continued to benefit greatly from the Standards Fund. 'The expansion of the service over that period of time was huge,' said Clemson. 'We were teaching in lots of schools we had never been in before – mainly due to the offer of free teaching.' Clemson went on to explain that, in response to what schools were asking for, a further, massive expansion took place in the teaching of non-orchestral instruments – guitar (including electric guitar), drum kit, steel pans and Asian instruments.

Upon Clemson's return to work as Acting Head of Service in September 2000, it soon became clear that his style of leadership was quite different to that of his predecessor, David Perkins. Whereas Perkins's approach had been firmly based on hierarchical line-management, with instructions coming from the top downwards, Clemson's style was more collaborative and collegiate, with people at different levels of the organization being listened to, and their views often helping to shape decisions that were being taken at the top. Clemson and I would spend many hours in his office discussing the developing ethos of the organization, as well as day-to-day management issues. It felt as though his views and mine were of equal value, as were the views of other colleagues – so the most senior person in the Music Service was no longer seen as the boss. This very much represented the start of a new era, with exciting, more modern approaches to leadership being developed that were to reach their fruition, I believe, in the early 2010s.

I would suggest, however, that the more authoritative management style adopted by Perkins was exactly what had been needed when he took over in 1991 – because of the horrendously difficult situation that he inherited and because, to use his own words, 'there was a culture of unprofessionalism that had to be quickly changed'. Many years later, my wife and I had the most terrifying experience of our lives when we were awakened in the middle of the night to find that our next-door neighbour's large garden shed had caught fire and was enveloped in flames, only a few inches from our house. We ran out of the house into the street and I phoned the fire brigade who arrived within a few minutes. We then stood on the opposite side of the road, watching in awe as firefighters extinguished what was, by then, a huge blaze. I was amazed by the calm efficiency with which those men and women handled the situation, as a result of which our own house did not catch fire. Throughout the operation it was obvious that there was one firefighter in the team, identified by a yellow helmet, who was clearly in charge – giving instructions that were immediately and unquestioningly followed by the others. In such a life-or-death situation, this kind of hierarchical, boss-led management style was clearly essential. If there had been consultation between different members of the fire-fighting team at each stage of the operation, I do not think our house would have survived. And I think that the Birmingham Music Service was probably in a similar situation when David Perkins took it over in 1991 – a major crisis was threatening the service's survival, so firm, quick decision-making was essential in order to get the organization back on track. Like the fire-fighting chief outside our house on that night, Perkins was extremely effective and efficient in quickly bringing an extremely dangerous situation under control and returning the Music Service to a state of calm and order.

Such had been the effectiveness of Perkins's work that, by the start of the new millennium, the service had become an extremely professional and confident organization, more highly regarded than ever in Birmingham schools. So, when Clemson took over in 2000, the time was right to start to develop a more distributed approach to leadership, in order to create a dynamic, collegiate organization with a culture of participation at all levels. Since Clemson's style was naturally democratic and consultative, I believe that he was exactly the right person to lead the service through this next period of important change in the areas of leadership and professional development.

I believe that I benefited, and the Music Service as a whole benefited, from an important decision taken by John Clemson towards the end of 2001. I had come to the conclusion, having been in the post of Acting Deputy Head of Service for just over a year, that I was unhappy in this role because the main part of my work was concerned with administration – in particular, the timetabling of instrumental teachers – which I found to be tedious and onerous. When I spoke to Clemson about my concern, he quickly came up with a solution. Because he knew that I was passionately interested in professional development, he suggested that that could become the main focus of my work, and that my job title could be changed to Head of Professional Support and Development. I was extremely happy with this suggestion and my new role came into effect almost immediately, with teachers' timetabling now being delegated to other members of staff. In 2004, John Clemson was appointed as Head of Service and, a year later, I was appointed Deputy Head of Service – both of these jobs now being on a permanent rather than an acting basis. In my new role, however, the professional development of staff continued to be my main responsibility, and this remained the case right up to my retirement in 2013.

One of Perkins's most important innovations as Head of Service, as explained in the last chapter, had been his introduction of professional support visits for teaching staff. Following each PSV, a written feedback report was completed by the visitor, a copy of which was then forwarded to the teacher who had been visited. This form included a box for the visitor to give an Ofsted grading for the lessons that had been observed: a score between 1 (excellent) and 7 (very poor). Ofsted, the government's inspection regime for schools, had been established only a few years earlier, so perhaps Perkins thought that it would appear rigorous and up to date to use their grading system on the form. One of the first things Clemson did upon taking over as Acting Head of Service, however, was to delete that part of the form. 'My feeling,' said Clemson, 'was that teachers used to fixate on the grade rather than thinking about the comments. So, if a teacher was given, say, a "2" following an observation, they might argue about that rather than discussing the actual quality of teaching.' This decision of Clemson's signalled an important change in direction. In the years ahead he was to play a crucial role in developing more meaningful approaches for assessing the work of teachers and pupils alike, which were based on conversation and the use of descriptive narrative, rather than on marks or grades.

Interestingly, Clemson was moving the Music Service in this direction just as the government was seeking to move the country's education system in exactly the opposite direction – through the introduction in 2000 of performance-related pay for teachers, along with a huge structure of mechanistic assessment systems to support this. In order to qualify for higher levels of pay, teachers now had to pass through a threshold procedure, demonstrating that they had met a large number of professional standards, mainly connected with pupil progress. And all teachers were now subject to annual performance-management meetings at which they would be set targets that were expected to be SMART (specific, measurable, achievable, realistic and time-measured).

I recall, as a Music Service manager at the time, devising an elaborate grid for each of the teachers whose performance management I was responsible for. Each grid comprised a series of tick boxes detailing targets that had been set, timescales for meeting these targets, criteria for assessing whether or not they had been met, and so on. And I remember compiling reams of paperwork giving evidence in support of my own application to pass through the threshold to the upper pay spine. There was a feeling of considerable irritation and cynicism at every level of the Music Service about these new procedures. We went along with them unquestioningly, however, for the best part of a decade – because we saw them as a statutory requirement and as hoops that had to be jumped through in order to gain increases in salary.

The Adviser's influence

The new spirit of collaboration embodied by John Clemson was demonstrated by the fact that, early on in his role as Acting Head of Service, he saw the value of linking up with Music Adviser Robert Bunting in a way that had not happened previously. Bunting was acknowledged as one of the country's leading thinkers on music education, with a huge range of high-level experience in the areas of both classroom and instrumental teaching, and Clemson saw a great opportunity for the Music Service to learn and benefit from this. So, as a result of meetings between John Clemson and Robert Bunting, arrangements were made early in the new millennium for Nancy Evans from the Birmingham Contemporary Music Group, working alongside Bunting, to lead a training session on composition for Music

Service teachers. And in 2004 Clemson listened to and acted upon advice given by Bunting in relation to appointing Advanced Skills Teachers (ASTs) within the Music Service. The AST was a new kind of promoted post for schoolteachers created by the Labour Government in 1998. It was intended as a way of acknowledging the professional status of very effective teachers by awarding them additional salary but, instead of moving up the management hierarchy within a school, the AST's role would be to work alongside other teachers in their school and in other schools, in order to share expertise. Clemson responded positively to Bunting's brilliant suggestion to import this structure from schools into the Music Service, whereupon AST posts were advertised internally within the service and, after a rigorous interview process, five members of staff were promoted to these positions: brass teachers Stuart Birnie, Bob Vivian and Tim Baptiste, woodwind teacher Ruth Cunningham, and violin teacher Heather Clemson (as Heather Doust was then known, following her marriage to John Clemson).

So, in response to requests from staff, the newly appointed ASTs made visits to instrumental teachers in schools, sometimes on a one-off basis and sometimes over a series of weeks – helping young, inexperienced staff as well as working alongside experienced teachers who might have wanted support, for example, in trying out new ideas with their pupils. The work of the ASTs was highly valued by staff and their visits were soon in very high demand. And, of course, they were leaders in the modern sense of the word – influencing others through working alongside them and sharing expertise, and doing so in a completely unthreatening way since they were not responsible for the management of the teachers they were supporting.

After the work of the ASTs had been established, John Clemson told me that he had known from the outset that it would be successful because he believed that I had effectively modelled that approach to supporting teachers in a jazz improvisation project I had undertaken in 2003. The project referred to by Clemson had grown out of a disillusionment I was beginning to feel with more conventional approaches to professional development. For much of my career I had spent a great deal of time running practical training sessions – in Birmingham and around the country – to support instrumental teachers in teaching jazz improvisation. I did this because jazz improvisation had always been an area of passionate interest for me – as a musician and as a teacher – and I believed that there might be some value in sharing with colleagues whatever expertise I had in that area. I eventually came to the realization, however, that although teachers seemed to enjoy the sessions, this method of professional development seemed to have little impact in terms of changing the ways in which teachers actually worked. So in 2003, in consultation with John Clemson, I decided to try a completely different approach within the Music Service. Instead of inviting groups of teachers to come together for training sessions, I offered – to any Music Service teacher who was interested – the opportunity for me to visit them at one of their own schools, in order to work alongside them at teaching jazz improvisation. The structure of the visits would be geared towards the needs of the individual teacher: it might be a one-off visit, or it might be a series of visits. Unlike the earlier training-day model, this new approach meant that I was working alongside teachers in their own schools with their own pupils, and sometimes over a period of several weeks. It worked! At last we saw teachers, from all kinds of different musical backgrounds, growing in confidence and beginning to give their pupils a real experience of playing jazz. And this was exactly the model of support that was to be used by the ASTs when they came into existence one year later.

In 2005 Robert Bunting once again made a creative suggestion to John Clemson, based on involving the Music Service in an initiative that had been designed for schools. Birmingham was one of six local authorities that had been invited to take part in piloting the Department for Education's new Secondary National Strategy for Music. Bunting had been asked to recommend seven Birmingham secondary schools to be part of the strategy's pilot project and, having gained Clemson's agreement, he responded by saying, 'Instead of having seven schools, let's have six schools plus the Music Service'. So the Birmingham Music Service became the only music service in the country to be involved in this groundbreaking project, with instrumental teachers Tim Baptiste, Ruth Cunningham and myself attending training sessions over a whole year alongside classroom music teachers from the six Birmingham schools involved. During the course of that year, the three of us learnt a great deal – particularly about new approaches to pupil composition – which we then shared with colleagues at Music Service training days. And, subsequently, Bunting and I visited music services in different parts of the country delivering training on the strategy.

By the mid-2000s managers in the Music Service, including myself, were continuing to deliver performance management to our teachers in the rather mechanistic, tick-box manner devised by the government, as described earlier. Around this time, I was chairing a meeting of Music Service managers, also attended by Robert Bunting, in which we were preparing for the forthcoming round of performance management review meetings. In hindsight, I believe that I was adopting a rather bossy, managerial approach, saying at one point, 'You shouldn't set someone a target based simply upon what that person enjoys doing.' Bunting immediately responded by asking,

'Why not?' This two-word challenge from Bunting set me thinking about some of the underlying assumptions behind performance management, and was one of the factors that helped to sow the seeds of change in our approach, although it would take several years before this change would come to fruition.

When I met up with Bunting many years later, as part of my research for this book, I reminded him about his comment during that meeting, whereupon he shared with me his reflections on the culture of performance management. 'At its worst,' he said, 'some schools have used it in a punitive way, with teachers being told, "You've got to get better at this, or else!" And, of course, that kind of approach doesn't help anybody.' Bunting explained that another danger of performance management, in his view, was that it could have a trivializing effect. 'For example,' he said, 'a headteacher might decide that a member of staff needs to improve their teaching by asking more questions. So, imagine that the headteacher watched a lesson in September when the teacher asked only three questions and then in January this has increased to six questions. So the teacher might have reached their target, but there's been no consideration as to what type of questions were being asked or what the teacher did with the answers, so the issue has been trivialized in order to make it easy to measure.'

In 2007 Bunting retired and was not replaced by the local authority, so he was the last in a line of seven Birmingham Music Advisers, going right back to Desmond MacMahon who had been appointed 70 years earlier. Following Bunting's retirement, however, I believe that his influence continued to be very strongly felt in the Music Service, particularly in the areas of leadership, Asian music teaching and pupil composition.

Around the same time that Robert Bunting retired from his role as Adviser, John Clemson created three new posts within the Music Service, which were to have a considerable effect in terms of flattening the hierarchy and widening leadership within the organization. These new posts were Assistants to Heads of Departments for the three largest Music Service Departments – Strings, Woodwind, and Guitar/Keyboard. The appointments were made internally and the people appointed did not receive any increments in salary but were given one day per week of non-teaching time in order to fulfil their new duties. The new Assistants helped their Heads of Departments with administrative matters, as well as assisting with the main professional development roles within their departments – undertaking PSVs and acting as mentors in performance-management meetings. But, like the ASTs, they were not considered to be part of the Music Service management team, so they contributed hugely to the organization's developing culture of peer review, as opposed to line management, as the backdrop to its professional development. Each Assistant's appointment lasted for one year only, so towards the end of each year the posts were re-advertised, and different members of staff were appointed for the following year. After stepping down from their posts after a year, however, the Assistants continued to act as mentors in performance-management meetings. This meant that each year the number of mentors increased by three so that, by September 2013, the number of mentors had risen to 27, a significant number of whom did not belong to the Music Service management team.

Rising with the Tide

One day during the autumn of 2009, as I was passing John Clemson in a corridor of the Martineau Education Centre, he briefly stopped me to suggest that I consider attending a course on leadership that he had just heard about. I then learnt that the course, Rising with the Tide, was being organized for music service managers by the Federation of Music Services. It was to be led by education consultant Andy Hind, and it would comprise ten days of training spread over a period of twelve months. I was initially reticent about signing up, because it seemed to me that it would involve a considerable commitment of time, when my working life was already extremely busy. When I met up with Clemson later that day, however, he strongly encouraged me to enrol, and I duly did so. That decision turned out to be one of the most important of my career – the course had a massive impact on my approach to leadership and professional development and a profound effect on the work of the Music Service – not just because of my own attendance but because, having made acquaintance with Andy Hind, I then arranged for him to run annual training sessions for the Music Service leadership team over three consecutive years.

The ten sessions of Rising with the Tide took place at the Beeches Management Centre, situated in the historic Birmingham suburb of Bournville – home of the Cadbury's chocolate business for 100 years and not far from the University of Birmingham. The participants consisted of approximately twenty senior managers from music services all over England, so it provided a wonderful opportunity for exchange of ideas between highly motivated people working for organizations that, in some respects, were very different to one another. Rising with the Tide introduced us to the 'coaching' approach to professional development – the idea of supportive, open-ended professional conversations between colleagues on a level playing field. We were encouraged to reflect on the differences between leadership and management, and on the importance of developing emotional intelligence within organizations. I remember to this day some of the comments made by Andy Hind that made a particularly strong impression upon me: 'the only person you can change is yourself'; 'leaders need to walk the talk'; 'feedback is something that you have done to you'; 'leadership teams are constantly changing whereas management teams remain the same until someone leaves'. (This last comment seemed particularly relevant to the Music Service in the light of its recent introduction of annually changing Assistants to Heads of Departments.)

Professional conversations

Early in 2011, after I had completed the course and Hind had led the first of his training sessions for Birmingham Music Service managers, John Clemson and I sat down together to talk about how we could apply some of what we had learnt in order to develop the Music Service's approach to professional development. We both felt that the top-down target-setting approach of performance management did not create the climate of trust that was necessary to fully unleash the creative and collaborative potential of our staff. We had come to believe that the danger of target-setting was that it encouraged people to focus on those areas that could be easily measured, rather than on the areas that were most important – exactly as described by Robert Bunting and quoted earlier in this chapter. Clemson and I quickly came to the conclusion that the only way to move forward was to get rid of the distraction of target-setting altogether. And we decided that the next stage in the process should be to discuss this idea with the rest of the leadership team at our annual awayday meeting in July at the Beeches Management Centre, with a view to agreeing a new approach that could be introduced the following September.

At the start of the awayday I passed around copies of 'When goal setting goes bad', in which Sean Silverthorne explores the research of Harvard Business School Professor Max Bazerman on the harmful side effects of target-setting: 'unethical behaviour, over-focus on one area while neglecting other parts of the business ... corrosion of organizational culture, and reduced intrinsic motivation' (Silverthorne, 2009). In the course of our discussion I related a story about an experience I had had a few weeks earlier upon entering a primary school classroom in Birmingham – the classroom teacher explained to me, pointing to a small group of children around one table, 'These are the children I'm concentrating on this year because my target is to increase the number of children attaining a Level 3 – the children on the other tables have either achieved this already or have no chance of achieving it.' So the teacher had decided to spend the whole year focusing on the work of just 6 children out of a class of 30, in order to achieve a measurable target. I also described what I considered to be the unhelpfulness of some of the targets that had been set for Music Service teachers in recent years, such as: to increase the number of pupils participating in a particular ensemble, or for a specified number of pupils to pass a particular graded examination. I explained that a teacher might fail to achieve the first of these targets for reasons beyond their control, such as transport difficulties. And they might succeed in achieving the second target by entering pupils for examinations for which they were unsuited. And I remember causing some amusement when I parodied the SMART acronym as meaning 'simplistic, mechanistic, anachronistic, reductionist and trite'. It was a lively, enthusiastic discussion that concluded with a unanimous endorsement of the proposal that target-setting should play no further part in the professional development of Music Service teachers.

So, in September 2011, the Music Service's new approach to professional development came into effect. We considered it important that the language used should reflect the change in ethos so, mindful of another quotation from Andy Hind, 'One person cannot manage the performance of another', we dropped the term 'performance management' altogether. From the start of that new academic year, each member of staff (including part-time teachers, non-salaried teachers and directors of ensembles) would now meet their mentor for a one-hour 'professional conversation'. The approach to this conversation was based on the coaching model, inspired by its well-documented use in the private sector, by the recently published report *Coaching for Teaching and Learning: A practical guide for schools* (Lofthouse *et al.*, 2010) and, most of all, by the training that colleagues in the Music Service had received from Andy Hind. The aim of the new approach was, first and foremost, that trust would be built between the mentor and the teacher because the meeting would be viewed, as far as possible, as a conversation between two colleagues on an equal level, rather than as a boss–employee conversation. This feeling was strengthened by the fact that the team of mentors included a significant number who did not have any line-management responsibility: the five Advanced Skills Teachers, the three Assistants to Heads of Departments, and the ever-increasing number of former Assistants to Heads of Departments.

The professional conversation was based on a style of questioning that was open-ended – so as to allow the teacher's own priorities and interests to emerge – but, at the same time, rigorous and challenging. The aim of the meeting was for a discussion to take place that would promote a deep level of reflection, and lead to the agreement of one or more areas for development (which we called 'focuses') for the member of staff to concentrate on during the year ahead. These agreed focuses would emerge solely from the professional conversation and would, therefore, be personalized as far as possible to the needs of the individual teacher, without being compromised by the distractions of target-setting or any externally imposed, predetermined criteria.

In the course of the professional conversation, agreement would also be reached on the kind of support that would most benefit the teacher in developing their focuses for the year. This agreed support might, for example, include team teaching or observing the work of another teacher and, crucially, it would very often include professional support visits, the outline of which would often be agreed during the professional conversation. At the conclusion of the professional conversation, a report would be written, summarizing the conversation and what had been agreed. And, since this report would simply be the summary of a meeting, and not one person's judgement of another, it could be written either by the mentor or by the teacher – yet another idea learnt from Andy Hind's training.

I believe that this new-style professional conversation resulted in more meaningful dialogue, more freedom for teachers to shape their professional development, the emergence of more creative and unpredicted ideas and, at the same time, teachers being held to account with greater rigour than ever before. I recall many occasions in my role as mentor when, by the end of the conversation, focuses had been agreed that neither the teacher nor I had thought of before the meeting, and that neither the teacher nor I would have thought of on our own. And there were many occasions where an agreed focus was to have an impact not only on the work of the teacher concerned but also more widely within the service. Tabla teacher Harjinder Matharu, for example, suggested in his professional conversation the setting up of a working party to develop resources for the teaching of Asian instruments. Matharu then duly established and chaired that working party, as a result of which new teaching materials were developed and shared across the World Music Department.

The response from teachers to the new-style professional conversations in 2011 was overwhelmingly positive. This was evident from the fact that 100 per cent of the staff attended, including the large number of hourly-paid teachers, for whom attendance was voluntary. In 2012 the Music Service produced a video for training purposes, consisting of a series of interviews with different members of staff, reflecting on the service's approach to professional development. At the start of the video John Clemson explains that changes had been introduced that were concerned with personalizing professional conversations for individual teachers, and that this reflected the developing ethos of the service. 'The move away from target-setting,' says Clemson, 'is because we are trying to change teachers' behaviours and attitudes, which you can't really measure by mechanistic targets.' Head of Strings Sally Hobbs goes on to describe the move away from targets as encouraging 'a much freer dialogue between the mentor and the member of staff, which tends to move naturally and organically towards a focus and a clear idea of how the year could move forward'. And woodwind teacher Jane Allin says, 'It doesn't seem as prescriptive as before ... It feels like a dialogue and a discussion rather than a directed conversation ... And I came up with ideas which I possibly wouldn't have done under the old style of performance management.'

The service's PSVs, ever since their introduction by David Perkins in 1991, had always been welcomed by teachers as an experience that was supportive rather than inspectorial. But from 2011 onwards they began to be viewed even more positively, because they were increasingly seen as being integral to teachers' continuing professional development – with staff being involved, during their professional conversations, in deciding on the time, place and purpose of the visits. Sally Hobbs expresses this clearly in the video: 'Staff responded very enthusiastically to the idea that any visit I made to them would be linked to the professional conversation ... The venue, the timing and the context of the visit would be by mutual arrangement, rather than just me deciding when to go out and see them.' And hourly-paid violin teacher Verena Lauer, talking about the idea that the PSV was a two-way process between teacher and visitor, says, 'It's really nice that the visit is not just for you to be judged, and not just to offer help, but also for the visitor to learn something from us as teachers ... you feel you have support when you ask for it but, at the same time, you feel that what you do is very much valued.'

In addition to this positive feedback from Music Service teachers, the new professional conversations also received recognition at a national level, including a very positive article by Michael Shaw in *The Times Educational Supplement* (Shaw, 2012). Following this article's publication, the Music Service received a congratulatory email from the city's then Chief Education Officer, Eleanor Brazil, as well as requests for support and advice from other educational institutions including one music service that, following a visit from myself, went on to adopt the Music Service's professional development model in its entirety – and with great success.

The Golden Thread and the Silver Service

From 2010, also in response to Andy Hind's Rising with the Tide course, the Music Service approach to staff training days began to change. The main focus of these sessions became more centred on staff talking to each other and learning from one another within small groups – often across different instrumental departments – rather than listening to presentations from Music Service managers or visiting speakers. Tabla teacher Harjinder Matharu summed up his response to this new approach: 'When we talk around the table it's a great way of getting people to learn from one another's experiences. Sometimes, just a simple idea that you pick up from another teacher can have a big effect on your teaching. The nature of our job is that we're quite isolated from other colleagues when we're going around schools, meaning that the training days are particularly valuable.'

This development was closely linked to another lesson from Rising with the Tide which was that, for an organization's stated values to have any meaning, they need to be agreed by the organization as a whole, rather than being imposed from above. Inspired by this, John Clemson and I decided to hold a full staff meeting in 2010, so that teachers could hold discussions leading to an agreement on what were the core learning principles of the Music Service. The meeting started off with small groups of teachers talking around tables in the Martineau Education Centre, and then feeding back to the rest of the room. The resulting outcome was an agreed set of four principles that became known as the Golden Thread: collaboration, creativity, understanding and skills. The term 'Golden Thread' was used because we believed that these principles represented a thread that should run through all of our teaching – whether in small groups, whole classes or ensembles, and regardless of instrument, attainment level or musical style. And, unlike the DfE's Teachers' Standards, introduced around the same time (Department for Education, 2013), the Golden Thread was based on broad philosophical principles, rather than being an attempt to reduce something infinitely complex to 43 tick boxes. Up until 2018 the Golden Thread was referred to on the Birmingham Music Service website under the heading 'Mission and Values', where it was explained as follows: '[The Golden Thread] means that young people are developing a deep understanding of how music works, the technical and other skills involved in becoming a musician, and this learning takes place through being imaginative and working with others.' And the interdependence of the Golden Thread's four principles was brilliantly depicted on the website by an image of four interlocking cogs (Figure 6.1).

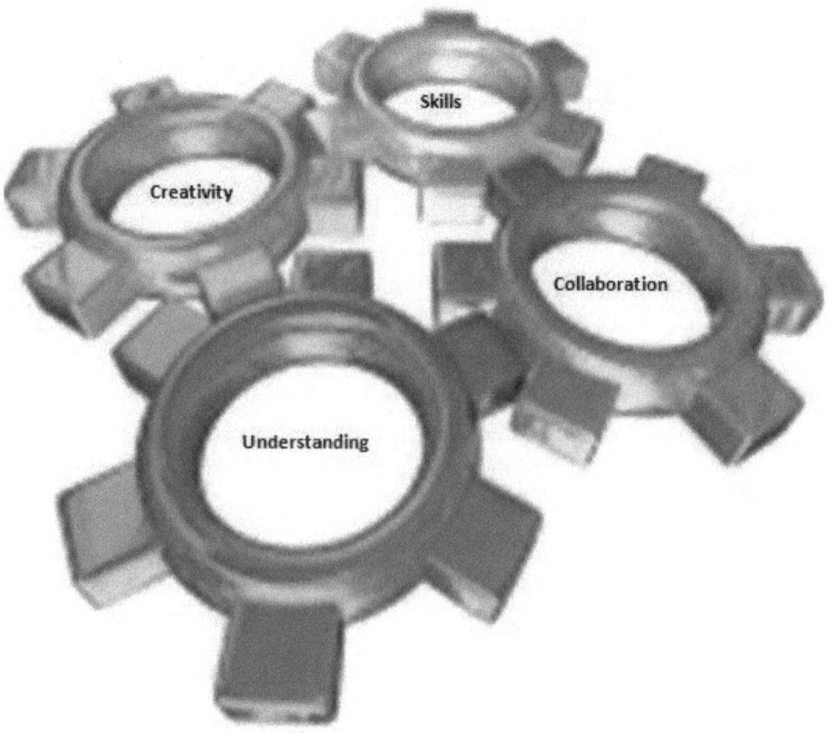

Figure 6.1: The Golden Thread

Shortly after establishing the Golden Thread, the Music Service's full team of teachers met once again – this time to agree a set of principles regarding the service's relationship with schools. At the conclusion of this meeting, three core principles were agreed and these became known as the 'Silver Service'. Like the Golden Thread, it appeared until 2018 on the Birmingham Music Service website, where it was described as follows:

- Communication – Music Service staff will make every effort to communicate effectively and respectfully with headteachers, school staff and pupils.
- Flexibility – Music Service staff will make every effort to be flexible and adaptable in responding to the needs of schools.
- Performances – Music Service staff will organize regular musical performances in schools as an essential aspect of their work, where possible combining with different instrumental departments and/or different schools.

As we have seen, both the Golden Thread and the Silver Service were developed and agreed through discussion among teachers at staff meetings, and it is for this reason, I believe, that they have been remembered by staff and have had a huge impact on the work of the Music Service. Within the Golden Thread's broad set of principles, teachers were expected to use their own judgement about what was taught and how it was taught – they were not required to follow schemes of work or achieve predetermined learning outcomes imposed from above. And an important aspect of both the Golden Thread and the Silver Service was that, far from being set in stone, there was an expectation that they would be subject to constant review by staff.

Community of Practice

As a result of the Birmingham Music Service's developing approach to leadership and professional development described above, I believe that a unique culture of collaboration was coming into being from 2010 onwards, albeit firmly rooted in work that had been going on for decades. As well as taking place within individual departments of the service, this collaboration was increasingly happening across different departments and influence was seen to be moving both upwards and downwards within the organization's hierarchy. This is exemplified by a story that starts off with a visit I made to observe the teaching of Head of Keyboard and Guitar, Nicola Walker. In what was a brilliant lesson, I was particularly impressed by Walker's use of the Latin American tune 'Sway' with a group of beginner keyboard pupils. I thought it was a beautiful piece of music, the main section of which was simple enough to be played by elementary pupils, and it was well known among young people at the time, due to recent hit recordings by Michael Bublé and by the Pussycat Dolls. So I stole Nicola Walker's idea and immediately started to use this tune in my own teaching, making an arrangement of it, for example, for the Broadway School Orchestra. Other teachers then heard my pupils playing 'Sway' and the next thing I knew was that the piece had 'gone viral' across the Music Service, being performed by pupils on many different instruments in different areas of the city. I later learnt that Walker had initially picked up the idea from a rank-and-file guitar teacher. So it had moved from a rank-and-file teacher to a Head of Department to the Deputy Head of the service, demonstrating a bottom-up learning process within the organization, and from a guitar teacher to a keyboard teacher to a woodwind teacher, demonstrating an exchange of ideas between different instrumental departments.

This experience strengthened my belief, more than ever, in the value of sharing ideas around the Music Service's different departments, and nurturing opportunities for leadership and influence to move in unexpected directions. So, increasingly, we were mixing staff up at meetings and training days: a keyboard teacher might be sitting next to and sharing ideas with a brass teacher; and a violin teacher might be sitting next to and sharing ideas with a tabla teacher. Harjinder Matharu commented to me, 'When you talk to someone from a different department you can bounce off ideas and you might think, "Yes, this could work for me", or "I could modify that idea and then use it." I think this makes the Birmingham Music Service unique and it's one of the reasons that the service has developed to such a high level.'

I had long considered the Music Service's Guitar Department to be the strongest group of teachers within the organization. The department's huge expansion from two teachers in 1984 to sixteen in 2014 was partly due to the increased interest in guitar playing in schools over that period of time but was also, I believe, due to the fantastic quality of teaching within that department. I found it interesting that when I met heads of music services from different areas of the country, they quite often complained that their guitar teachers were the most difficult to manage. But maybe the problem in those music services was that they were trying to over-manage their guitar teachers, or manage them as though they taught orchestral instruments. One head of service said to me that his guitar teachers did not enter sufficient pupils for graded examinations. This comment brought to my mind one of the Birmingham Music Service's strongest guitar teachers who was a rock musician and did not read musical notation, so would have been unable to prepare pupils for examinations. But this did not prevent his pupils from enjoying a rich tapestry of musical experiences in accordance with the Golden Thread, and developing into highly accomplished guitarists. Because our guitar teachers were part of a combined department that also included keyboard teachers, and the head of that department was herself a keyboard teacher, they were often left to look after themselves at training days and staff meetings. It was partly because of this, I believe, that they developed such a strong sense of responsibility and a culture of sharing ideas and supporting one another. And these teachers covered a huge variety of musical styles and experiences: some were classically trained whereas others came from backgrounds in flamenco, jazz or rock music; some had a university or conservatoire training whereas others had a background of performing music in pubs and clubs; and most read musical notation, but some did not. What was most important, however, was that they all worked together, enthusiastically sharing their varied skills and expertise with one another. At the end of the Music Service training day at the Martineau Education Centre on the last day of the summer term in 2011, a group of guitar teachers invited me to join them for an end-of-term drink at the

Court Oak public house. I arrived there somewhat later than the guitar teachers because it had been my responsibility to tidy up the room at the end of the training session. As I entered the pub, I saw about ten of them seated around a couple of tables, deep in conversation. I walked over, expecting to hear them sharing their plans for the forthcoming summer holidays. But when I sat down, I found that they were discussing their department's curriculum and the most effective strategies for developing guitar technique within different musical styles. I considered this to be a wonderful demonstration of their commitment as musicians and teachers, as well as being a great example of the Community of Practice model of learning – a concept developed by Étienne Wenger and Jean Lave, described as 'groups of people who share a concern or a passion for something they do and learn how to do it better as they interact regularly' (Wenger-Trayner and Wenger-Trayner, 2015).

Record of Musical Achievement

We have seen how, in the 2010s, the Music Service built on the crucial foundations laid by David Perkins some twenty years earlier in order to develop new approaches to leadership and professional development. Another area in which the service built on Perkins's foundations concerned the methods used for reporting to parents on pupils' achievement. The developments in this area were similar to those in the area of professional development in that they were concerned with focusing on what was meaningful and supportive, rather than on what was measurable. In the early 1990s, shortly after taking over as Acting Head of Service, Perkins established the Pupil Profile. This was a single sheet of paper completed by teachers for each pupil at the end of an academic year, giving information on performance and ensemble activities the pupil had been involved in, and including written comments by both teacher and pupil on achievements over the year and areas for future development. There was no use of tick boxes, grades, phrase banks or subheadings (such as effort, technique or sight-reading), which characterized the reports of many other music services. There were simply large boxes on the form for both teacher and pupil to write down their reflections, using their own words. The risk of this approach was that some teachers might use poor grammar or spelling (in particular, the words 'practice' and 'practise' were often incorrectly spelt), or they might simply fail to write down anything that was useful. And, since the number of reports totalled several thousand, no effective monitoring by managers was possible. Notwithstanding these risks, I believe that it was a very effective and meaningful reporting process that was highly valued by pupils, schools and parents. (Some years later, following my retirement, an instrumental music teacher from Sandwell Music and Arts Service suggested to me a brilliant way of reducing the risks referred to above. Her suggestion was that instrumental teachers could meet up in pairs in order to read and give feedback to one another on their reports, before sending them out to parents. I wished I had thought of that while I was still working for the Birmingham Music Service.)

The autumn of 2012 was a time when much debate was taking place nationally about methods of assessment and reporting within education, and when many old assumptions in these areas were being challenged. This debate had been partly prompted by the huge public outcry and High Court legal challenge in response to errors in the marking of English GCSE examinations in August of that year, resulting in 45,000 pupils needing to re-sit examinations. Following this, Tim Brighouse described GCSEs as '"smoke and mirror" exams with at least a 10 per cent error and a confused mixture of normative and criterion referencing' (Sutcliffe, 2012). And September 2012 saw the publication of the final report of the Burgess Implementation Steering Group. This was a report on the introductory trials of the Higher Education Achievement Report (HEAR) – a new way of recording the achievements of university students by providing a fuller, descriptive account of their work, including participation in non-academic areas such as sports, clubs and music. According to Robert Burgess, Vice Chancellor of the University of Leicester, who had chaired the group that recommended the introduction of the HEAR, 'We have long needed a new way of measuring and recording student achievement ... the classification system alone is no longer fit for purpose in the twenty-first century. It simply cannot give students, employers and institutions the range and depth of information they need to make the right decisions for their futures' (Burgess, 2012).

Later that year, I was touring university open days with my teenage daughter, Ailsa, who was considering applying for a degree course in art and design. At Goldsmiths University of London open day, Ailsa asked a tutor in the art department, 'What BTEC grades would I need to get in here?' 'We're not interested in your grades,' came the reply. 'We'd look at your portfolio of work and talk to you, to find out if you're the kind of person we're looking for.' That reminded me of my own interview at Goldsmiths music department nearly forty years earlier when I played a movement from a Brahms Sonata on the clarinet and Charlie Parker's 'Ornithology' on the saxophone, following which I was given the unconditional offer of a place on the BMus course. I later learnt that Goldsmiths music department was, at that time, seeking to broaden the range of musical styles they covered, so perhaps they felt that I had something to offer the department as a jazz musician. I believe that the response of Goldsmiths – to both my daughter and myself – was consistent with the fact that the principal way in which artists and musicians have demonstrated their work to others has always been through showing their portfolios of work, or playing their musical instruments.

Reflecting on all of these thoughts towards the end of 2012 reinforced my belief that the Music Service Pupil Profile, based as it was on descriptive narrative, represented a move in the right direction compared with the reporting systems of many other music services, which were based on tick boxes and grades. I began to wonder, however, if there were ways in which we could develop our reporting system still further, making it even more meaningful, and perhaps making use of modern technological developments as Robert Burgess had done with the HEAR, which existed in the form of an electronic document. So, in the summer of 2013, after consultations between Music Service managers, the Pupil Profile was replaced by the Record of Musical Achievement (ROMA) – a new style of form, with some important new features. First of all, the new form included a section where teachers were encouraged to insert electronic links to audio recordings of pupils' work – ideally being drawn from different stages of the school year in order to show progress over time. At Broadway School, for example, where I was the visiting woodwind teacher, recorded examples of pupils' work were uploaded to the school's FROG Virtual Learning Environment, making it particularly easy for these to be accessed by parents and pupils (through the link on the ROMA).

'Distributed cognition' is a theory of learning developed by Edwin Hutchins and others during the 1990s which, like the Community of Practice model referred to earlier, emphasizes the essentially social quality of learning. Describing the concept of 'distributed cognition', Gavriel Salomon wrote, 'it is based on the notion that the distributed system of cognitions is more than the sum of its components; thus its operations cannot be understood by examination of its isolated parts, and the system should be examined as a whole' (Salomon, 1993: 120). It could be argued that this idea is particularly relevant to music education, since music is essentially a collective activity where the whole is certainly greater than the sum of its parts. At the end of a symphony orchestra concert, for example, our main reflections will tend to be on the sound of the orchestra as a whole, and on how well the musicians played together, rather than on the achievement of the second violinist in the back row. On this basis, I would suggest that we can only give a true account of music learning by looking at the social context in which it takes place. So, to report as meaningfully as possible on the work of students learning in a group, we may need to talk about the achievements of the group as a whole, rather than the achievements of each individual within the group. In accordance with this principle it was decided that, when the work of a group of pupils was being reported on in the ROMA, a single report could be written for the group as a whole, with additional, individual reports being written if and when this was considered appropriate. I had recently experienced exactly this type of reporting in relation to my teenage son Cian's attendance at an outdoor-activities excursion organized by his school as part of the Duke of Edinburgh's Award scheme. After the event, I received a report for parents, written by the school's headteacher, summarizing the achievements of the group of students as a whole during the trip. This report told me everything I needed to know as a parent and I trusted that, had there been anything additional that I needed to know about my son's work as an individual, then the school would also have passed on that information to me.

In the new ROMA form, we decided to delete the separate box for pupil's comments on the basis that, rather than asking teacher and pupil to write their comments separately, teacher and pupil would be encouraged to discuss the pupil's achievements and then write down their shared reflections. This, of course, mirrored the way that professional conversations were now developing in the Music Service, where the written report was a summary of what had been agreed by both parties.

It was proposed that, in future years, the ROMA could be rolled out to include not just small-group instrumental teaching, but also whole-class Wider Opportunities teaching and membership of Area and Central Ensembles. This meant that, across the full breadth of the Music Service's work, the same process would be used for reporting to parents on pupils' music-making, in just the same way as the professional conversation and the Golden Thread were applied to every teaching situation. I recall that, shortly before my retirement from the Birmingham Music Service, Martin Orgill, Director of the Birmingham Schools' Brass Band, piloted the ROMA for parents of band members. Within the form Orgill included a link to a YouTube video clip showing the band's recent School Prom performance at the Royal Albert Hall. As a colleague commented to me at the time, 'What a wonderful opportunity for pupils and parents to be able to relive that unique experience!'

Chapter 7

Wider opportunities in the new millennium

'Over time, all pupils in primary schools who wish to do so should have the opportunity to learn a musical instrument.' This statement, delivered by Secretary of State for Education and Skills, David Blunkett, in 2000, ushered in what was, in my view, the most exciting development to take place within English music services since their inception nearly fifty years earlier. Following this, in 2002, twelve local education authorities were invited by the Department for Education and Skills to participate in pilot projects in teaching instrumental music to whole classes of primary school children. This new approach, which became known as Wider Opportunities, was considered very radical at the time and was viewed initially with extreme scepticism by many in the instrumental music-teaching profession. After all, the teaching of musical instruments in this country, and in many parts of the world, had traditionally been carried out on a one-to-one basis. Even small-group teaching was still regarded by many in the profession as a second-best option that had been forced on them by economic necessity.

Following the conclusion of the Wider Opportunities pilot projects in 2004, music services throughout England began to introduce this new approach to instrumental teaching in primary schools – because they knew that their future government funding would depend upon this. The Birmingham Music Service, however, decided to delay its introduction of Wider Opportunities. 'We started this later than some other music services,' said John Clemson, 'because, at the time, I was struggling with the concept. In 2004 I went to a concert at The Barbican in London demonstrating the work of the pilot projects, and I couldn't believe how bad it was. There were children playing the trombone with their cheeks bulging out, and instruments pointing in all the wrong directions. The noise was indescribable, so I thought, "I'm not having that!"' But over the next two years Clemson visited a number of music services where he saw some very good examples of Wider Opportunities, including some particularly impressive whole-class strings teaching in the London Borough of Croydon. That experience, combined with increasing pressure at a national level, provided Clemson with the encouragement he needed to introduce Wider Opportunities teaching in Birmingham schools from 2007.

Figure 7.1: Wider Opportunities brass class from Water Mill Primary School performing (with their class teacher) to Birmingham Music Service teachers at the Martineau Education Centre, *c.*2008 (Photo: Michael Bates, Birmingham Music Service)

Having made that decision, five schools including Water Mill Primary School were identified for piloting the project in Birmingham and Music Service teachers were invited to volunteer to be involved (Figure 7.1). 'The five schools,' said Clemson, 'were in deprived, challenging areas of the city and were schools which had had very little, if any, prior contact with the Music Service. And the staff involved, who would be working in pairs, included some of our strongest teachers, such as brass teachers Bob Vivian and Tim Baptiste, woodwind teacher Sandy Hay and guitar teacher Frances Griffin.' Clemson went on to explain that three guiding principles were agreed before the project started. 'These were based on what I'd learnt from my experience at The Barbican,' said Clemson, 'that children should establish good posture, hold and technique right from the start so that, if they chose to continue with small-group lessons after the first year of whole-class work, then they'd be able to do so without having to start all over again.' The Music Service's pilot project was extremely successful. The instrumental teachers worked in close collaboration with the schools concerned and established an effective model that would soon form the basis for the development of Wider Opportunities teaching more widely across the city – within ten years it would be taking place in over 100 Birmingham schools. At the end of the project's first year, the five classes came together to give an extremely impressive performance at Birmingham's Adrian Boult Hall, at which Clemson's three guiding principles – good posture, hold and technique – were clearly in evidence. The concert was attended by Tony Howells, who had taken over as the city's Chief Education Officer following Tim Brighouse's retirement in 2002. Shortly after this event, Howells once again demonstrated his support for the Music Service when he attended a conference on Wider Opportunities teaching at London's Southbank Centre, organized by Trinity College London, at which the Birmingham Music Service had been asked to make the main contribution of the day. Woodwind teacher Sandy Hay opened the presentation, giving his perspective of Birmingham's Wider Opportunities from the point of view of an instrumental teacher. I then spoke from the point of view of a music service manager, following which Tony Howells spoke on behalf of the local education authority. In travelling to London to show his support for the Music Service in this way, Howells was following in the footsteps of his local authority predecessors who, as we have seen, established the tradition of civic pride in relation to Birmingham's music education. Sadly, however, this was a tradition whose days were now numbered. Only a few years later, that most fruitful of relationships, between Birmingham City Council and the Music Service, which had flourished for half a century, was to be severed.

In the Music Service's piloting of Wider Opportunities, each class was taught by a pair of instrumental teachers working together alongside the classroom teacher. In the second year of the project, that pair of instrumental teachers split up, with each member of the pair then working alongside a new teacher. This arrangement enabled twice as many schools to be visited in the second year and it meant that each time a new teacher joined the project they would be working alongside an experienced teacher. During the initial phase of Wider Opportunities, it continued to be rolled out in this way from one year to the next, resulting in an annual doubling of the number of schools involved, and of the number of instrumental teachers involved. Many years later John Clemson reflected that, when he took over as Acting Head of Service in 2000, the Music Service was teaching 7,000 pupils per week, and by the time he retired, 14 years later, that figure had increased to 33,000 – largely due to the roll-out of Wider Opportunities. 'And the vast majority of those 33,000 pupils,' said Clemson, 'were getting a much better musical experience then than had ever been the case before.' Clemson went on to say that, by the time he retired, many pupils who had started off having lessons through Wider Opportunities were developing to high levels of playing, often ending up as members of the Central Ensembles. And, in stark contrast to Clemson's observations at the start of his career, many of these children were from disadvantaged areas of the city.

Towards the end of the 2000s Robert Bunting, although he had then retired from his post as Adviser, was continuing to work closely with the Music Service in supporting the development of Wider Opportunities. 'I think the service tackled this brilliantly,' said Bunting, 'particularly when you compare it with what was happening in some other parts of the country. In Birmingham it was a full year's experience for children on one particular instrument, whereas in some music services children learnt a different instrument each term, meaning that they'd just be getting started on one instrument when it was time to switch to something else.' Bunting went on to say that in Birmingham there was a real understanding that Wider Opportunities was part of a broad music curriculum. 'So pupils weren't just learning which valves to press down on the trumpet and learning to read crotchets and quavers,' said Bunting. 'They were also improvising, singing and listening to music.' And Bunting told me that he had seen clear evidence in schools showing the social development of children that had resulted from Wider Opportunities. 'So it was about far more than just music,' he said.

In my opinion, the most valuable professional learning that ever took place within the history of the Birmingham Music Service arose when Wider Opportunities teaching was being led by pairs of instrumental teachers working alongside each other and alongside classroom teachers. Such collaboration was, of course, a new experience for instrumental music teachers who, hitherto, had tended to work in quite an isolated way. Many instrumental teachers commented to me upon how much they had learnt from working in this collaborative way and many classroom teachers, who were not music specialists, told me about how much they had learnt about music education through this experience. Robert Bunting summed this up by saying, 'When you're working beside a partner, you share ideas with one another and, week by week, things develop and grow – and, through all of this, you've got the support of a colleague.' And Harjinder Matharu, referring to his Wider Opportunities percussion teaching alongside Bethan Jones, said, 'It's amazing how much you learn when you're working alongside another professional over a period of weeks and months. My specialism is teaching the dhol and improvisation whereas Bethan's is teaching djembe and singing, so we've picked up things from one another in all these different areas.'

Looking back, it is now clear that the Birmingham Music Service's approach to the introduction of Wider Opportunities was an exemplary model for the management of change within an organization. First of all, the introduction of the project was delayed for three years in order to allow opportunities to observe and reflect on models elsewhere in the country. The project then started off in a collaborative way, on a small scale, gradually growing from one year to the next, and allowing time for feedback and further reflection. And, throughout the first few years of Wider Opportunities, the main emphasis was on *how* it should be taught, rather than on *what* should be taught. So there were no predetermined lists of learning outcomes, for example, but rather, a lively, continuous discussion taking place between teachers about which strategies worked best. And, given that Music Service teachers were, for the first time in their careers, working in uncharted waters, the Clemson principle of 'establishing good posture, hold and technique' proved to be an extremely helpful reference point. As Wider Opportunities became better established and partnerships with schools developed, Music Service teachers then began to develop an awareness of wider educational issues going far beyond the teaching of instrumental technique – as described by Robert Bunting above.

The early years of the new millennium were a time of great change in English primary education, described to me by one Birmingham schoolteacher as 'an era of implementation overload'. This teacher was referring to the introduction of the National Strategies in mathematics, English and other subjects, and to the top-down manner in which these government-imposed schemes were introduced. In contrast to this, Birmingham's Wider Opportunities model was based on a set of guiding principles agreed by the teachers concerned, with thinking being developed, in the course of the project, on the basis of feedback from those teachers working in collaboration.

By the mid-2010s, for financial reasons, Wider Opportunities sessions were increasingly being led by instrumental teachers working on their own, rather than in pairs. And also by this time, schools were buying in Wider Opportunities as a way of releasing teachers from the classroom for their statutory entitlement to planning, preparation and assessment (PPA) time, and this meant that classroom teachers were often absent from the sessions. Sadly, therefore, the great opportunities for collaborative professional learning that were seen in the early days of Wider Opportunities were diminishing. This was exemplified for me on an occasion when I entered a classroom to lead a Wider Opportunities session in 2015, after my retirement from full-time teaching. I approached the classroom teacher to ask for advice on a couple of struggling pupils, whereupon she started walking out of the room, saying, 'I can't speak now – this is my PPA time.'

'You wouldn't be allowed to drop out of maths or English after one year, would you?'

An exciting exception to this trend, however, and in my view one of the most successful examples of Wider Opportunities teaching anywhere in Birmingham, was taking place and, at the time of writing, continues to take place, at Rookery School – a primary school in the inner-city area of Handsworth. Rookery already had a well-established history of small-group instrumental teaching provided by the Music Service when, in 2013, the decision was made to start Wider Opportunities cello teaching for the school's two classes of 8 year olds. According to my wife, Debbie Loane, Partner Headteacher at Rookery School:

> Right from the start of our Wider Opportunities teaching we saw a huge impact on certain children who, up to then, had found it difficult to concentrate and to collaborate. Many of these children were now focusing and working effectively with others for the first time, and were achieving outcomes in their music which they were really proud of. I think it was the discipline of large group performance that encouraged this and, once the children knew what this felt like, it began to transfer to other areas of their learning.

The normal model for Wider Opportunities in Birmingham and around the country has been that, after the first year of whole-class teaching, pupils would decide individually whether or not they wished to continue for a second year of teaching, which would be in small groups. But such had been the success for all 60 of the children involved in that first year of cello playing at Rookery, that the school decided they would like to continue the project into its second year for all of those children – with no opting out.

Although this model did not appear on the Music Service's menu of services, the service supported the school's request and continued to do so subsequently, when the school requested that the project should carry on into its third and fourth years on the same basis. This meant that the same 60 children continued with their full-class cello teaching for four years, right up to the end of their time at primary school – the only example of its kind anywhere in the country, as far as I am aware. In 2016, as part of my research for this book, I interviewed Julian Lloyd Webber, the newly appointed Principal of the newly named Royal Birmingham Conservatoire.

When I told Lloyd Webber about Rookery's 60 cellists – by then into their fourth year of learning – he was so excited that he quickly arranged a visit to the school to hear them perform. Commenting on the fact that all 60 children had been expected to continue their cello playing for four years, Lloyd Webber said, 'It's a great idea – well, you wouldn't be allowed to drop out of maths or English after one year, would you?' And Partner Headteacher Debbie Loane said, 'With everyone carrying on over four years, we found that some children, who were slower at picking it up at the start, were pulled along by the others and eventually developed a passion for playing the cello. In the traditional model of Wider Opportunities, those children would probably have dropped out after the first year, and if it had been small-group teaching, they would probably never have been selected in the first place.' Debbie went on to say, 'Playing the cello became what was special about that year group. It became their signature and they were soon regarded as the most senior musicians in the school and the backbone of our school orchestra.' Following the huge success of this project at Rookery, the school took the decision to replace all of its small-group instrumental teaching with whole-class teaching. 'Small-group teaching was never really consistent with our ethos of inclusion,' said Debbie Loane. 'Everyone should have the chance to play a musical instrument, not just a select group.' So, at the time of writing, the school benefits from whole-class teaching of violin, cello, clarinet and guitar, with each instrument being played by a different year group who started their lessons aged 8, and continue until their final year at the school, aged 11.

Debbie told me that she believed an important factor in the success of Wider Opportunities at Rookery was the fact that classroom teachers were always present during the teaching sessions, providing support in areas such as differentiation, and sometimes learning to play the instruments alongside the children. Another factor, she said, was the fact that, through Wider Opportunities teaching, instrumental teachers were increasingly seen as an integral part of the school. 'For example,' said Debbie, 'our cello teacher Kate Sidhu arrives half an hour before her teaching session begins and has lunch with our teachers. And because she's meeting our staff once a week in a collaborative teaching situation, professional relationships are being built in a way that didn't happen with small-group teaching.' Debbie Loane went on to say, 'With Wider Opportunities, the pupils' progress between one performance and the next is much more evident than it ever was with small group teaching. And the outcomes are much more impressive – hearing sixty children playing together, as opposed to four or five, creates an excitement that inspires the whole school.' And Debbie said that since Wider

Opportunities had become strongly established at the school, the audiences of pupils had become much more attentive. 'I think this is because they are all musicians now – they know more about music than the teachers do!'

Area Ensembles

We have seen that in the 1970s Peter Davies created an embryonic structure of non-auditioned ensembles, known as Consortium Orchestras, for beginner pupils in different areas of the city, in order to support the BSSO and other Central Ensembles. From the early 1990s onwards this structure of non-auditioned ensembles – now known as Area Ensembles – grew massively, both in number and in importance, to the extent that, early in the new millennium, an annual series of concerts at the Adrian Boult Hall was established, giving opportunities for all of these groups to perform in a prestigious city centre venue. The Area Ensembles were now seen as highly valued groups in their own right, and not merely as a training ground for the higher-level Central Ensembles. And, as well as orchestras, wind bands and brass bands, the Area Ensembles now included Asian music groups, steel bands and rock bands.

Martin Fautley, whose work as a Birmingham music teacher was referred to in Chapter 3, left the city in 1984 in order to develop his academic career, but returned again in 2004 to take up a post as lecturer in music education at the University of Central England (formerly Birmingham Polytechnic and soon to be renamed Birmingham City University). Commenting on the change in the Music Service's ensemble provision during the time he was away from Birmingham, Fautley said, 'In the 1970s the ensembles were mainly centralized activities which you had to be at a minimum standard to take part in. But now the Area Ensembles take place throughout the suburbs, and they are open to a far wider group of pupils. So you don't have to be almost an expert before you can take part, and that's made a huge difference.' Talking about the work of the Music Service more generally, Fautley said that when he returned to Birmingham he found that 'the Music Service had changed beyond recognition. It's now a different organization for a different time. It's no longer just concerned with Mozart, which is good because, after all, this is Birmingham!' Fautley said that, in the 1970s, Consortium Music Teacher Paul Slater had been very much a lone voice within the service in advocating the use of pop, rock and jazz within teaching. 'But by the time I returned to Birmingham,' he said, 'these were recognized by the Music Service as important styles of music – as well as world music, of course.'

Robert Bunting, commenting on the Area Ensembles, said, 'The way they work is visionary – they involve kids in a freer way, with much of the work being done aurally, rather than through notation. After all, you can't learn to read music unless your ear is already ticking over – if you can't imagine what it's going to sound like, then you can't play it. So teaching kids to play by ear leads towards playing from notation and that's what the Area Ensembles are doing, which is brilliant.' Making a similar point, Martin Fautley said, 'It is now established that notation is not the primary mode of thinking in music. It is a secondary symbol system, and this is something which is fully understood by Birmingham Music Service teachers. For example,' he said, 'I spoke to one of the service's violin teachers who said to me, "It's hard enough just playing the instrument without having to read all those symbols at the same time." In other words: "Let's just get on with making music, and we can learn about the notation later."'

Sadly, however, this understanding about the role of notation in music-making was not shared by Ofsted which, in 2013, published *Music in Schools: What hubs must do* – a report on 'the role of hubs in promoting an effective day-to-day music curriculum in schools for all pupils' (Ofsted, 2013). The report expresses concern about the rehearsal of a primary school choir because 'the pupils were only shown the song words and not the notation. Good opportunities for pupils to understand melody shape, rhythm, beats and rests were missed.' The writer was perhaps unaware that musical notation is a secondary symbol system, and also unaware that there are jazz musicians, Indian classical musicians, gospel singers, and many others who have a deep understanding of the components of their music, without recourse to musical notation. Or perhaps the message of the Ofsted report merely represented a regression to the view of Stanley Adams that Western symphonic music – which does have a dependence on notation – was superior to other musical styles. Such regressive thinking within the educational establishment was brought home to me not long after the report's publication, when I was teaching in a primary school on a day when it received a visit from a Department for Education minister. After spending ten minutes listening to an African drumming workshop in the school hall, the minister walked into a practice room where a pupil of mine was performing a piece of classical music from notation. 'Now, this is what I call music,' said the minister.

From the early years of the twenty-first century, Birmingham's Area Ensembles began reaching out to children from a wider range of backgrounds than ever before, increasingly providing opportunities in less advantaged areas of the city and including children from ethnic minorities. An example of this was the Handsworth Area Ensemble, which was established in 2011, meeting for weekly rehearsals at Grove Primary School and providing ensemble opportunities for young musicians in that challenged, inner-city area. As director of that ensemble I remember, in the first year of its existence, making an arrangement of Dave Brubeck's 'Take Five', to feature a very promising 13-year-old alto saxophone player Xhosa Cole. Seven years later, after progressing to membership of the Midland Youth Jazz Orchestra as a saxophonist and the Birmingham Schools' Symphony Orchestra as a flautist, and having established a reputation as one of Birmingham's up-and-coming young jazz saxophonists, Handsworth-born Cole received national acclaim when he was announced as the winner of BBC Young Jazz Musician 2018.

In 2012, four of the Area Ensembles embarked on a two-year composition project entitled Imagine Compose, organized by the Birmingham Contemporary Music Group (BCMG) and led by composer Liz Johnson. The project consisted of professional development sessions for Music Service teachers alongside emerging professional composers, and workshops in composition for pupils in the Area Ensembles. Imagine Compose culminated in concerts in the Adrian Boult Hall at which the young musicians gave performances of compositions that they themselves had created collectively in the course of the project. As directors of the Handsworth Area Ensemble at that time, cello teacher Kate Sidhu and I were directly involved in Imagine Compose and I consider it to have been one of the most rewarding experiences of my career. I have two particular memories of the project that will always remain with me. The first concerns a young musician in the Handsworth Area Ensemble who had found it very difficult to concentrate at rehearsals during the weeks leading up to the project. As soon as Imagine Compose started, however, and Liz Johnson asked him to suggest ideas for a group composition, he became completely engaged in the activity and ended up taking a leading role in the compositional process. My second memory is the feeling of inspiration as I watched BCMG's clarinettist Mark O'Brien and cellist Ulrich Heinen – two of the country's finest classical musicians – sitting side by side with, and exploring musical ideas with, the young musicians of Handsworth, just as Simon Rattle had done in his pioneering educational work in Birmingham thirty years earlier. Commenting on Imagine Compose, Martin Fautley said, 'I thought that the Music Service teachers were significant in their openness to the challenge of this project – they were happy to take it on, keen to develop it and very concerned about the development of their own pupils as musicians.'

Diversity

From conversations with colleagues, and from my own observation, it would appear that the Music Service Central Ensembles have also moved in the direction of including children from a wider range of backgrounds, but that they have travelled less far in this direction than the Area Ensembles. Bob Vivian told me, 'Over the 30 years that I have been conducting the BSCO, the number of parents requesting financial assistance for children to attend residential courses and foreign trips has increased hugely. This suggests that over that period of time the Music Service has made great strides in reaching out to children from poorer backgrounds.' David Perkins, however, said that, although the demographic make-up of the Central Ensembles had broadened during the new millennium, 'children from Pakistani and Bangladeshi backgrounds are still under-represented. This might be because we haven't yet given them the skills they need or because we're trying to squeeze them into a pattern of ensembles which is not appropriate for them. We haven't cracked that one yet.'

Notwithstanding this under-representation of certain groups within the Central Ensembles, there can be no doubt that, from the start of the twenty-first century, the Music Service was successful in reaching a wider cross-section of children within school-based musical activities. In July 2000, for example, Moira Foster-Brown, headteacher at Birchfield Community School, made the decision to buy in instrumental teaching from the Music Service. Birchfield was a primary school in the Perry Barr area of North Birmingham where over 90 per cent of the pupils were from Pakistani or Bangladeshi backgrounds. What began in September 2000 as half a day of woodwind teaching per week had grown, by the start of the next decade, to include the teaching of violin, cello, woodwind, brass, guitar, keyboard, sitar, tabla and djembe. And by 2013 the school boasted a 50-strong orchestra that gave regular performances in school and in the local community. A large proportion of the young musicians from Birchfield transferred at the age of 11 to Broadway School and, partly as a result, Broadway also saw a huge growth in their instrumental music teaching at that time. So in 2009 I was spending two hours per week teaching woodwind instruments at Broadway, but by 2011 this had increased to one whole day per week and, in addition, I was directing the school orchestra, made up of pupils playing all the instruments being taught at the school: violin, flute, clarinet, brass, guitar, sitar and tabla. A sign of the high esteem in which music was held at Broadway School was the fact that, in 2011, the headteacher invited the school orchestra to perform at a celebration marking the opening, by the Duke of Kent, of the school's new building.

Around the same time, Robert Bunting embarked on a unique educational project with the aim of raising awareness of Islamic music within Birmingham schools and increasing the involvement of Muslim children in school music-making. Bunting was prompted to set up this project in response to a visit he had made as Adviser to one of the city's Islamic schools a few years earlier, where he was told by a member of staff, 'We don't have music on our curriculum because Muslims don't do music.' 'I then started to do some research,' said Bunting, 'and learnt about the incredibly rich musical tradition within Islam.' Bunting then got together with one of Birmingham's leading Islamic musicians, Amran Elahi, and the Music Service's Head of World Music and Percussion, Harjit Singh, and, working together, they started to lead training sessions for secondary school music teachers on Islamic music. This resulted in some extremely successful composition work being undertaken by pupils in a number of schools, inspired by Islamic musical traditions, and an awakening of interest in school music-making among many of Birmingham's Muslim children.

'No ceiling on what can be achieved'

Although there are concerns, which have been referred to above, regarding the representation of minority ethnic groups within the Music Service Central Ensembles, there can be no doubt that in the new millennium these groups continued to move forward in the standard of their music-making. In 2001 the BSSO embarked on a concert tour in Japan. 'The BSSO was at a low ebb that year,' said Peter Bridle, 'but once they started doing concerts in Japan they were on a high, and playing better than ever! More than anything else,' he said, 'the experience of touring abroad serves to bring an orchestra together, both socially and musically.' And following that tour the BSSO gave concerts in Birmingham, which included stunning performances of Ravel's *Bolero*, Bartok's Concerto for Orchestra and Brahms's Piano Concerto No. 2, with Peter Donohoe as the soloist. In 2006, after a 20-year tenure characterized by extraordinary musical achievement, Peter Bridle stood down as conductor of the BSSO. Reflecting on those twenty years, Bridle told me, 'The thing I loved most about BSSO was that it was so encompassing – it catered for kids from all different backgrounds and for many of those kids it gave them an experience they wouldn't have had otherwise, and it changed their lives.'

In 2007 Bridle was succeeded as conductor of the BSSO by Michael Seal (Figure 7.2) – highly acclaimed for his work as the CBSO's Assistant Conductor, as well as his work with other major orchestras in Britain and around the world. In addition to this experience, Seal had a passionate commitment to getting the best out of young musicians and, under his conductorship, the BSSO was to attain standards of professionalism in its performance that had not previously been imagined. I believe this was partly due to Seal's own level of professional experience, meaning that he had extremely high musical expectations. In the words of a colleague, 'Mike Seal puts no ceiling on what can be achieved by young musicians.' In particular, I believe that Seal brought to the BSSO levels of interdependence and spontaneity that are not typically found within youth orchestras. On occasions when I sat in on rehearsals, I often heard Seal telling the young musicians to be less reliant upon him as the conductor and more reliant upon one another. I remember him once saying to the orchestra's woodwind section, for example, 'Don't follow me at bar 99. Follow the cellos – they've got the tune!' And on another occasion, he said to the violin section, 'If you're not sure how to play that bit, look at someone you trust and copy them.' And I remember Seal saying to the orchestra at a final rehearsal before an Adrian Boult Hall concert, 'I conducted it that way just now, but we might do it differently tonight – it just depends on how I'm feeling!' I believe it was this way of working that gave BSSO performances under Seal a feeling of 'on the edge of your seat' excitement, which can characterize the work of top professional orchestras but is rare among youth orchestras. The BSSO had certainly travelled a long way since those days when the local authority music adviser waved his baton in front of them on Saturday mornings – drilling them in the same repertoire 'until any spontaneity in the performance had long expired,' as a colleague was quoted as saying. During the early 2010s Seal was assisted in his work with the BSSO by the young, up-and-coming conductor Alpesh Chauhan. Chauhan's passion for music had been ignited when, as a pupil at Hall Green Junior School, he started having cello lessons with Birmingham Music Service teacher Veronica Raven. He then worked his way through the service's progression of Central Ensembles, before going on to study cello and conducting at Manchester's Royal Northern College of Music. At the time of writing Chauhan is Principal Conductor of the Filarmonica Arturo Toscanini in Parma, Italy, and is considered to be one of Europe's most promising young conductors – sometimes referred to as 'the next Simon Rattle'.

Figure 7.2: Michael Seal conducting a rehearsal of the Birmingham Schools' Symphony Orchestra in Weimar, while on tour in Germany, 2014 (Photo: Michael Bates, Birmingham Music Service)

The Birmingham Schools' Gala Concert on 17 July 1996 was the last public performance at Birmingham Town Hall before the building's long period of closure for refurbishment. It was not until 2007 that the Town Hall finally re-opened, following a £35 million programme of renovation. Most strikingly, the main hall had now been restored to its original 1834 single-balcony structure (removing the second balcony, which had been added in 1927), and the hall's beautiful plasterwork and ceiling design had been restored to their original appearance. Also, the building had now been brought fully up to date in terms of the main hall's acoustics, and public ease of access to all the different areas. The Town Hall celebrated its re-opening in October 2007 with a three-week festival featuring some of the city's leading musicians: the City of Birmingham Symphony Orchestra, the Ex Cathedra choir, jazz musicians Soweto Kinch and Andy Hamilton, and rock musicians Steve Gibbons and Trevor Burton. And, demonstrating the city's continuing civic pride in relation to its music education, the festival's concert on 18 October consisted entirely of performances given by Birmingham Music Service ensembles – the Suzuki Violin Ensemble directed by Heather Clemson, the Birmingham Schools' Brass Ensemble directed by

Bob Vivian and the Birmingham Schools' Symphony Orchestra directed by their new conductor Michael Seal. And the Music Service's ever-broadening commitment to diversity was represented by the Birmingham Schools' Azaad Dhol Ensemble directed by Harjit Singh, the North Birmingham Steel Band directed by Stephon Phillip, the Feadóg Tin Whistle Ensemble directed by Pat Brennan, and the Town Hall Festival Gospel Choir directed by Claudia Prince. This concert demonstrated that, in the new millennium, the Birmingham Music Service was continuing to present performances by young musicians in Birmingham's most prestigious venues – and at a higher standard than ever before. It also demonstrated that the huge range of Music Service ensembles reflected Birmingham's rich, multicultural heritage.

Chapter 8
Exit from the local authority

Following the huge expansion of English music services that had taken place since the election of the Labour Government in 1997 – largely due to the Standards Fund – the general election of 2010 led to the formation of a Conservative-Liberal Coalition Government, signalling a major turning point for English music education. The Standards Fund continued for the first year of the new government, during which Darren Henley, Managing Director of Classic FM, was commissioned by the Department for Education (DfE) to undertake a review of English music education, resulting in the publication of the National Plan for Music Education in 2011. The National Plan set out the DfE's expectations for schools, local authorities, arts organizations, private teachers, and the new Music Education Hubs that were to be established in 2012. The Music Education Hubs were groups of organizations set up in different local authority areas, each comprising the local music service as well as community groups and arts organizations, with each partner in the hub having a particular responsibility in relation to delivering the National Plan. In accordance with the National Plan, the government funding for music services would now be allocated through the hubs on a three-year basis, and would come through Arts Council England, rather than through the Federation of Music Services as before. And the new level of funding represented a significant decrease compared with the budgets for music services since 1997.

In addition to the reduced government funding for music services, it also became clear, following the election of the 2010 Coalition Government, that funding of local authorities was likely to be cut back and that this could pose a further threat to music services. This fear was shown to have been well grounded when, in 2011, Birmingham Education Authority took the decision to withdraw all funding from the Music Service. This meant that the Music Service ensembles, which up to then had been funded by the local authority, now had to be paid for entirely from central government funding – since the Music Service was adamant that parents should not be charged for this provision. In response to these financial threats, and allied with a desire to break free from perceived local authority bureaucracy, conversations started taking place during 2011 involving the managers of five different teams from Birmingham Education Authority to explore the possibility of moving outside the council as a joint, private organization. The teams represented in these talks were the Music Service, Learning and Assessment Service (advisory teachers), Health Education Service, Outdoor Learning Service and Cityserve (school meals providers).

Around the same time, presumably also symptomatic of the reduced funding of local government, Birmingham City Council took the decision to sell the site of the Martineau Education Centre to private property developers. This caused considerable sadness among the hundreds of local authority employees based there, and among local residents who greatly valued the resources that the centre offered them, such as adult education classes and room hire for private functions. And sadly, this decision of the city council signalled the end of the Martineau Centre's 60-year history – first of all in Edgbaston, and then in Harborne – as a local authority administrative base and as a social and professional meeting place for Birmingham teachers. So, early in 2012, local education authority employees moved out of the Martineau Education Centre in preparation for the demolition of all but the centre's historic clock tower building, in order to make way for the building of a new housing estate. At this point the Music Service, along with other teams from the Martineau Education Centre, moved to the Portland Centre in Edgbaston – formerly Portland Road School. (Neither my colleagues nor I were aware at the time of the significance of that building for the Music Service: through my research for this book I learnt that, nearly fifty years earlier, Portland Road School had been one of, if not *the* first rehearsal venue for the newly formed Birmingham Schools' Symphony Orchestra.)

In the course of 2012, the Music Service continued to be involved in discussions with a view to forming a private organization outside the city council. By this stage, however, the plan was that this new organization would be made up of just three teams – the Music Service, Health Education Service, and Learning and Assessment – since these were considered to be the most viable commercially. By the summer of 2012, arrangements for these three teams to leave the local authority and operate as a single charitable company were agreed, in principle, with the council. So, in September 2012, Services for Education (S4E) was established and began trading independently from the council. I recall the meeting for all S4E staff that took place at the Edgbaston Cricket Ground on the first day of that new academic year, celebrating the launch of the new company (although S4E would have to wait a further twelve months before formally moving outside the Council, due to protracted discussions regarding pension schemes). At that inaugural meeting the staff were addressed by the organization's chief executive, David Perkins, who spoke positively and optimistically about the future of S4E outside the city council. It was no surprise that Perkins occupied the position of chief executive since in the preceding few years he had been the city council's line manager of the three teams that now constituted S4E. At the conclusion of this meeting staff were invited, as they left the room, to collect a Services for Education mug inscribed with the new organization's name and logo – a pink circle. I remember feeling a sense of sadness as I picked up my S4E mug, which, for me, symbolized the Music Service's departure from a city council that, for 75 years, had done so much to transform the lives of Birmingham schoolchildren through music education. The S4E promotional mug also symbolized for me the move towards a culture of marketization within education that, I feared, would increasingly characterize the Music Service's work in the years ahead.

A few weeks later, on 9 October, I was driving into the car park at the Portland Centre and was surprised to see a large group of staff standing outside the building. A glum-faced David Perkins walked over to my car to explain that I would need to work from home that day. Apparently the building was not safe to enter, due to a major fire that had taken place during the early hours of that morning. It later transpired that vandals had broken into the Portland Centre, stealing a number of laptops and then starting several fires on the ground floor, resulting in the destruction of musical instruments belonging to the Music Service to the value of £300,000. Since the Music Service was still formally part of the local authority, we were immediately rehoused – in a small number of rooms that were available at the North Area City Learning Centre, situated in the former Josiah Mason Sixth Form College in Erdington. And, after a lengthy, bureaucratic delay, the city council paid £300,000 to the Music Service as reimbursement for the lost instruments.

Towards the end of the autumn term in 2012 the Music Service, along with its S4E partner Learning and Assessment, moved into new, very comfortable and spacious accommodation at Warwick House, Edward Street, in Birmingham's city centre. So, for the first time in its history, the Birmingham Music Service was now based in a modern, purpose-built office, as opposed to a former school building. I consider myself fortunate to have worked in all five of the Music Service's different locations up to that point. Although I missed the Martineau Education Centre's opportunities for interaction with a huge team of local authority employees, I enjoyed the pleasant, working environment at Warwick House. I also enjoyed being able to walk along the canal-side to the International Convention Centre for a sandwich during lunch breaks, and being able to travel to work by train on the days of heavy snow during that first bleak winter at Warwick House.

During the academic year 2012/13, not only were S4E managers involved in intense discussions leading to the organization's final departure from the local authority, but they were also simultaneously involved in complex negotiations regarding the setting up of the Birmingham Music Education Hub. By September 2013 all of these conversations had been successfully concluded and S4E was able to start the new academic year having achieved its aim of complete independence from the city council, and with the Music Service now established as the lead partner within the newly formed Birmingham Music Education Hub. The other organizations in the hub were the CBSO, BCMG, Ex Cathedra, Symphony Hall and the community music charity Sound It Out.

When I spoke to John Clemson following his retirement from the Music Service, he told me that the service's move outside the local authority suddenly gave the organization new freedoms, such as being able to create a much better website. 'And for many years,' said Clemson, 'we had been asking the council's HR [Human Resources] department to prepare a contract for our hourly-paid teachers. Finally, on the day we left the authority, we were able to establish this ourselves – so leaving the authority enabled us to get things done much more quickly.' According to Clemson, the Music Service did not lose any security through leaving the council. 'Because by that time,' he said, 'the security had disappeared anyway – we were no longer receiving any funding from the council, and the authority, due to increasing budget pressures, was making people redundant.' According to Clemson, 'The local authority, at that time, was characterized by inertia and inefficient systems so we were better off outside it.' Clemson explained that, in his view, the secret to S4E's successful move from the council was that this was led by heads of services, rather than by city council officers. It was because of this, he said, that the Music Service was able to hold on to its central ethos of providing the highest-quality education for the greatest number of children. 'We weren't just going to find the profitable bits and dump the rest,' said Clemson, 'whereas in some areas of the country, music services had been unceremoniously dumped by the local authority, and they had to become extremely commercial in order to survive.'

'A new generation of leaders'

In December 2013, after 29 very happy years with the Birmingham Music Service, I retired from my post as Deputy Head of Service in order to spend more time as a performing jazz musician. Part of the reason for my retirement was that a large part of my fulfilment as a teacher throughout my career – both in London and in Birmingham – had been rooted in the deep satisfaction I felt from working in forward-looking, democratically accountable local education authorities. And, as far as the Birmingham Music Service was concerned, and many other music services around the country, those days were now behind us. I also felt uncomfortable with the increasing government pressure on teachers and pupils to conform to assumptions whereby the infinite complexity of human learning was reduced to sets of predicted, externally imposed, measurable outcomes – getting in the way of creativity. When my successor as Deputy Head of Service, Heather Clemson, retired in 2017, the post of Deputy, with its primary focus on professional development, ceased to exist.

In 2005 I had interviewed a very enthusiastic 24-year old clarinettist, Ciaran O'Donnell, for work as an hourly-paid woodwind teacher for the Music Service. As part of his interview O'Donnell gave a beautiful rendition of the slow movement from Mozart's Clarinet Concerto, and he was duly given a place on our register of sessional teachers. O'Donnell had gained a degree in music from Queen's University Belfast, before undertaking postgraduate studies at the Birmingham Conservatoire and performing with the Orchestra of the Swan and the Royal Philharmonic Orchestra. After proving himself to be an excellent instrumental teacher, O'Donnell went on to become the Music Service's Head of Woodwind in 2009, and his meteoric rise within the management team culminated, in September 2014, in his appointment as Head of Service, taking over from John Clemson upon his retirement.

One of the first challenges facing O'Donnell in his new role as Head of Service was the implementation of a salary cut for Music Service teachers. From the birth of the Birmingham Music Service in the 1960s its instrumental music teachers, as public employees, had been paid in accordance with the nationally agreed School Teachers' Pay and Conditions. Ciaran O'Donnell explained to me that by 2015 – only two years after S4E's departure from the city council – the organization could no longer afford to maintain this pay structure for its teachers. According to O'Donnell this was because 'there had been a standstill in national funding since 2014; increased payments had to be made into the teachers' pension scheme and national insurance; and there had been a decrease in the number of hours being ordered by schools'. So, in 2015, Music Service teachers were moved outside School Teachers' Pay and Conditions and, for the first time in the organization's history, suffered a cut in salary. 'The only alternative,' said O'Donnell, 'would have been to start charging parents – either for the loan of musical instruments or for membership of ensembles. And that would have restricted access to those families that could afford it.' Four years later, at the time of writing, the Music Service continues to uphold its policy of providing the free loan of instruments to pupils and free membership of ensembles – features that, now more than ever, set the service apart from many music services elsewhere in the country.

In the summer of 2016, it felt like a hugely important era of Birmingham Music Service development was about to come to an end when, to the surprise of many of us, David Perkins announced that he was to retire from his post as S4E's chief executive. This meant that, within the space of less than three years, the three most senior managers in the Music Service since the 1990s – Perkins, Clemson and myself – would have retired. The time had come to hand over to a new generation of leaders. When I asked David Perkins, after the event, about the reasons for his retirement, he told me that 'the pressures on school budgets had increased enormously since 2010 and music services were having to take radical measures to reduce their costs in order to remain affordable to schools'. According to Perkins, music services were having to adopt increasingly commercial methods of organizing themselves and, in Birmingham, the move outside the council had been the first step in that process. Perkins said that the freedom from local authority control had allowed S4E to make itself more efficient and responsive while, at the same time, maintaining what he described as 'its public service ethos'. But by 2016 Perkins felt that he had moved S4E as far as he could in this direction and yet, because financial pressures were continuing to mount, he saw the need for still further commercialization. 'My own background,' said Perkins, 'had been in music, in education and in public service, and the time had now come for others, with a greater commercial acuity, to move the company into its next phase. The challenge now for S4E – and for all music services – is to maintain the balance between this new commercialism, forced upon them by market forces, and what they know to be their moral duty which is to provide high-quality, diverse and inclusive music education for young people.'

'Captain of the ship'

Upon Perkins's retirement in September 2016, Charles Elvin was appointed to replace him as chief executive at S4E. Elvin's fast-moving international career up to that point had included teaching English as a foreign language in Japan, senior roles with blue-chip companies RM and UBS, work in Malaysia for the CfBT Education Trust, consultancy work in the USA, directorships for the British Standards Institution and The Open University and, most recently, chief executive at the Institute of Leadership and Management. Elvin's appointment to S4E meant that, for the first time in the history of the Birmingham Music Service, instrumental teachers found themselves to be responsible to someone who did not have a background in music education – an issue that will be returned to later in this chapter.

Like many others, I was shocked to learn in October 2017 that, after only one year in the post, Elvin had resigned from S4E – in order to become chief executive of the Independent Schools Inspectorate. Our shock at the short duration of Elvin's tenure in Birmingham was presumably rooted in the fact that every previous Music Service boss had remained in post for a number of years so, as far as teachers were concerned, that duration of commitment had become an expectation. When looked at in the context of Elvin's overall career, however, his short tenure in Birmingham was far from untypical. And perhaps his decision to continue living fifty miles away at his home in Oxfordshire – rather than moving to Birmingham – could have been seen as an indicator that he might not stay very long.

Towards the end of Charles Elvin's time in Birmingham, but before he had announced his resignation, I met up with him at his S4E office in Warwick House. When I asked Elvin to describe his initial impressions of the Birmingham Music Service, he told me, 'The first thing I was struck by was the sheer scale of the organization – the fact that there were 27,000 instruments on loan to schools and 287 teachers. Getting the right teachers into schools with the right instruments is quite a feat of planning. And most schools are very happy with what they get and see it as an important part of an holistic education for their pupils.' Elvin went on to say, 'Because of Birmingham's incredible diversity, music has a particularly important role to play in the city – as a common language through which children can work together.' Interestingly, Elvin then echoed a remark made by Tim Brighouse, commenting on his own first impressions of Birmingham over twenty years earlier, and quoted in Chapter 5. Brighouse had said, 'Brummies have got an underlying degree of self-doubt and tend not to shout about their achievements.' Elvin, expressing a similar view, said, 'The Music Service is probably Birmingham's best-kept secret.' He went on to say that he believed the service had probably done itself no favours by remaining so quiet. 'I think the service is taken too much for granted,' he said, 'which is not what you want in the modern world where everything is marketized. We have to fight our corner, because we have lots of competitors. These competitors are not other music services – it might be to do with a school deciding whether to spend its money on a visiting PE teacher or on a visiting music teacher. We have to make people aware that we're not free,' he said. 'We're a charity, and if they don't support us, we will disappear.' Elvin explained that when Music Service teachers organize concerts in schools, they are now asked to place promotional leaflets on the seats and explain to parents that the organization is a charity that depends upon their support. Elvin then expressed agreement with a long-held view of mine that an organization like the Birmingham Music Service could only have been born within the framework of a local authority. 'It would be a bizarre private sector enterprise,' he said, 'if only because of the sheer cost of purchasing musical instruments. You certainly wouldn't start an organization like this from scratch.' And when I asked Elvin whether he believed the Music Service was sustainable in the current economic climate, he said, 'Yes, with a number of caveats. We are very generously supported by the Arts Council – without that funding we're completely non-viable. And we depend upon continued support from schools and from the community.'

Ciaran O'Donnell explained to me that, at the time Charles Elvin took over as chief executive at S4E, it was becoming clear that the budget that had been prepared for the year ahead was no longer realistic. This was because the Music Service was suffering an unexpected drop in its income, resulting from a 10 per cent reduction in orders from schools – largely due, in O'Donnell's opinion, to cuts in schools' funding and the introduction of the English Baccalaureate (EBacc). The EBacc was a performance measure for secondary schools introduced by the government in 2015, based on the percentages of pupils gaining high GCSE grades in a combination of subjects that did not include music or other arts subjects. As a result, according to O'Donnell, less music was then being taught in secondary schools, fewer children were taking GCSE music, and fewer children were having instrumental music lessons. So, when Elvin took over as chief executive, he found that the levels of expenditure that had been planned would have put the company into deficit. Straight away, therefore, he decided that S4E would have to find ways to cut its costs. 'There had already been salary cuts for instrumental teachers in 2015,' said O'Donnell, 'so it was now time to look at different ways to make savings.' O'Donnell decided that, by reducing the number of Central Ensembles rehearsals and the number of staff training days, it would be possible to make savings within the Music Service without compromising standards. Reflecting on these decisions when I interviewed him two years after the event, however, he said, 'With the benefit of hindsight, I think that cutting back on training days was possibly the biggest mistake I made during my four years in the post, because if you're not investing in the staff, then the quality drops and the goodwill can change. We've restored the training days now, but the attendance isn't as good as it used to be, because it only takes one year to break the continuity – it's going to take some time to get back to where we were.' Such open acknowledgement by O'Donnell of a mistake that he believed he had made and learnt from demonstrates, in my view, a level of confidence and integrity not always seen in the leaders of our organizations, but which certainly characterized O'Donnell's work with the Birmingham Music Service.

Speaking about the budgetary challenges he faced as soon as he started his post with S4E, Charles Elvin told me that a number of quick decisions had to be taken in order to reduce the organization's internal costs. One such decision was to close down the Learning Technologies Division (a team of IT specialists established by Perkins a few years earlier) because this was not economically viable. 'It was to do with becoming more efficient and spending less money,' said Elvin, 'and these matters weren't open to negotiation because you don't negotiate with the captain of the ship in the middle of a storm – it was a case of taking control and issuing instructions. We went through a difficult time, having to spend less money, but now we're in calm waters again.' And, referring to the continuing cuts to schools' budgets expected from 2018 onwards, Elvin said, 'We are tailoring what we do to what schools can afford, and keeping the quality high because quality is what sells. But there are still things that need to change – we need to be more agile and give schools a greater range of options that are affordable to them and viable for us. The challenge for the future is: "How do we retain the quality of experience for children at a price that we can sustain?" This is what we've been working on for the last year and we're making good progress.'

Many Music Service teachers I interviewed spoke in very negative terms about the impact of leaving the city council and the impact of Charles Elvin's leadership style. A senior manager in the service said to me, 'Elvin left the organization in a more secure financial position but with morale much lower. During his time, the Music Service became a business rather than an education service, with children no longer being at the centre of the company's ethos.' Another manager said, 'Elvin wasn't a musician and he never really understood our philosophy as music educators.' And one of the service's most highly respected and longest-serving members of staff said to me, 'I enjoy my teaching as much as ever but everything else has now become a burden. It's all about business – there are never-ending requests for data and we've now been asked to read a script promoting the Music Service at our concerts. Well, I'm not doing that – the way I promote the service is through my work, and that should speak for itself.'

The most common concern expressed to me by Music Service teachers, and the one that was expressed most vehemently, was that Elvin did not attend Music Service concerts. This was not strictly true because he was seen to attend at least one of the Summer Gala Concerts at the Symphony Hall shortly before the end of his tenure in Birmingham. It is true, however, that he did not maintain the tradition of regular concert attendance that had been demonstrated by Music Service bosses over the decades, and which instrumental teachers had come to expect. We have seen that during the 1970s, Education Committee Chairman Neil Scrimshaw attended almost every BSSO concert, even including those that took place in Germany; in 1988 Head of Service Keith Allen drove all the way to London to support a Birmingham Schools' Jazz Orchestra performance; around the turn of the millennium, education authority leaders Tim Brighouse and Mick Waters were frequently seen at Music Service events; and probably the greatest concert attender of all was Elvin's immediate predecessor, David Perkins. Not only was it unheard of for Perkins to miss any Music Service performance at the Symphony Hall or Adrian Boult Hall, but he was also a regular supporter of individual school concerts including, for example, the last two such events I was involved in before my retirement in 2013 – at Birchfield Community School and Broadway School. Looking back now, and on the basis of my interviews with teachers, it is clear that this kind of support from Music Service managers was vital for teachers' morale, and when it was missing, albeit temporarily, morale was seen to suffer. A senior Music Service manager at the time said to me, 'The fact Elvin did not attend concerts really wobbled the morale of the staff – because if the person at the top is not seen to be engaged with the work that's happening on the ground at a time when cuts are being made, then people begin to wonder how secure their jobs are.' Interestingly, the infrequency of Elvin's concert attendance seemed to cause much greater anger among staff than the cut in salary they suffered a year earlier under David Perkins's leadership. Perhaps it was *because* Perkins was seen to be so supportive in terms of his concert attendance, for example, that he was able to effectively manage that salary cut.

Two important changes took place for S4E towards the start of the autumn term in 2017. First of all, following substantial increases in rental payments for its Warwick House office, the organization moved to new accommodation at the Birmingham Science Park – a vibrant, developing area of the city that was also, by then, home to Birmingham City University and the Royal Birmingham Conservatoire. And in October 2017, upon the departure of Charles Elvin, his place as chief executive was taken by

Martyn Collin. Collin had already enjoyed a long and happy association with the Music Service and with S4E: in his role as Principal Primary Adviser for Birmingham Education Authority in the early 2000s he worked closely with the Music Service in promoting the new Wider Opportunities project in schools, and from 2014 he worked as Acting Head of S4E's Schools Support Service. (Collin was to remain in his post as S4E's chief executive until his retirement in September 2019, whereupon he was succeeded by the former Group Vice Principal at Warwickshire College Group, Sharon Bell.)

O'Donnell – the innovator

Despite the financial challenges and the wavering of staff morale described above, there can be no doubt that, in the years following S4E's move outside the city council, under the leadership of Ciaran O'Donnell the Birmingham Music Service continued to develop its long tradition of expanding and broadening its provision for Birmingham children. We have seen throughout this story that, at every stage of the Music Service's development, its leaders built on the work of their forebears, thinking creatively in order to move the city's music education forward in new, unexpected directions. So, after Desmond MacMahon had established the tradition of children's choral concerts at Birmingham Town Hall, Stanley Adams created a children's symphony orchestra to perform there and introduced instrumental music teaching in schools in order to support that orchestra. Then Peter Davies expanded this teaching to include tuition on non-orchestral instruments, and greatly increased the range of ensemble provision for young people. Linda Gilbert developed the quality and creativity of music teaching in the classroom and, in the new millennium, under the leadership of John Clemson, Wider Opportunities introduced the possibility for every primary school child to learn to play a musical instrument. And when Ciaran O'Donnell took over as Head of Service, there were three key areas of music education that he was determined to develop: rock and pop music, music for children with special educational needs and disability (SEND), and music for Early Years and Foundation Stage children.

So, in 2015, within his first few months in the job, O'Donnell established four rock and pop academies for pupils to attend at the end of the school day at secondary schools in different areas of the city. These were based on the then well-established Area Ensemble model and, to support this new project, the service purchased 200 electric guitars, 100 bass guitars and 100 amplifiers. Around the same time, the Music Service established a partnership with South and City College so that young rock musicians could avail of the college's authentic rock performance venue – a stage with tiered seating, along with professional lighting and recording equipment. 'The service has always been concerned with providing authentic musical experiences,' said O'Donnell, 'so that we are replicating the music profession for our students. And performing in appropriate venues is a large part of that.' When the British and Irish Modern Music Institute and the Academy of Contemporary Music opened branches in Birmingham in 2016, the Music Service immediately started to develop relationships with those institutions as well – making the most of every available opportunity for developing their rock and pop education. All of this work demonstrates the immense distance travelled by the Music Service since its early days when not even the saxophone was regarded as a serious musical instrument, let alone the electric guitar or drum kit.

Under Ciaran O'Donnell's leadership the Music Service made great strides in providing musical opportunities for children with SEND. O'Donnell appointed Sophie Gray as the Music Service's first SEND Adviser to co-ordinate this work and in 2015 a partnership was established with the One-Handed Musical Instrument Trust to pilot a teaching and research project whereby children in mainstream schools with upper limb disabilities received tuition on adapted recorders and trumpets. The great success of this project, in which the Birmingham Music Service led the way nationally, resulted in the formation of the One-Handed Ensemble, which was to take part in high-profile Music Service concerts. Through its hub partnership with the CBSO, the Music Service arranged free CBSO performances for special school pupils at the Adrian Boult Hall, with groups of CBSO players making visits to special schools to give performances, in cases where pupils were unable to travel. And a partnership was established with the University of Roehampton through which a fully accredited course in SEND teaching was established for Music Service teachers, with sessions taking place locally at the Midlands Arts Centre. O'Donnell also established a partnership between the Music Service and the Birmingham and Solihull Mental Health NHS Foundation Trust, so that counsellors could recommend musical activities for school pupils who might particularly benefit from these. And in 2018 the Music Service demonstrated its commitment both to mental health and to lifelong learning when it established the BBC WM Dementia Choir in collaboration with BBC WM and Wolverhampton City Council. After six weeks of rehearsals the choir performed at Birmingham's Symphony Hall as part of the Music Service's Youth Prom concerts. 'I see it as one of the aims of the Music Service,' said O'Donnell, 'that we are involved not just with school learning but with lifelong learning, so this includes working with preschool children and with adults.' And to develop the music provision for Early Years and Foundation Stage children, O'Donnell introduced Soundtots – visits by Music Service teachers to preschools, nurseries and reception classes, providing musical experiences for children up to the age of 5.

Notwithstanding the cancellation of some teacher training days, referred to earlier, O'Donnell's tenure as Head of Service saw significant, continued advances in professional development opportunities for Music Service staff. In 2016, as a young, technologically aware leader, O'Donnell was able to exploit the possibilities of the new digital era in a way that none of his predecessors could have imagined, creating a transformative training resource called ReelMusic. This innovation – the first of its kind in the country – consisted of over 200 six-minute video clips showing examples of instrumental teachers' work. These clips, recorded in Birmingham schools, covered many different aspects of music teaching including, for example, room layout, classroom management, questioning and warm-up. And, in the well-established Birmingham Music Service tradition, ReelMusic was not just a selection of videos to be watched by teachers, but its online tools enabled personalization of the resources to meet the needs of individual teachers, as well as encouraging conversation and debate among colleagues. ReelMusic was established by the Music Service in collaboration with technology company ReelLearning and film company Vyka and, in the year of its creation, was shortlisted for the Best Digital Innovation category of the Royal Television Society Midlands Awards. More recently S4E has sold access to ReelMusic to other music services. 'So this is one example,' said O'Donnell, 'of us creating a new income stream to supplement what we receive from the Arts Council and from schools.' Ever conscious, however, of the need for face-to-face as well as online interaction, O'Donnell also established weekly, after-school, collaborative training sessions for instrumental teachers. These were known as CCCCC events – cake, coffee, curriculum, chat, clinic – and O'Donnell told me that they were regularly attended on a voluntary basis by between 20 and 30 members of staff. And, to conclude the autumn term in December 2016, O'Donnell arranged a three-course Christmas dinner for all Music Service staff because, in his words, 'a dispersed workforce needs time to talk and to feel part of a team'.

In the summer of 2018 Ciaran O'Donnell announced that he would be leaving the Birmingham Music Service at the end of that academic year in order to become a successor to Robert Bunting as Head of the Wolverhampton Music Service. Shortly before his departure from Birmingham I met up with O'Donnell once again, asking him to share with me his final reflections before departing for Wolverhampton. First of all, he explained that between 2016 and 2017 the number of Music Service pupils at intermediate level and above who were receiving one-to-one tuition in schools had dropped from 3,000 to 1,300. According to O'Donnell, this was largely due to the introduction of the EBacc, which had led to a move away from music in secondary schools and which, in turn, had led to many parents moving their children's instrumental lessons to private providers outside school. 'So the Music Service was doing most of the preparatory work in primary schools,' said O'Donnell, 'but then we were losing many of those children when they moved to secondary school. And we want to take children all the way from the bottom to the top.' To counter this loss of work and the resulting drop in revenue, O'Donnell decided that, from October 2018, the Music Service would establish two music schools to provide tuition for intermediate and advanced level pupils – one at Bishop Vesey's Grammar School in Sutton Coldfield and the other at Bournville School in the south of the city. These music schools would operate outside the school day, from 5.30 to 7.30 p.m., providing 30-minute individual lessons for which parents would be charged at the rate of £19.00 per lesson – slightly lower than the standard charge in the private market. But, in contrast to the private market, pupils would benefit from the free loan of a musical instrument, from the full structure of Music Service support including practice diaries and reports, and from S4E regulation in terms of safeguarding and quality. Furthermore, in accordance with the Music Service's new commitment to lifelong learning, these lessons would be open to adults as well as to children. 'Increasingly,' said O'Donnell, 'there are secondary schools now with only one music teacher who might be spending half the timetable teaching music and the other half teaching French, for example, and not running any extra-curricular activities. In a school like that, music is obviously not highly valued, so that creates a space where the Music Service can step in – through our ensembles and our music schools.'

O'Donnell said to me, 'Over the last year my job has been like running a business. For example, I had to work out how much money we'd have to make in order for the new music schools to break even. These are matters that heads of music services would not have had to think about in the past.' O'Donnell explained that the DfE funding received by S4E to run the Music Education Hub was £2 million – amounting to £9.90 for each school-age child in Birmingham. 'That's not enough to provide music education for every child as outlined in the National Plan,' he said, 'so we are relying on schools buying in our services. But because schools are suffering budget cuts at the moment, that limits how much we can charge, so we now need to get money through fundraising as well.' O'Donnell went on to explain that S4E now had a full-time fundraising manager and £200,000 per year was being generated in that way – from parental contributions, from local businesses and from trusts and foundations. 'Our ensemble membership remains free,' he said, 'which is a key part of our philosophy, and is one of the drivers for our fundraising success – telling people that without fundraising we'd have to charge for ensemble membership.' Ciaran O'Donnell told me that he believed the Music Service's future was now extremely secure in financial terms. 'Over the last two years,' he said, 'our buy-back reduced from 3,000 hours to 2,500 hours but I think we've now hit the lowest point and I predict an increase of 4 per cent next year. It's building up again because we've helped schools to set up contracts for charging parents, so many schools are now getting all the money back that they're spending on instrumental teaching. And with our new music schools opening soon, I think we'll start to poach some work back from the private market.'

O'Donnell rounded off our conversation telling me that he was looking forward to starting his new post as Head of the Wolverhampton Music Service because he was excited at the prospect of leading a thriving local education authority music service, which was going to be a new experience for him. He felt that because of this, and the much smaller scale of the organization, he would find more time to spend with his young daughter and, instead of 'running a business', he would now be able to 'get back to some more direct involvement with music education'. Upon his departure from Birmingham, Ciaran O'Donnell was succeeded in his post as Head of Service by former CBSO tuba player and Birmingham Music Service Assistant Head, Stuart Birnie, who was appointed initially on an interim basis and, from May 2019, on a permanent basis.

New heights of performance

Despite the challenges faced by S4E as a business from 2015 onwards, there can be no doubt that the performance standard of the Music Service ensembles continued to grow to higher levels than ever before. Nowhere was this more evident than in a concert given by the Birmingham Schools' Symphony Orchestra at Symphony Hall on 20 May 2017. Under the direction of Michael Seal, the BSSO, working alongside the City of Birmingham Choir, performed William Walton's *Belshazzar's Feast* – an incredibly challenging work for a youth orchestra. Music critic Christopher Morley, writing in the *Birmingham Post and Mail,* described the performance as 'the undiluted highlight of my reviewing year ... crackling, confident, assured, colourful and dramatic ... with no less an accompanying band than the peerless Birmingham Schools' Symphony Orchestra' (Morley, 2017).

And John Clemson, who had been listening to BSSO performances since the start of his career over forty years earlier, described it as 'their finest performance ever'.

On 31 March 2019 I attended the Ruddock Performing Arts Centre at King Edward's School in order to hear the final performance in a series of nine Music Service Area Gala Concerts. I believe that this concert reflected the cultural diversity of England's second city more fully than any of the several hundred Music Service concerts I had attended in the preceding 35 years. I was delighted to hear the Handsworth Area Ensemble, which I had established eight years earlier, performing with more assurance than ever; the St Brigid's Area String Orchestra played beautifully and with impeccable bowing; and the Sparkhill and Sparkbrook Area Dhol Ensemble gave a rousing performance. The quality and confidence of all the music-making was outstanding. And, as Music Service Head of Strings Sally Hobbs said, while compering the concert, this was in no small measure due to the hard work of the teachers in preparing bespoke arrangements for their respective groups of young musicians. In the course of the nine Area Gala Concerts, in addition to the more conventional string orchestras, wind bands and brass bands, performances were given by seven rock bands, six Asian music ensembles and two steel bands. Many of these groups were based in challenged areas of the inner city and outer suburbs, and Birmingham's ethnic minority communities were clearly well represented. What a transformation since Peter Davies established the Consortium Orchestras, based predominantly in the city's leafy suburbs, some 40 years earlier. And, in a conversation after the concert with the Music Service's Interim Deputy Head, Paul Douglas, I was assured that all nine concerts had demonstrated the same exceptionally high standard of performance.

Afterword

Improvising in an unfamiliar landscape

At the time of writing, English music services find themselves operating in a political and educational landscape that has changed beyond recognition since the second half of the twentieth century. Many have moved outside their local authorities to form private organizations, and even among those that remain within local authorities, only a very small number continue to receive local authority funding. So nearly all music services now, whether they are part of local authorities or not, depend for their existence entirely upon continued buy-back from schools and funding from the DfE through Arts Council grants. Towards the start of 2019 I interviewed Bridget Whyte, chief executive of Music Mark (as the Federation of Music Services became known, following its merger with the National Association of Music Educators). Referring to those music services that had 'spun out' from their local authorities to form private organizations, Whyte told me that 'some jumped, and some were pushed,' and that 'although most of them are settling down OK, some are struggling'. Whyte went on to explain that, in recent years, some music services had been forced to drastically cut back on their provision, because schools had stopped buying in individual and small-group teaching from them. 'In these cases,' she said, 'the music services may just be providing Whole Class Ensemble Teaching [as Wider Opportunities had then become known], because this is what their DfE funding is for – in accordance with the National Plan.' And she told me that at least one of these music services was now acting as an agency for small-group and individual teaching – keeping a database of accredited organizations and individual teachers whom they would recommend to schools, instead of providing that teaching themselves. Commenting on this reduction in music service provision John Clemson, in a conversation a few months earlier, told me that this represented a fracturing of the system. 'The pyramid of teaching that existed in the 1970s and 1980s was small-based but went quite high,' he said, 'whereas now, if a music service only provides Whole-Class Ensemble Teaching, the base may be much broader but the lessons might come to an end after one or two years.'

Up until the twenty-first-century privatization of many music services, the tradition had been that most instrumental music teachers were employed by local authorities in accordance with School Teachers' Pay and Conditions (on the qualified or unqualified salary scale), with a small number being employed on an hourly-paid basis. But now, according to Bridget Whyte, the landscape of instrumental teachers' pay and conditions has become very disparate, varying hugely from one area of the country to another. Some music services still employ their teachers on School Teachers' Pay and Conditions, but many private music services (as well as some local authority ones) have now established their own rates of pay and conditions of service. And there are some music services, including local-authority ones, that made all of their salaried teachers redundant and then re-employed them on a freelance basis. Whyte told me that many music services now struggled to recruit suitably qualified staff – due to their geographical location, their low rates of pay, their inability to advertise full-time posts, and the failure of some conservatoires and universities to adapt their training of students to meet the needs of the twenty-first century. Bridget Whyte told me: 'There's less public money than there used to be for music services and the money that is available is allocated for specific activities in accordance with the National Plan; the costs for music services are going up because of increases in teachers' pay, pension contributions and rent; schools are struggling to pay for instrumental music because of budget cuts, and parents don't always have the means to pay.' Whyte said that, although these conditions had the potential to create 'a perfect storm', music services were finding innovative ways to solve these problems. According to Whyte, they were becoming more resilient, more businesslike and entrepreneurial, and Music Mark was providing training for them in all of those areas. 'There's money out there,' she said, 'but finding ways to access this is not something that heads of music services have necessarily had to do in the past.'

Despite these challenges, many English music services at the time of writing continue to thrive in terms of the quality of music education they provide, and continue to believe that their financial futures are secure. The Birmingham Music Service is one such example. According to Ciaran O'Donnell, the service's financial security is the result of a strong educational ethos, built up over many years. 'Some music services try to game the system,' he said, 'so their philosophy is determined by the National Plan. But in Birmingham we had a strong philosophy long before there was a National Plan and we've stuck with that.' O'Donnell continued: 'Decades ago the Birmingham Music Service was way ahead of its time in terms of building relationships with schools, investing in teachers, thinking strategically about the curriculum and doing creative music-making. So what we've got now is built on all those foundations. And at this time of massive, turbulent change in education, it's more important than ever that we don't get distracted from this philosophy.' O'Donnell's suggestion that some music services 'game the system' accords with a concern expressed by Mick Waters in *Thinking Allowed on Schooling*. According to Waters, the current preoccupation in many schools with data, league table position, inspection and the EBacc has encouraged a culture of 'game theory' whereby 'pupils gradually become the currency for the school rather than the beneficiaries of education' (Waters, 2013: 104).

The extent to which national, top-down policies have become the determining factor for the work of many schools and music services, as described by O'Donnell and Waters above, represents, in my view, the polar opposite to the culture that gave birth to music services and saw their rapid development during the 1960s and 1970s. At that time, to quote a colleague of mine who worked as a music teacher during the 1970s, 'There wasn't a plan in sight!' Music services were coming into being and growing, simply as a result of conversations taking place locally between politicians, local authority officers, musicians and teachers, and through exchanges of ideas between these people in different parts of the country – exactly as described by Tim Brighouse in the Foreword to this book. I would suggest that, to use a musical metaphor, these people were improvising – making it up as they went along – and that the theme upon which this improvisation was based was their core belief in providing the best possible musical experiences for young people in their communities.

In my conversation with Ciaran O'Donnell he cited what he believed to be an example of the Birmingham Music Service's philosophy, which for me encapsulates the integrity and depth of thinking within the organization:

> There is a view that progression in music education is an upward movement – that it's to do with learning to play more notes or learning to play them faster. And this view is reflected, for example, in the graded examination system. Our view, however, is that progression in music is to do with your skills, understanding and musicianship becoming deeper over time. So, a pupil might revisit 'Twinkle, Twinkle, Little Star' and play it with better tone quality, better phrasing or greater depth of understanding.

I recall this exact view being articulated at a Music Service training day a few years earlier by Keith Swanwick, Emeritus Professor at the Institute of Education, University of London. To hear it being repeated with such conviction by O'Donnell in 2018 was extremely heartening. O'Donnell, like Swanwick before him, was acknowledging the complexity of musical learning at a time when there is such an emphasis on valuing what is measurable in education – an approach reflected in the preoccupation of many music services with numerical data such as graded examination results.

Another feature lying at the heart of the Birmingham Music Service philosophy, referred to by Ciaran O'Donnell in Chapter 8, is the emphasis on authenticity in children's musical experiences – through, for example, opportunities to perform in genuine, professional-type situations. Again, this accords with the thoughts of Mick Waters expressed in *Thinking Allowed on Schooling*, where the author describes some powerful examples of authentic learning that he had witnessed:

> From the school in Bradford with its splendid garden to the school in Cornwall with its farm, ... to the school in Stockport that has produced a full-scale film depicting local history, to the schools that produce newspapers, websites and exhibitions for their communities to enjoy. They all know that authentic learning strikes a chord. (Waters, 2013: 207)

I believe it is highly appropriate that Waters's quotation concludes with a musical metaphor, since the work of music services, in Birmingham and around the country, surely represents another great model of authentic learning and, if that teaching ceased to flourish, then that model would sadly be lost.

John Clemson told me he believed that, in the first two decades of the twenty-first century, the music services that had survived best were those that had compromised least in terms of their educational philosophy. 'Those that have gone down very commercial routes,' he said, 'have done less well because, at the end of the day, headteachers want to see educational benefit for their pupils and if they see this, they'll pay for it. So the educational philosophy at the centre of the Birmingham Music Service is also its best commercial prospect.' Clemson said that he believed the success of the Birmingham Music Service had been built on 'an absolute emphasis on quality, and on becoming a partner with schools – rather than it being a relationship of customer and provider. This is particularly evident,' he said, 'when it comes to Wider Opportunities – there is a shared educational purpose, with quality as its background – and that's always the best hope for survival.' John Clemson concluded his reflections by recalling a visit he had made to a primary school, while Head of Service, to attend a Wider Opportunities performance. 'The school hall was full of pupils, teachers and parents', he said, 'and it was a fantastic experience for everyone concerned.' At the end of the concert, however, after expressing his huge appreciation for the Music Service's work, the headteacher said to Clemson, 'There's one instrumental teacher we've got who no one has ever seen – he comes in, doesn't speak to anybody, and then leaves again. So we'd rather not have him back again next year, if that's ok.' 'This,' said John Clemson, 'brought home to me the huge value of the new, partnership approach to instrumental teaching, as opposed to the old-fashioned method, where the teacher came in, worked with some individual pupils and then went off again.'

When I asked Bridget Whyte whether, in view of the challenges she had described to me, she still saw a future for English music services, she responded very optimistically. She described three developments due to take place at a national level that she believed would have a positive impact. First of all, she believed that the new Model Music Curriculum, to be published by the DfE in 2019 would raise the status of music in schools. (The release of this document, however, was delayed by the DfE – by the start of 2020, there was still no sign of its publication.) Second, the planned 'refresh' of the National Plan for Music Education, to be published in 2020, would hopefully extend the period of government funding for music services. And third, Whyte explained that the new Ofsted inspection framework, due to come into effect in 2019, would focus on the need for a 'broad and balanced curriculum'. 'So schools which have removed music from their curriculum,' she said, 'will now need to bring it back again if they want to get an 'Outstanding' grade from Ofsted – so they'll be coming back to music services again for support.'

If, however, schools were to buy in instrumental teaching merely to satisfy an Ofsted requirement – to tick a box – then this, arguably, would represent a return to 'game theory', as described by Mick Waters and referred to earlier in this chapter. And, if this were the case, I would suggest that there may not be sufficient depth of commitment to the project within schools to meet the needs of our young musicians. Furthermore, if a school in the current financial climate decided that they wished to increase their instrumental music provision, this would depend upon the school having sufficient reserves of funding available, and upon the local music service having the necessary resources. Otherwise, the school might turn to a private provider instead and might find that the level of commitment and pedagogical understanding that they had come to expect from a music service was now lacking.

While Whyte described three areas of government policy as possible saviours of English music services, it could be argued that the most serious, fundamental, current threat to music services is the increased level of government control at the expense of those fruitful, creative relationships between musicians, teachers and local authorities that gave birth to music services in the first place. The most obvious benefit of the local authority link in the past was the safety net of financial security. This was summed up by Bridget Whyte when she told me, 'In the past, heads of music services would have gone to their local councillors and said, "this is the amount of money we'll need this year", and the councillors would have said, "OK".' And John Clemson said to me, 'The emasculation of local government has broken the crucial connection between pride within a local community and the funding that went with it. So, where you might have had local councillors who were proud of the Birmingham Schools' Symphony Orchestra and would vote for its continued funding, that link no longer exists. So music services have now had to attach themselves to central government instead, and that's much more risky because there isn't the local connection anymore.' John Clemson went on to say that he thought government funding for music services might come to an end in the near future, and that if that happened the Birmingham Music Service would almost certainly have to close down their ensembles. 'Because,' he said, 'the ensembles are currently supported entirely by government money and there's no other way to fund them unless you started charging parents about £300 per year for each child. And with the increasing cuts to school budgets,' he said, 'a small primary school, for example, might now have to decide between cutting their number of teaching assistants or getting rid of their violin teacher. So it's possible that we may be reaching the end of music service provision in this country.'

David Perkins was similarly less than optimistic about the future of music services. 'No doubt some will survive,' he said, 'and will continue to offer high-quality teaching and ensemble opportunities.' But Perkins said it was unclear as to what extent schools would continue to be directly involved in this provision. 'And without the involvement of schools,' he said, 'who would ensure that opportunities were available to all young people, including those from "the wrong side of the tracks"?' He went on to say, however, that if any music service continued to succeed, he was sure the Birmingham Music Service would, 'because its teachers and leaders have been committed to a clear vision for many years, and they won't let that go easily'.

These concerns expressed by Perkins regarding the possible reduction of school involvement in instrumental music accord with the concerns expressed by Ciaran O'Donnell and referred to in the last chapter. And the Birmingham Music Service's introduction of music schools in 2018 reflects this move away from school involvement, as well as a move away from equality of provision, since parents are expected to pay nearly the market rate for these lessons. In the words of O'Donnell himself, in reference to the music schools, 'The downside of getting money from charging parents is that tuition can become the preserve of those who can afford it.' (And, since the music schools are predominantly concerned with providing one-to-one rather than group tuition, they also serve, perhaps, to reinforce the old assumption that individual teaching is the ideal.) O'Donnell's concern about musical opportunities becoming 'the preserve of those who can afford it' was articulated by many people I interviewed who feared that increasingly, across the country, parents would be expected to pay for their children's instrumental music teaching and ensemble membership. When I asked Bridget Whyte about this, she said, 'Yes, the postcode lottery is a real worry. The remissions pot is getting smaller, so in the London Borough of Tower Hamlets, for example – one of the poorest areas in the country – the music service is struggling to provide teaching for children who cannot afford to pay. And often it is a challenge for music services to find the funding to provide progression for children following on from Whole-Class Ensemble Teaching.'

Roderick Dunk and Anneke Scott, two highly successful professional musicians and alumni of the Birmingham Music Service, whose stories were told earlier in the book, both expressed their concerns on this matter. Dunk said, 'There is a much bigger percentage of people coming into the music profession now from public-school backgrounds. So we are going back to the way things were in the 1960s and earlier when it was the more privileged classes who got the opportunity to learn musical instruments. I saw things balancing out class-wise in the course of my career, but now I can see it going the other way again.' And Scott said, 'It deeply saddens me that future generations might not get what I got. Had the Birmingham Music Service not existed, my parents might have found me a private teacher, but I still wouldn't have ended up doing what I'm doing now, because I wouldn't have had the social experiences of ensembles and concerts. But for children from a less advantaged background – what chance would they have without a music service?'

When Robert Bunting shared with me his reflections on his time as Adviser for Music in Birmingham he said that he believed a great loss would be suffered through music services moving outside local authorities. 'As a local authority adviser,' he said, 'it was a great experience for me to be working alongside a literacy consultant, a religious studies adviser and a special educational needs adviser. When I met with the Music Service, I was able to share some of the richness of those different perspectives – and I think that breadth of educational understanding helped the service to flourish. The great thing about the local authority was that you felt you were part of a big network across the city and that you were all working together. But the danger now is that a private music service, working on its own just to provide music, would find it much harder to encompass that breadth.' In describing the huge educational value of a music service being part of a local education authority, I believe Bunting was echoing the words of Mick Waters, quoted in Chapter 5: 'There was a tradition within the Birmingham Music Service that the teachers were brought together for training, not just in music, but in the latest educational thinking. So people in the service knew the bigger picture … ' And Bridget Whyte explained that, 'Many music services now struggle to provide appropriate professional development for their staff – particularly those services that employ freelance teachers who would expect additional payment to attend training.'

When I asked Julian Lloyd Webber in 2016 for his reflections on the present state of music education in England, he said:

> The narrowing of the school curriculum is potentially a disaster for education in this country, because if you're going to take arts subjects out of schools, then fewer and fewer state school children are going to get access to the arts, which is so short-sighted. And if we were to destroy the fabric of music education in this country by getting rid of instrumental music teachers, how would we suddenly get them back again if we changed our minds? It would be so easy to destroy this system but so hard to bring it back again. The impact of the work of music services in this country over the years has been fantastic – that's why there should not be any question of them being threatened. What they contribute in relation to what they receive represents the best possible value for money. The danger is that, in this country, we tend to take things for granted and think that if something is there then it will always be there – but one day we might find that it isn't. So people need to be kept constantly aware of how valuable the work of our music services is, and how sad it would be if we didn't have them anymore.

I consider myself extremely fortunate to have worked as a teacher and manager with the Birmingham Music Service for most of my career. It feels like a great privilege to have followed in the footsteps of the 'wartime giants' of education, described by Tim Brighouse in the Foreword, who did so much to establish music and the creative arts as an essential part of children's education in England. And it has been a particular privilege to work alongside Birmingham's musicians, teachers and politicians who, in line with the city's motto, 'Forward', have continued to create new, exciting musical opportunities for young people over many decades. As suggested by Julian Lloyd Webber above, I believe it is now more important than ever that we celebrate the story of the Birmingham Music Service, remind ourselves of the extraordinary value of such organizations, and do everything within our power to ensure that future generations of children will continue to have their lives enriched through music.

References

Berliner, W. (2002) 'A great crusade'. *The Guardian*, 9 April. Online. https://tinyurl.com/rdpdyv8 (accessed 12 November 2019).

Biddulph, F. (1985) 'Woodwind Festival '85'. *Keynotes*, Spring, 16.

Birmingham Mail (1949) 'Our debt to Dr D. MacMahon', 2, 16 November.

Birmingham Mail (1952) 'TV in the schools', 3, 22 January.

Birmingham Post (1950) 'Festival of Music at the Town Hall', 3, 19 December.

Birmingham Post (1953) 'Desmond MacMahon's songs', 5, 17 July.

Brighouse, T. and Woods, D. (1999) *How to Improve Your School*. London: Routledge.

Burgess, R. (2012) 'The HEAR: A richer record of student achievement'. *Leicester Exchanges*, 9 October. Online. http://leicesterexchanges.com/2012/10/09/the-hear/ (accessed 30 May 2019).

City of Birmingham Education Department (1987) *Instrumental Music Teaching – A forward look*. Birmingham: City of Birmingham Education Department.

Davies, P. (1990) '1975–83: The "Middle" Years'. *BSSO 25th Anniversary Concert* (Programme notes).

DfE (Department for Education) (2013) *Teachers' Standards: Guidance for school leaders, school staff and governing bodies*. London: Department for Education. Online. https://tinyurl.com/y8tpu3rh (accessed 12 November 2019).

Duckett, R. (1988) *Team Brass*. London: International Music Publications.

Loane, B. (1987) 'Understanding Children's Music'. Ph.D. diss. University of York, UK.

Loane, C. and Duckett, R. (1991) *Team Woodwind*. London: International Music Publications.

Lofthouse, R., Leat, D. and Towler, C. (2010) *Coaching for Teaching and Learning: A practical guide for schools: Guidance report*. Reading: CfBT Education Trust. Online. https://tinyurl.com/roeslu6 (accessed 12 November 2019).

MacMahon, D. (1938) *The New National and Folk Song Book – Part 1*. London: Thomas Nelson and Sons.

Mann, P.O. (1991) 'The Development of Music Education in the West Riding of Yorkshire Education Authority: 1935–74'. Unpublished PhD thesis, University of Leeds.

Martineau Gardens (n.d.) 'Mollie Martineau (1-9-26 to 15-8-15)'. Online. https://tinyurl.com/t8bheu9 (accessed 12 November 2019).

Massey, R. (n.d.) 'Famous Moseleians: Dr Roy Massey MBE'. Online. www.moseleians.co.uk/people/famous-moseleians/ (accessed 30 May 2019).

Ministry of Education (1949) *Story of a School: A headmaster's experiences with children aged seven to eleven* (Ministry of Education Pamphlet No. 14). London: HMSO. Online. https://tinyurl.com/wpttw5u (accessed 12 November 2019).

Morant, R.W. (1978) 'Re-appraising the role of teachers' centres'. *Journal of In-Service Education*, 4 (3), 199–205.

Morley, C. (2017) 'Notes from a great year on classical and choral scene: Christopher Morley rounds up his personal highlights from a busy 2017'. *Birmingham Post*, 28 December. Online. https://tinyurl.com/t9ybk88 (accessed 12 November 2019).

Ofsted (2013) *Music in Schools: What hubs must do*. Manchester: Ofsted. Online. https://tinyurl.com/y2bsezfd (accessed 12 November 2019).

Paynter, J. and Aston, P. (1970) *Sound and Silence: Classroom projects in creative music*. Cambridge: Cambridge University Press.

Preston, J. (2003) 'Welcome to Britain's poshest prison'. *The Telegraph*, 28 January. Online. https://tinyurl.com/qqcjw7s (accessed 12 November 2019).

Radio Times (1924) 'Mr Desmond MacMahon'. *Radio Times*, 20 June. Online. https://tinyurl.com/vh3rf5k (accessed 12 November 2019).

Radio Times (1937) 'Songs for Schools'. *Radio Times*, 8 October. Online. https://tinyurl.com/uk4sm77 (accessed 12 November 2019).

Robinson, K. (ed.) (1982) *The Arts in Schools: Principles, practice and provision*. London: Calouste Gulbenkian Foundation.

Salomon, G. (ed.) (1993) *Distributed Cognitions: Psychological and educational considerations*. Cambridge: Cambridge University Press.

Shaw, M. (2012) 'Replacing appraisals with a "professional conversation" that puts bosses and staff on an equal footing'. *TESpro*, 6 April, 11.

Silverthorne, S. (2009) 'When goal setting goes bad'. *Working Knowledge*, 2 March. Online. https://hbswk.hbs.edu/item/when-goal-setting-goes-bad (accessed 31 May 2019).

Stephens, J. (1982) 'Roles in in-service education'. *British Journal of In-Service Education*, 9 (1), 47–52.

Sutcliffe, J. (2012) '2015 and beyond: What's next for school reform?'. *The Guardian*, 22 October. Online. https://tinyurl.com/s7n7dpf (accessed 12 November 2019).

Waters, M. (2013) *Thinking Allowed on Schooling*. Carmarthen: Independent Thinking Press.

Wenger-Trayner, E. and Wenger-Trayner, B. (2015) 'Introduction to communities of practice: A brief overview of the concept and its uses'. Online. https://tinyurl.com/y38k5fyh (accessed 12 November 2019).

Wheatley, M.J. (1999) *Leadership and the New Science: Discovering order in a chaotic world*. 2nd ed. San Francisco: Berrett-Koehler Publishers.

Whittock, C. (1985) 'City of Birmingham Schools Orchestra'. *Birmingham Evening Mail*, 26 June, 7.

Index